Library of
Davidson College

Garland Studies in Historical Demography

Stuart Bruchey

Allan Nevins Professor Emeritus
American Economic History
Columbia University

GENERAL EDITOR

A Garland Series

Historical Demography of the Pima and Maricopa Indians of Arizona, 1846–1974

VOLUME ONE

Cary Walter Meister

GARLAND PUBLISHING, INC.
New York   London
1989

Copyright © 1989 by CaryWalter Meister.

Library of Congress Cataloging-in-Publication Data

Meister, Cary Walter.
Historical demography of the Pima and Maricopa Indians of Arizona, 1846—1974 / Cary Walter Meister.
p. cm. — (Garland studies in historical demography)
Thesis (Ph. D.) University of Michigan, 1975.
Includes bibliographical references.
ISBN 0-8240-3364-7 (alk. paper)
1. Pima Indians—Census. 2. Maricopa Indians—Census. 3. Pima Indians—History. 4. Maricopa Indians—History.
I. Title. II. Series.
E99.P6M45 1989
979.1'004974—dc20   89-16970

Printed on acid-free, 250-year-life paper

Manufactured in the United States of America

ACKNOWLEDGMENTS

In the course of the 3 years during which I have been collecting data and writing this dissertation, a considerable number of persons have assisted me in one way or another, and some in multiple ways.

Academically, I wish to thank all those who have served on my dissertation committee or who agreed to attend the dissertation defense in place of a committee member. They include Joseph G. Jorgensen, Conrad P. Kottak, and Aram Yengoyan, who have served as co-chairmen, and Frank Livingstone, Roy Rappaport, and Maris Vinovskis.

My debt to these people goes beyond the dissertation. Dr. Joseph G. Jorgensen, my original committee chairman, agreed to see this project through to completion (and beyond) even though he has left the University of Michigan and is now Director of the Program in Comparative Culture at the University of California, Irvine. The encouragement that he has given me has played an important part in this dissertation ever getting written, and his conscientious and thorough criticisms and suggestions have been of the highest value to me in revision. It was by taking Joe's course on contemporary reservation and urban American Indians and his lucid account of how American Indians have come to occupy the position they do in the United States economy that my interest in American Indians was reawakened, and my intellectual debt to him is great.

Dr. Aram Yengoyan also read the draft of the dissertation, and his detailed comments and criticisms as well as his knowledge of demography and Australian Aborgines have been of great value to me. He is truly a friend of the student, and his constant urgings to wrap up this study have played an important part in its finally being completed.

Dr. Conrad P. Kottak also read and commented on the draft and took on the burden of co-charmanship. I especially appreciate his work in arranging the defense, as well as the interest that he has always shown in my work. I hope that eventually our plans to engage in research in Madagascar will come to pass.

These persons have always been available for consultation, criticism, and encouragement, and I could not have hoped for three more conscientious and stimulating advisors.

The National Science Foundation provided financial support for my research expenses through NSF Grant GS-30151.

I am grateful to the utmost to my wife, Nancy, who has helped in almost every way at every point in producing the dissertation. She has provided financial support so that I could carry out this research full time and has put up with several changes in topic and other delays. As dietitian at the Sacaton Hospital of the Indian Health Service on the Gila River Reservation, her knowledge of the reservation has helped me in the writing of the dissertation and her comments on and criticism of my ideas, both through discussions and reading the dissertation, has been most valuable to me. Somehow, even with a more than full-time job, she also found some time to help me tabulate census rolls and type all the tables and much of the text of the dissertation. If she ever decides to write a dissertation or book, the least I can do is as much for her.

My father, Dr. Arnold G. Meister, helped in many ways by assisting me with understanding mathematics, loan of his calculator, and helping me in drawing figures. Discussions with him on the content of this work proved extremely valuable. My mother, Bernice M. Meister, I thank for encouragement and support.

The collection of data took me to several libraries and government agencies, and I wish to collectively thank all persons who have helped me at those places. More specifically, the Hayden Library of Arizona State University provided me with full library privileges, without which this dissertation could not have been completed. I thank Mrs. Clarice Mondo,

Circulation, and several divisions of the library.

All personnel in the Documents Service were most helpful in locating government documents. Debbie Lantz and Hazel Wegener went beyond helping me to find books and brought a number of references to my attention as well as letting me know of any new publications received on American Indian population.

In the Arizona Room, I thank all the persons who made me feel at home (and in fact as one of the staff) while I spent several weeks tabulating microfilms of census rolls. Eleanor Ferrall, Assistant Librarian, saw that all my needs for publications and work space were taken care of. Susie Sato provided me with cookies and coffee to keep me going. Joan Gregory, a fellow anthropologist temporarily in exile provided most valuable discussions when I became weary of tabulating.

The Inter-Library Loan personnel diligently searched out a holder of the microfilms of Bureau of Indian Affairs census rolls, without which this study would have been much less accurate and useful. I wish to thank Fort Lewis College, possessor of microfilms of the rolls, for allowing me use of them through Inter-Library Loan.

Personnel at the Arizona State Library and Archives were also most helpful. Wilma Smallwood, Head Reference Librarian, immediately located any holding in the library and guided me to some obscure sources on Arizona Indian population, such as newspaper clippings. Carol Downey, Historical Records, also helped me locate publications. In the documents division, Mary Sanders, Federal Documents Librarian, Lowell Tausend, Federal Documents Assistant, and Annette Fry, Federal Documents Clerk, all promptly responded to my numerous and time-consuming requests. My time in the documents section of the Arizona State Library was not only valuable to this study, but to me as well, as I gained three new friends and have pleasant memories of hiking through some of the same places that are described in this work.

    I am indebted to the Division of Health Records and Statistics of the Arizona State Department of Health for almost all of the vital statistics data in this study. All persons I contacted were most helpful. Ramona Tager could not have been more diligent in providing me with the data I needed. Were it not for the work of her and the key punch staff on coding Indian vital statistics, it would have been much more difficult and time-consuming to obtain vital statistics by reservation. Don Schoen also was most helpful in providing me with what I needed. Discussions with both Ramona and Don about demography and Arizona vital statistics have been of great value to me amd they were always ready to answer any questions I had about the data. I thank Ramona for instructing me in use of two of the revisions of the International Classification of Diseases, and some of its pitfalls. Were all keepers of government data as conscientious as Ramona Tager, there would be no need for the Freedom of Information Act, because data would be available for legitimate purposes yet the right to privacy of individuals would be respected.

While I was tabulating a considerable amount of data at the Arizona State Health Department, Dr. R. Frank Reider, M.D., D.P.H., Assistant Commissioner, Epidemiology and Program Design, graciously allowed me to use some space in his office. His Secretary, Hilda Motta, kept me supplied with coffee and cookies as well as conversation when I became weary of work. I consider myself truly fortunate in having come to know Hilda, who always brightened my day.

Finally, Clinton M. Pattea of the Arizona Commission of Indian Affairs was most helpful in providing information and in allowing me to interview him in his capacity as Executive Secretary.

I should also mention others who made my work go easier, but who do not know it: Giacomo Puccini, Murice Ravel, Claude Debussy, Heitor Villa-Lobos, Ralph Vaughan Williams, Richard Wagner, and Georges Bizet. Also <u>Auriparus flaviceps</u>, the verdin, and most importantly, all Pima and Maricopa who have put up with census-taking so that there are some data to analyze.

This is as good a point as any to introduce a

note on plant and animal nomenclature. Both scientific and common names have been used as in the following sources:

    Trees: Little (1950)

    Cacti: Benson (1969)

    Other wild plants: Kearney and Peebles (1960)

    Domesticated Plants: Castetter and Bell (1942); Hedrick (1919)

    Native vertebrates: Lowe (1964).

TABLE OF CONTENTS

VOLUME I

ACKNOWLEDGMENTS iii

LIST OF TABLES xii

LIST OF ILLUSTRATIONS xix

LIST OF APPENDICES xx

LIST OF ABBREVIATIONS xxi

INTRODUCTION 1

CHAPTER ONE: THE ENVIRONMENT, EARLY HISTORY, AND CULTURE OF THE PIMA AND MARICOPA 19

CHAPTER TWO: FROM THE BEGINNINGS OF SUSTAINED ANGLO CONTACT THROUGH THE FIRST CENSUS (1846-58) 77

CHAPTER THREE: ESTABLISHMENT OF THE GILA RIVER INDIAN RESERVATION TO THE BEGINNING OF OFF-RESERVATION MIGRATION (1859-69) 109

CHAPTER FOUR: THE BEGINNING OF OFF-RESERVATION MIGRATION TO THE END OF SELF-SUFFICIENCY (1869-89) . . . 144

CHAPTER FIVE: FROM THE LOSS OF THE WHEAT CROP TO ALLOTMENT (1890-1910) 195

CHAPTER SIX: FROM ALLOTMENT THROUGH THE DEPRESSION (1910-40) 223

CHAPTER SEVEN: FROM THE SECOND WORLD WAR TO THE PRESENT (1940-74) 256

CHAPTER EIGHT: SUMMARY, COMPARISONS, DISCUSSION, AND CONCLUSIONS 288

VOLUME II

TABLES	349
FIGURES	507
REFERENCES	515
APPENDICES	547

LIST OF TABLES

1. Maricopa Total Population, 1846-58 349
2. Pima Total Population, 1846-58 350
3. Pima and Maricopa Combined Total Population, 1846-58 351
4. Pima and Maricopa Warrior and Non-Warrior Population, 1846-58 352
5. Pima Total Population, 1859-69 353
6. Pima and Maricopa Child-Woman Ratio, Mean Family Size and Persons per Occupied Dwelling, 1860 354
7. Maricopa Population by Village, Aged 0-9 in 1860 355
8. Pima and Maricopa Median Age by Village in 1860 356
9. Maricopa Total Population, 1859-69 357
10. Age Distribution of Pima Population by Sex in 1860 358
11. Age Distribution of Maricopa Population by Sex in 1860 360
12. Age-Specific Death Rates for Infants and Young Children of Selected Populations 362
13. Infant and Child Mortality for Selected Populations 363
14. Pima and Maricopa Population by Sex, 1859-68 . . 364
15. Pima Total Population, 1870-89 366
16. Maricopa Total Population, 1870-89 369
17. Pima and Maricopa Combined Total Population, 1870-89 371

18.	Pima and Maricopa Population for Selected Years	374
19.	Adjusted Pima and Maricopa Populations, 1870-90	375
20.	Pima and Maricopa Child-Woman Ratio	376
21.	Number of Pima-Maricopa Adults and Children	377
22.	Number of Pima and Maricopa Adults, Children, and Children of School Age by Geographic Area, 1887	378
23.	Pima and Maricopa Population by Sex, 1870-89	379
24.	1870 Village Population by Ethnic Group, Gila River Reservation	381
25.	Enumerated and Adjusted Population for Selected Years, 1890-1910	384
26.	Pima Total Population, 1890-1910	385
27.	Maricopa Total Population, 1890-1910	387
28.	Pima and Maricopa Combined Total Population, 1890-1910	389
29.	Geographic Distribution of Combined Pima and Maricopa Population	392
30.	Pima and Maricopa Median Age	393
31.	Pima and Maricopa Combined Population by Age and Cohort Survival Ratios, 1890 and 1895	394
32.	Population by Tribe by Reservation, 1911-50	396
33.	De Jure (Enrolled) Population by Sex by Reservation, 1911-37	398
34.	Vital Rates by Reservation, 1928-31 Combined Data	400
35.	Pima-Maricopa Adjusted De Jure Population by Reservation of Enrollment	401
36.	1970 Indian Population by Age, Gila River and Salt River Reservations	402
37.	Reported and Estimated Population by Reservation and Reported Indian Population for Maricopa and Pinal Counties, 1910-40	404

38. Population (All Races) of Gila River Indian Reservation by County, 1910 and 1920 405

39. Proportion of Estimated Enrolled Population Residing On-Reservation 406

40. Sex Ratio of Enrolled Population by Reservation, 1911-28 407

41. Sex Ratio and Probability by Reservation, Enrolled and On-Reservation Population, 1930-37 408

42. Sex Ratio and Probability for Indian Population, Maricopa and Pinal Counties 409

43. Enrolled (BIA) and Enumerated (Census Bureau) De Jure Pima-Maricopa Population by Age, 1930 . 410

44. Estimated Pima-Maricopa On-Reservation Population and Annual Growth Rate by Reservation, 1940-72 413

45. Gila River Reservation Reported Indian Population, 1950-74 414

46. Salt River Reservation Reported Indian Population, 1950-74 418

47. Indian Resident Deaths by Selected Age Groups, Gila River and Salt River-Fort McDowell Reservations, 1969-71 421

48. Seven Leading Classes of Death, Gila River-Salt River Indian Population, 1 April 1928-31 March 1931 and Indians on Reservations in Maricopa and Pinal Counties, 1959-61 422

49. Residence in 1955 of Nonwhite Persons 5 Years Old and Over Resident in 1960 at Gila River and Salt River-Fort McDowell Indian Reservations . 424

50. Place of Work, Gila River and Salt River-Fort McDowell Reservations Populations, 1970 426

51. Automobiles Available to Household, Gila River and Salt River-Fort McDowell Reservations, 1970 428

52. Pima and Maricopa Adjusted Population and Annual Growth Rate, 1700-1972 429

53. Pueblo Indian Population, 1600-1967 431

54.	Navajo Population, 1600-1973	432
55.	Ute Population, 1800-1968	433
56.	California Indian Population, 1770-1955	434
57.	Australian Aboriginal Population, 1788-1961 . . .	435
58.	Contact and Nadir Populations for Selected Groups of American Indians, and Australian Aborigines	436
59.	Comparison of Pima-Maricopa and Navajo Population Growth, 1800-1973	437
60.	Number of Pima and Maricopa Institutions or Traits Predicted from Population Size	438
61.	Age Distribution by Sex, Pima and Maricopa, 1860	439
62.	Calculation of Myers' Index, Pima and Maricopa, 1860	441
63.	Myers' Measure of Residual Heaping in Age Group Data, Pima and Maricopa, 1860	444
64.	United Nations Accuracy Test for Census Age Distributions Tabulated in Five-Year Groups, Pima and Maricopa, 1860	445
65.	Pima and Maricopa Combined Total Population, 1859-69	447
66.	Number of Deaths and Death Rates by Village, Pima and Maricopa, 1860	449
67.	Pima and Maricopa Population by Village and Percent Change since Previous Census, 1858, 1859, and 1860	450
68.	Pima and Maricopa Population by Village: 1860 Census as Reported by Different Sources	452
69.	Pima and Maricopa Village Population by Sex, 1859 and 1860	453
70.	Sex Ratios by Village and Probability of Occurrence by Chance, 1859 and 1860	455
71.	Children by Single Years of Age 0-10, Pima and Maricopa Combined, 1860	457

72. Selected Pima-Maricopa Birth Cohort Populations, Censuses of 1860, 1890, and 1895 458

73. Selected Pima-Maricopa Cohort Survival Ratios, Censuses of 1860, 1890, and 1895 459

74. Graduation of Pima and Maricopa Combined 1860 Census Population Age Data by Various Methods . 460

75. Geographic Distribution of Population by Ethnic Group in Various Reports of the Census of 1887 463

76. Pima and Maricopa Distribution by Age 0-9, 1890 and 1895 464

77. Age-Specific Sex Ratios, Pima and Maricopa Combined, 1890 and 1895 465

78. Pima Population by Sex, Sex Ratio, and Probability of Occurrence of Sex Ratio by Chance, 1890-1910 466

79. Pima and Maricopa Population by Village, 1894-96 468

80. Maricopa Population by Sex, Sex Ratio, and Probability of Occurrence of Sex Ratio by Chance, 1890-1910 470

81. Pima Distribution by Broad Age Groups, 1890, 1895, and 1910 471

82. Maricopa Distribution by Broad Age Groups, 1890, 1895, and 1910 472

83. Reservation ("At Jurisdiction") Population by Sex, 1930-37 473

84. Indian Population by Sex, Maricopa and Pinal Counties, 1930 and 1940 474

85. Gila River Pima and Maricopa De Jure (Enrolled) Population 475

86. Median Age of De Jure Pima-Maricopa Population . 476

87. Reported and Expected Births to Enrolled Population by Period of Occurrence 477

88. Reported and Expected Deaths in Enrolled Population by Period of Occurrence 479

89.	Leading Causes of Death by Reservation, 1 April 1928-31 March 1931	481
90.	1960 Gila River Indian Reservation Total Population Estimates Using School Enrollment Data	483
91.	Vital Rates at Assumed Degrees of Underenumeration, Pinal County Indian Population, 1960	484
92.	School Enrollment, Pima and Salt River Agencies, 1960-72	485
93.	1970 and 1972 Gila River Indian Reservation Total Population Estimates Using School Enrollment Data	487
94.	Vital Rates at Assumed Rates of Underenumeration, Gila River Reservation Indian Population, 1970	488
95.	1960 Salt River Indian Reservation Total Indian Population Estimates Using School Enrollment Data	489
96.	1964 Salt River Indian Reservation Total Indian Population Estimates Using School Enrollment Data	490
97.	Population by Sex by Reservation, 1950-70	491
98.	Salt River Indian Reservation Population by Age, 1964	493
99.	Nonwhite Population by Age, Salt River and Fort McDowell Indian Reservations, 1960	494
100.	Nonwhite Population by Age, Gila River Indian Reservation (Maricopa County Part), 1960	495
101.	Indian Population by Age, Pinal and Cochise Counties, 1960	496
102.	Indian Population by Age, Pima Indian Agency Area, 1950	497
103.	1970 Census Population in Complete Count and Sample Enumerations	498
104.	1970 Census Population by Sex in Complete Count and Sample Enumerations	499

105. 1970 Indian Population by Age, Gila River
     Reservation (20% Sample Data) 500

106. Indian Births to Residents 501

107. Deaths to Indian Residents 502

108. Reported Deaths to Indian Residents by Age, Gila
     River Indian Reservation, 1969-71 503

109. Deaths by Class, Indians Residing on Reservations
     in Maricopa and Pinal Counties 504

LIST OF ILLUSTRATIONS

1. Map of Arizona 507
2. Map of Pima-Maricopa Indian Reservations and Adjacent Area 508
3. Pima and Maricopa Population by Single Years of Age, 1860 509
4. Pima and Maricopa Population by Single Years of Age, 1890 510
5. Pima and Maricopa Population by Single Years of Age, 1895 511
6. Pima and Maricopa De Jure (Enrolled) Population by Single Years of Age, 1930 512
7. Indian Resident Births and Deaths, Pinal and Maricopa Counties, 1950-71 513
8. Population as Percent of Population at Contact . . 514

LIST OF APPENDICES

Appendix A. Demographic Definitions and Methods . . . 547

Appendix B. Evaluation of Accuracy of Population
             Data, 1859-69 566

Appendix C. Evaluation of Accuracy of Population
             Data, 1870-89 622

Appendix D. Evaluation of Accuracy of Population
             Data, 1890-1910 648

Appendix E. Evaluation of Accuracy of Population
             Data, 1910-40 682

Appendix F. Evaluation of Accuracy of Population
             Data, 1940-74 703

LIST OF ABBREVIATIONS

BIA	U.S. Bureau of Indian Affairs
ICD	International Classification of Diseases; see World Health Organization (1967, 1969)
RBIC	<u>Report of the Board of Indian Commissioners</u>
RCIA	<u>Report of the Commissioner of Indian Affairs</u>
RITINT	<u>Report on Indians Taxed and Indians Not Taxed</u>; see USOC (1894a)
RSI	<u>Report of the Secretary of the Interior</u>
USBC	U.S. Bureau of the Census
USDC-EDA	U.S. Department of Commerce, Economic Development Administration
USDI	U.S. Department of the Interior
USOC	U.S. Office of the Census
USOIA	U.S. Office of Indian Affairs
USOIA-AZ	U.S. Office of Indian Affairs, Arizona Superintendency
USOIA-NM	U.S. Office of Indian Affairs, New Mexico Superintendency
USOIA-PA	U.S. Office of Indian Affairs, Pima Agency
USPHS	U.S. Public Health Service

In the Library of Congress Main Catalog there are--under the heading Indians of North America-- 12 drawers of cards. Twelve drawers contain approximately 18,000 cards and of this number only 16 cards are under the subheading Statistics and 11 cards under the subheading Census. Yet under the subheadings Pottery and Legends there are 103 for the former and 314 for the latter. Under the subheadings Population and Income there are no cards at all. The only reason for this observation is to point out that a person with an interest in the American Indian can get much more information on subjects such as pottery and legends than he can on the income or educational attainment, land, etc., of the American Indian today.

>   Stephen Langone, A Statistical Profile of the Indian: The Lack of Numbers

INTRODUCTION

The present dearth of demographic studies of North American Indian populations is surprising, given the professions of comprehensiveness and holism which have accompanied many studies of Native Americans. In that until recently anthropologists were the predominant group engaged in studies of North American Indians, it is anthropologists who are largely responsible for the lack of North American Indian population studies. Moreover, the initial problem facing a researcher in North American Indian demography is not that data are nonexistent, but rather that the existing data, extending back over a century, remain largely unanalyzed. Most abundant for the latter half of the nineteenth century, these data are readily available to anyone who consults the series known as the <u>Report of the Commissioner of Indian Affairs</u> or the various and numerous publications of the Bureau (formerly Office) of the Census.

In my zeal to promote use of the large body of demographic data on American Indians, I do not intend to ignore the problems the data present. A major portion of this study is devoted to evaluating the accuracy of the demographic data on the Pima and Maricopa, the two ethnic groups which I have chosen for this study. However, there has long been a prejudice in anthropology against using data collected by government or other non-anthropological sources. This attitude has been especially successful in hindering demographic studies of American Indians, since few anthropologists had the time, money, or interest to undertake by themselves an enumeration of the ethnic group they were studying. Even those anthropologists who did take a census often ignored existing data which they knew were available. In her article <u>Census Data from Two Hopi Villages</u>, Pearl Beaglehole (1935) could have provided an important comparison of the consistency of her data with the government tribal roll of the two villages. Unfortunately, Beaglehole (1935:41) dismissed the government census data with prejudice rather than comparison: "I have not used the government census material because this, I think, is of more than doubtful accuracy." How are we (and she) to know if she does not compare the government data with her data?

Having heard and read so many unfavorable comments about demographic data on American Indians, I started this study intending to evaluate for accuracy all available demographic data for the Pima and Maricopa, and if the data warranted it, write a historical demographic study. Besides evaluating for accuracy all demographic data available to me for the Pima and Maricopa from 1846-1974, this study describes and explicates Pima and Maricopa population change and its components. This study is proof of my conviction that historical demographic studies of not only the Pima and Maricopa, but almost all North American Indian populations can be written, as the major data sources are largely the same. Conclusions from this study will be used to evaluate certain statements by anthropologists regarding population, especially of American Indians, as well as generalizations from demography. These topics, and others, mainly discussed in Chapter 8, include the following:

    1. Do demographic data support qualitative statements about population in ethnographies? For example, are statements concerning severity of warfare or gain of captives verified by the population data?

    2. Methodology. What methods are appropriate to evaluate the accuracy of demographic data on American Indians? What measures are appropriate to summarize these data? These methods should be applicable to any group of American Indians, since the major data sources are largely the same, and thus the same types of data are available, collected in relatively the same way.

    3. Assessment of the effects of European and Euro-American contact and policies on American Indian populations. Major factors of interest will be the introduction of previously unknown diseases, warfare, and the acquisition or destruction of Native American

resources, such as land, water, and the biota.

4. The effect of population size on sociocultural evolution. For American Indian populations after European contact, we will be more concerned with devolution than evolution, and can attempt to determine the extent of loss of cultural traits or social institutions that can be ascribed to population loss alone.

5. The present political and economic condition of American Indian reservations resembles the less developed countries in that Indian reservations are satellites providing resources and labor and consumers for the benefit of distant centers of political and economic power in a larger, ultimately global economy (Jorgensen 1971). These satellite societies are characterized by high unemployment and underemployment, low income, poor housing, little schooling, few public facilities, and an overall lack of autonomy in economic and political affairs. This is, of course, the state known as poverty, and such populations are not realizing their potential economically or demographically. In that population growth is related to social and economic factors, we may expect American Indian populations to resemble those of the less developed countries in measures such as birth rate, death rate, net increase, and age structure. At the same time, there are demographic, economic, and social variations among American Indian reservations. Thus, when enough demographic studies

of American Indian populations appear for comparisons to be made, cross-cultural studies based on them should provide some valid generalizations about American Indian population which can then be tested on a worldwide scale in order to arrive at generalizations about population regardless of geographic area. Data on American Indians are extremely valuable because they are much more comparable than data from a number of different countries, where not only will accuracy vary more, but the variables are often defined differently from one country to another.

6. Because of the importance to demography of the ideas of the demographic transition and Malthus, their veracity and utility will be examined through the conclusions of this study.

7. Finally, this study should have a practical value to persons outside anthropology and demography. From it may be assessed the effects of particular programs, especially health, and projections can be made using the information collected here. Although I had hoped to project Pima-Maricopa population, time limitations prevented doing so. It should be added as a historical note that an administering group will adopt different policies toward a subject group depending upon whether the administering group thinks the population of the subject group is increasing or decreasing. Thus, as long as whites believed that American Indians were headed for extinction, programs were considered stopgap measures to

make the last days of the native population easier to bear (e.g., rations, religion, and subsistence farming).

Previous Studies of North American Indian Demography

The large body of ethnographies of Native American cultures produced by anthropologists generally includes some population figures. Usually these are perfunctory statements of the population before European contact or at the time of European contact and the population at the time of research or writing. The "contemporary" figure is often obtained locally from the Bureau of Indian Affairs, and is usually stated without evaluation. The intention of most of these ethnographies was to describe the "aboriginal" culture, and previous studies of North American Indian population also reflect this interest. Many of these studies estimate only the aggregate precontact population for North America or for the Americas. Although earlier estimates exist, Mooney's (1928) paper, written 1908-9, is the starting point for most discussions of precontact Native North American populations. The virtue of Mooney's work is that it includes estimates by ethnic group, which make his North American total much more subject to verification than estimates of only the North American aggregate population. Several other well-known studies of precontact Native American population include Dobyns (1966), whose article was afforded Current Anthropology treatment, Kroeber (1934, 1939), Rosenblat (1954, 1967), Smith (1928), and Spinden (1928).

All these studies compare an estimated precontact population with the population at the date of writing or the nadir population. If one is attempting to determine the degree of depopulation as a result of contact, the nadir population is obviously superior to the population at the time of writing, which may or may not be at nadir. This point is emphasized by Dobyns (1966). However, to compare two population figures from distant points in time, without knowing what happened in between assumes a continuous decline (although not necessarily at a constant rate), and thus tells only a small part of the story. Consequently, to go beyond general statements regarding the degree of depopulation experienced by American Indians (and to tell of what has happened since a population hit its nadir), it is necessary to take a historical perspective. Very few studies have attempted to trace what happened in the years between the time of contact and nadir for a specific ethnic group, and only Rosenblat (1954) has attempted to do this for the Americas as an aggregate population.

Only with the development of ethnohistory has interest in American Indian population developed historical depth. Perhaps the earliest study of an American Indian population with a historical perspective is Wissler's work on Northern Plains Indians (Wissler 1936a, b, c). Another important early study is an account of the vital history of San Juan Pueblo by Aberle, Watkins, and Pitney (1940). However, to date, the only person who has devoted a lifetime of research to the study of American Indian population is Sherburne F. Cook. Cook not only has always taken a historical perspective in his studies of California and Mexican Indian population, but has always attempted to evaluate and use all available data.

California has probably been the area of most intensive research into American Indian population, at least north of Mexico. Controversy began when Merriam (1905) rejected Powers's (1877) higher estimates. Merriam's figures were reduced in turn by Kroeber (1925: 880-91, 1934:1). Cook (1943a:4, 194, 1964[1971:72]) has once again increased the estimate, but in his work, the assumptions are clearly stated and the estimates rest on firmer ground. Cook (1940, 1943e, 1955a, b, 1956, 1957) produced many publications on California Indian population, his magnum opus being the four volume study The Conflict between the California Indian and White Civilization (Cook 1943a, b, c, d). Even Cook, however, did not cover the Anglo period of California Indian population history as fully as the Hispanic period. Certainly, the fascination of Cook and his co-workers with Mexican Indian population is understandable (Borah and Cook 1960, 1963; Cook 1949a, b; Cook and Borah 1960,

1968, 1971, 1974; Cook and Simpson 1948), for not only is the subject interesting in itself, but there are also better data for Mexican Indian and mestizo populations, at least in central Mexico. A large part of Cook's energies were thus devoted to this subject.

Turning to the Southwestern United States, of which the Pima and Maricopa are a part, we find no S. F. Cook, but Johnston's (1966) study of Navajo population from contact to the early 1960s stands out as the major demographic work on any Southwestern United States Indian population. More recently, Kunitz (1973, 1974) has taken a historical perspective in examining differences in population growth between the Navajo and Hopi. Zubrow's (1974) recent study of the population of all New Mexico Pueblos is also historical, but is hampered by not evaluating the data for accuracy.

Turning to the Papago, practically nothing has been done in a historical perspective. A number of studies covering the period since the Second World War have appeared, largely based on the Papago Population Register (Hackenberg 1967). The most notable of these are Kelly (1963) and a special issue of Human Organization edited by Hackenberg (1972). Finally, the Hispanic period[1] of Pima-Maricopa population history has been covered by Dobyns (1962, 1963), Ezell (1961, 1963), and Sauer (1935). Other Southwestern Indians appear to remain unstudied in terms of historical demography, including the Apache.

Choice of Populations and Time Period

I originally intended to carry out a comparative study of the historical demography of all Native American ethnic groups in what became Arizona, but restricted to the Anglo period.[1] While I still intend to produce a monograph on each group and a comparative summary volume on the historical demography of Indians in Arizona, in order to complete the dissertation within a reasonable length of time, I found it necessary to restrict myself to two related groups of Indians, the Pima and Maricopa of south central Arizona. I chose the Pima and Maricopa because they offered certain advantages for a first study (on my part) of a Southwestern Indian population. Because the Pima and Maricopa were on one of the main routes to California, they were in earlier contact with Europeans and Euro-Americans, and thus there are historical records of greater depth for the Pima and Maricopa compared with most other Indian ethnic groups in Arizona. Moreover, the Pima and Maricopa, being mainly sedentary farmers, were easier to count than less sedentary groups such as the Navajo and Apache. Finally, the Pima and Maricopa were never involved in armed conflict with either the United States Army or white citizens. This should have promoted obtaining a more accurate count, compared with the Apache, whose relations with the United States soon became mutually hostile. I also felt that looking into the demography of two groups that had never been in armed conflict with the United States (and only briefly with Spain) would be useful to compare with other groups that had, in order to assess the effects of Euro-American contact on population when deaths from warfare were not a significant factor. This subject is covered more fully in Chapter 8.

The time period I have chosen for this study is 1846-1974. I omitted the Hispanic period for several reasons. First, data became much more abundant as the United States extended control over the Southwest. Besides this, Dobyns (1962, 1963), Ezell (1961, 1963), and Sauer (1935) have already examined published and archival sources from the Hispanic period and published the results of their investigations as they relate to population. I have summarized and synthesized their work in Chapter 1. Before the Hispanic period, 1400-1700 has been considered a problem in southern Arizona archaeology, as sites are few and some archaeologists are reluctant to wholeheartedly commit themselves to linking the Pima of 1700 to the Hohokam of before 1400.

I have included both the Pima and Maricopa because during the Anglo period they have lived adjacent to each other and thus have often been grouped together, especially in population figures, by whites unaware of the separate identities of the two groups. To this day, no one has studied how this distinction is maintained, and unfortunately, this subject cannot be considered here.

Much of the time, especially in the twentieth century, I was obliged to treat the Pima and Maricopa as a combined population since population figures were not available separately, or the enumerators were so hopelessly confused that their classifications were shown to be inconsistent from one census to the next. To the extent that it is possible, Pima and Maricopa are treated as separate populations.

Sources of Data Inaccuracy

There are a number of factors which cause inaccuracies in demographic data on the Pima and Maricopa. Obviously, with an estimate of population not based on census data, accuracy is merely a matter of how good a guess the estimator made. There are a number of ways to reduce error in estimates, one of which would be counting the number of houses in a village, multiplying by the number of villages, and multiplying again by the estimated mean household population.

In a census, other factors act to create inaccuracy. The population may not be completely enumerated or may be overenumerated. Enumerators may miss a particular area inhabited by the population, or underenumeration may be selective for certain age groups or by sex. There is really no incentive for American Indians to be counted in most cases; the most accurate censuses of American Indians are probably those taken in connection with rations, distributions of goods, annuity payments, and land allotments.

Cultural differences between the enumerator and the enumerated also create inaccuracy. Communication will be difficult if the enumerator and enumerated speak different languages. Even if an interpreter is available, the enumerator and enumerated may have different ideas as to what constitutes a family or household, as well as who is the head of the household. Furthermore, a person may have more than one name.

A further difficulty concerning the accuracy of American Indian population data is that many American Indian populations are small. The smaller the population is, the greater the variation expected by chance in the sex ratio and age distribution. This makes it difficult at times to determine when population data are inaccurate, and when extreme sex ratios or unusual age distributions are a result of small population size. Fortunately, there are some techniques to deal with this.

Consequently, evaluation of the accuracy of population data is very important to this, and any other study of American Indian population. In this study, I have evaluated for accuracy every total population figure and sex ratio, by tribe when available. Demographic terms and the methods of evaluation are defined and discussed in Appendix A, while the population figures, including age distributions, are evaluated in Appendices B-F. The evaluations of data accuracy have been put into appendices so as not to break up the main account of Pima-Maricopa population history, but ideally each appendix should be read in conjunction with the chapter it refers to, as this should answer many of the questions readers will have as to the accuracy of the data I have accepted, or how I have adjusted the data.

General Assumptions of This Study

Throughout this study, I have employed several general assumptions about data accuracy, which are stated here.

1. Qualitative statements about population are more accurate than quantitative statements. This is based on Cook (1956:81), who gives as an example that a person is more likely to remember village names than how many villages there were. In my case, I have used this assumption to test qualitative data against quantitative data for consistency, as will be discussed below.

2. A census is more amenable to evaluation, and hence establishing its degree of inaccuracy, than an estimate. By a census, I mean an enumeration of names of individuals on a form or schedule. This information is usually accompanied by data on sex, age, marital status, and sometimes occupation for each person. An estimate is a guess, or may have some quantitative basis, but at some point relies on a guess, such as of mean household size

where the number of houses and villages is known. A census, however, is based on an actual count of individuals, and one must only determine who has been left out or erroneously included. This is, of course, more difficult than it sounds, and can only be done well when tabulations by sex and age are available.

3. All censuses of the Pima and Maricopa reflect some underenumeration. I feel this to be so because there was no incentive for Pima and Maricopa to be counted except for land allotment in 1912-20, and I doubt that there were a significant number of double enrollments at that time. Furthermore, there were no extended periods of rations or distributions of goods. Moreover, the censuses were usually taken and always administered by non-Indians. Consequently, with the Pima and Maricopa, adjusting census data is a problem of determining the degree of underenumeration.

Plan of the Study

This introduction is intended to present the background and purposes of the study. Chapter 1 contains preliminary material on the environment, early history, and culture of the Pima and Maricopa, as well as an account of Pima and Maricopa population during the Hispanic period (ca. 1700-1846). Chapters 2-7 present and explicate evaluated data on Pima and Maricopa population. The data are mainly total population, sex distribution, annual growth rate, and when available, age distribution. Data on fertility, mortality, migration, and the net increase or decrease in population are quite scarce, but are included when available. In each of Chapters 2-7, I first present and discuss qualitative data on population. These are reports on factors such as epidemics, famines, floods, raids, and battles, among others. After that, I compare the trends suggested by the qualitative data with the trends determined from the evaluated quantitative data, discovering whether the trends of the two sets of data coincide, and if not why, and which set of data is incorrect.

There are a few exceptions to this plan. In Chapter 2, there are so few useful data, these being mainly estimates of wide range, that I present the unevaluated data in the chapter, dismiss most of it, accept the trends of the qualitative data, and retroject population figures from the first census taken in 1858. In Chapter 7, the opposite situation occurs. There are practically no qualitative data, so I use quantitative data to infer events. In each chapter, I generally present all of the qualitative data before comparing them with the qunatitative data for consistency, but if only one factor appears to have an overwhelming effect on some aspect of population (e.g., the child-woman ratio), I discuss the appropriate type of quantitative data in the qualitative data section.

Chapter 8 is composed of three parts. First, I summarize Pima-Maricopa total population dynamics from 1700-1972, highlighting the main factors responsible for population change. Second, I compare Pima-Maricopa population change with other American Indian populations and Australian Aborigines, as well as examine certain generalizations of anthropology and demography concerning population. Finally, I state my general conclusions resulting from this study.

Notes to Introduction

1. For the Pima and Maricopa, the Hispanic period refers to about 1700-1846, when Spain and Mexico claimed the territory, and the Anglo period refers to 1846 and after, when the United States claimed the territory. Neither Hispanic nor Anglo is an accurate term, since a fair number of the priests during the Hispanic period were in fact Germanic or from other European countries, while during the Anglo period many of the immigrants to Arizona were not descended from a specific group of residents of England, but from Europeans, Africans, Chinese, Japanese, and others. However, as these terms are widely in use and I can not think of any better, the terms are employed throughout the study. Ezell (1961) has referred to the Anglo period as the American period, which is no more inaccurate.

CHAPTER ONE

THE ENVIRONMENT, EARLY HISTORY, AND CULTURE
OF THE PIMA AND MARICOPA

This chapter is included for two purposes. First, it is a brief introduction to the Pima and Maricopa for persons unfamiliar with them. Second, it is a summary of Pima and Maricopa culture traits which could have had an influence on population, such as by affecting the birth rate, death rate, or migration rate. Thus the chapter does not attempt to exhaustively describe Pima and Maricopa culture, history, or environment. Persons desiring further information will find it necessary to consult the standard ethnographies. For the Pima, these are Castetter and Bell (1942), Curtin (1949), Ezell (1961), and Russell (1908). For the Maricopa, the major sources are Ezell (1963) and Spier (1933).

The Pima and Maricopa of the desert of southern Arizona (USA) are presently found in greatest numbers on two Indian reservations near Phoenix, the Gila River Indian Reservation and the Salt River Indian Reservation (see Figures 1 and 2 for these and other locations mentioned in the dissertation). Although Pima and Maricopa have resided adjacent to each other for over 100 years, they have maintained their separate identities. Many of the cultural differences described below no longer occur, but the Pima and Maricopa today maintain their respective identities linguistically and spatially, in spite of a probable greater than ten to one numerical advantage for the Pima. Linguistically, the Pima speak a language of the Uto-Aztecan family, while the Maricopa speak a language of the Yuman family (Voegelin and Voegelin 1966). Spatially, the Maricopa are found mainly in restricted areas on both the Gila River and Salt River Reservations. An undetermined number of Pima and Maricopa live off-reservation, presumably mainly in the Phoenix area, but also in other cities such as Tucson, Albuquerque, Los Angeles, San Francisco, Portland, Seattle, Chicago, and New York.

Environment

In that since 1846 the Pima and Maricopa core area of residence is covered by the present reservation boundaries, a description of the two reservations, allowing for certain changes since 1846, will suffice to describe the Pima-Maricopa environment throughout the period covered by this study.

The Gila River Indian Reservation is located south and southeast of Phoenix (Figure 2) and contains 371,933 acres (150,633 ha) (ACIA 1973-74). It is generally bisected by the Gila River, now a dry bed except after periods of heavy rain. The reservation consists largely of the valley of the Gila River, and is generally flat or of gentle slope, descending from about 1500 feet (450 m) where the river enters the reservation on the southeast to about 1000 feet (300 m) at the point where the river leaves the reservation on the northwest. A few isolated buttes interrupt the generally level valley floor, while the valley is bounded by several groups of mountains, mainly of low elevation. The Sierra Estrella forms the approximate western boundary of the reservation, rising to over 4500 feet (1375 m). This range is quite rugged, with several jagged peaks. On the north, South Mountain (formerly the Salt River Mountains) forms a barrier between the reservation and the Phoenix metropolitan area (population of Phoenix Urbanized Area 863,357 in 1970; USBC 1971b: Table 16). However, the Phoenix metropolitan area is beginning to spread around the east end of South Mountain toward the Gila River Reservation. South Mountain generally lies north of the reservation boundary and rises to a maximum height of about 2500 feet (760 m). At the northwest corner of the reservation, the Sierra Estrella and South Mountain come quite close to each other, creating a constriction in the river bed where underground river flow formerly came to the surface.

On the east side of the reservation are the Santan Mountains and the Sacaton Mountains, with summits of 2000-2500 feet (600-760 m). Here also the river flows between the mountains, and the constriction also produces an area where underground river flow formerly rose to the surface. Between the mountains and the river valley is a sloping area known as the bajada. It is in this area that the native vegetation attains its greatest abundance.

There are a number of communities on the Gila River Reservation, generally near the river bed. The government offices, both federal and local (the Gila River Indian Community) are located in Sacaton, which is off the major highways through the reservation. Interstate 10 crosses the reservation from northwest to southeast, and is the main route between Phoenix and Tucson as well as Los Angeles and the southern United States. Several state highways cross the reservation from north to south.

The Salt River Indian Reservation is located east of Phoenix and Scottsdale and north of Mesa. It contains 49,294 acres (19,964 ha). The Phoenix urban area has extended until it is adjacent to the reservation, and is beginning to extend onto the reservation through long-term leases from the governing body, the Salt River Pima-Maricopa Indian Community Council. The reservation is generally on the right (northwest) bank of the Salt River, but at one point, known as Lehi, extends across the river to include an area on the left bank. As with the Gila River, the Salt is normally dry as a result of several dams built upriver.

The southern and western parts of the reservation are generally flat or of gentle slope, while the northern and eastern parts are hilly or mountainous. Much of the reservation bordering the Phoenix metropolitan area is excellent irrigated farmland, and has been leased for this purpose. Along the river, elevation is generally 1100-1300 feet (335-400 m), while the mountains rise to approximately 2500 feet (760 m). There are two main areas of settlement on the Salt River Reservation. Population is scattered over the western part of the reservation, extending back from the right bank of the river. Lehi is the other important area of residence, on the left bank of the river.

The climate of both reservations is that of a subtropical desert. Some characterize it as a torrid desert climate (Kroeber 1939:Map 24) because of the hot summers. The mean annual temperature for Sacaton is 68.7° F (20.4° C), while the monthly mean temperature ranges from a low of 49.0° F (9.4° C) in January to a high of 89.5° F (32.0° C) in July. In Phoenix, the normal extremes in January are a high of 64° F (18° C) and a low of 35° F (1.7° C), while in July the normal daily extremes are a high of 105° F (40.6° C) and a low of 75° F (23.9° C). Thus, throughout the year there is a considerable range between the high and low temperature (Kangieser 1966:9, 10). The high temperatures are moderated considerably by low humidity. At all hours of the day, humidity is generally below 50%, and readings below 10% are not uncommon in the dry period in June.

Precipitation, as would be expected, is low. At Sacaton, the mean annual precipitation is 8.5 inches

(21.6 cm) (Kangieser 1966:9). Moreover, what rain falls is concentrated into several favored months. From July through September, 41% of the mean annual rainfall at Sacaton occurs, while an additional 30% falls from December through February. Thus, nearly 75% of the mean annual precipitation occurs during six months of the year. The two rainy periods differ in character, however. During the summer, rain falls in greater quantity during sometimes violent and abrupt thunderstorms. The storm will often produce only dust or wind, and one area may be saturated with rain while another several miles away remains dry. These storms, which originate in the Gulf of Mexico, are responsible for flash floods, but the storms are of brief duration, usually only several hours. During the winter, the storms originate in the Pacific Ocean. These storms are much less violent, usually without thunder, lightning, wind, and dust, and often produce an overcast lasting several days, as well as a gentle rain. Because of the biseasonality of rainfall, the desert of south and central Arizona is uniquely favored for maximum development of xerophytic plant life. To the west, along the Colorado River, summer precipitation is not as important, and annual rainfall is less than half that of the south and central Arizona desert. To the east, summer rainfall predominates, and while this is not always associated with lower annual rainfall, the biseasonal precipitation of the south and central Arizona desert permits the growth of ephemeral plants restricted to either winter or summer, but which will not grow in the opposite season (Jaeger 1957:63). It is in this south and central Arizona desert that cacti of the United States grow in greatest abundance and variety. In Sacaton, the growing season is 250 days (mean days between 32° F or 0° C lows), and Phoenix has 211 clear days a year, with 86% of possible sunshine (Kangieser 1966:7, 10). Thus, with plants adapted to take advantage of moisture when it is available, and only a short time when frosts occur, the desert area occupied by the Pima and Maricopa is far from a barren wasteland. Along the rivers, such as the Gila and Salt, there was a permanent supply of water capable of supporting deciduous trees such as the Fremont cottonwood (Populus fremontii) and Goodding willow (Salix gooddingi). Mesquite (Prosopis juliflora) thickets were also common along streams. More recently, the introduced salt cedar or French tamarisk (Tamarix gallica = T. pentandra) has replaced many of the native trees. A considerable variety of other vegetation, such as shrubs and grasses, also grew along permanent water courses.

On the desert plains away from the river, there is much less vegetation. The most common plant is the creosote bush (Larrea divaricata), a shrub of less than 10 feet (3 m). In areas of high salinity, creosote bush is replaced by saltbush (Atriplex spp.), but a few cacti and other plants are also found in the plains. On the bajada, the characteristic xerophytic vegetation attains its greatest development. There are a number of species of cacti, including the giant saguaro (Cereus giganteus) and several species of cholla (Opuntia spp.). Also common are the green-limbed palo verde tree (Cercidium microphyllum) and the spindly shrub known as ocotillo (Fouquieria splendens). Grasses and numerous ephemeral flowering plants are abundant after rain, at which time favored areas may be carpeted with plants. Thus, while food and water were not abundant and it was necessary to cope with hot summers, the Pima and Maricopa still possessed an area with significant wild plant resources, as well as a relatively secure permanent water supply in the Gila River (Ezell 1961:10).

Prehistory and Ethnohistory

Because the Pima and Maricopa lived some distance apart until slightly before the middle of the nineteenth century, it is necessary to discuss them separately. The consensus now appears to be that the Pima are a continuation of the Hohokam, a Mexican-influenced group that inhabited the valleys of the Gila, Salt, San Pedro, and Santa Cruz Rivers for about 1500 years. However, no site has been found definitely linking the Hohokam to the Pima (Gladwin et al. 1937:18; Haury 1945:212). The Hohokam were a rather complex culture of irrigation farmers of maize, beans, squash, and cotton who possessed some multistory buildings, ball courts related to but less developed than those found in Mexico, mounds, pottery, effigy stonework, acid etching, and copper bells obtained through trade links that extended deep into Mexico.

About 1700, when the Pima were first contacted by Spanish missionaries, they were reported to be living in farming villages at scattered points along the Gila River from the Casa Grande ruin to Gila Bend (Ezell 1961:9, 131). They were also exploiting a wider area for wild plants and animals. By 1846, although there were still as many, if not more, villages, the area of settlement had contracted to an area from 15 miles (24 km) below the Casa Grande ruin to a point 20 miles (32 km) farther down the river (Ezell 1961:15). This appears to have been a response to pressure from Apache and Yavapai raids and serious population losses from epidemics. Much of this contraction had apparently occurred by 1775 (Ezell 1961:109).

Besides the Pima along the Gila River, other Piman speakers lived along two tributaries of the Gila, the San Pedro and the Santa Cruz. These people, especially those along the San Pedro River, have often been referred to as Sobaipuri (Dobyns 1962:27, 1963:181; Ezell 1961:9). By 1762, the Sobaipuri had abandoned the San Pedro River Valley, some joining the Gila River Pima, others joining those along the Santa Cruz (Dobyns 1963:175; Ezell 1961:21). By 1800, the Santa Cruz River Valley was the home of only a few Pima or Sobaipuri, the others having died from epidemics or moved to the Gila River in response to Apache raids, epidemics, and possibly increased water salinity (Dobyns 1962:28; Ezell 1961:21; Winter 1973:72). Thus, from 1700-1800, the Pima experienced overall contraction of territory resulting from epidemics and Apache-Yavapai raids. The population data for this period are presented and discussed in the last section of this chapter.

The prehistoric origins of the Maricopa appear to lie along the lower Colorado and lower Gila Rivers. Their predecessors have been called the Hakataya or Patayan (J. Hayden 1970:92; Schroeder 1965, 1966; Wormington 1947: 167). However, the extent of area held by the Hakataya and the dates of occupation are in dispute. The Maricopa as they are known today (and as they were known in 1846) are made up of five constituent groups originating along the lower Colorado and lower Gila. Two of the component groups came from the lower Gila River, the Opa and Cocomaricopa (Ezell 1963:26; Spier 1933:ix-x, 37). The Opa lived farther upstream than the Cocomaricopa. As the Pima moved upstream along the Gila from 1700-1800, the Opa filled in the vacated area from Gila Bend to the Gila-Salt River confluence, while the Cocomaricopa occupied the area from Gila Bend downstream about halfway to the Colorado River. By 1825-30, the Opa occupied an area upstream from the Gila-Salt confluence, quite close to the Pima, while the Cocomaricopa occupied the area from the Gila-Salt confluence to no farther downstream than Gila Bend. By

1849, all Opa and Cocomaricopa resided above the Gila-Salt confluence (Ezell 1961:21) extending to a point 30 miles (48 km) upstream at Pima Butte (Spier 1933:x). Some time later, the territory became smaller through further movement upstream from the Gila-Salt confluence and no corresponding movement upstream at the eastern end (Pima Butte) because the Pima were immediately adjacent.

Three of the constituent groups of Maricopa originated on the lower Colorado River: the Halchidhoma, Kohuana, and Halyikwamai. The Halchidhoma, who had been at war with the Mohave and Quechan, also Yuman-speakers along the lower Colorado River, left the area below Parker in 1825-30, fleeing to an unknown location in what is now the Mexican state of Sonora. In 1833, some Halchidhoma moved to join the Opa-Cocomaricopa on the Gila River, and by 1838, all Halchidhoma had moved to the Gila River (Spier 1933:x, 12, 14, 40). The Kohuana and Halyikwamai, who first lived south, then north of the Quechan on the Colorado River, had in the meantime coalesced, and directly joined the Opa-Cocomaricopa-Halchidhoma in 1838-39 (Spier 1933:10, 16, 40). Although all these groups were known to the Spanish, by the time Anglos arrived in significant numbers, all five groups were living together and of largely similar culture, and Anglos did not or could not distinguish among them.

Before continuing, I must mention that Kaveltcadom is another name referring to certain Yuman-speakers of the lower Gila River. However, it is not clear whether the Kaveltcadom are to be considered the Cocomaricopa, as Ezell (1963:26) would prefer, or the Opa, as Spier (1933:37) contends. Ezell's (1963) careful evaluation of the Spanish documents on the Opa-Cocomaricopa lead me to believe that his identification is much more plausible.

European contact with the Pima began in 1539 with the Spanish priest Marcos de Niza, and continued in 1540 with the Coronado exploring expedition. These initial contacts were not sustained, and were relatively insignificant. Spanish contacts can only be briefly noted here and are covered in more detail in Bancroft (1888: 344-407) and Dobyns (1962). In 1694, the Jesuit priest Kino began relatively sustained contact with the Pima, mainly those along the Santa Cruz River. Throughout the eighteenth century contact was maintained sporadically by priests in missions at Bac, Tumacacori, and Guevavi on the Santa Cruz River (Dobyns 1962). No missions were established among the Gila River Pima, although priests occasionally visited them. After the Santa Cruz Pima revolted against the missions in 1751, Spanish troops were stationed in the area along with the returning priests. Eventually a few civilians moved in, and the Spanish settlements of Tucson and Tubac began. Overall, however, what became southern Arizona was never as important an area of Spanish settlement as California or the Rio Grande Valley of New Mexico.

After 1821, newly independent Mexico administered the territory which became Arizona, but there was in fact little Mexican government control over the area, being the frontier. Apache raiding has been credited with limiting both Spanish and Mexican expansion into the area. During the Mexican period (1821-53) Anglo trappers began to exploit the Gila River, especially for beaver, which were becoming scarce farther to the north. That Anglos could move relatively unhampered in Mexico emphasizes the limited control over the area exercised by the Mexican government and hence the considerable autonomy which the Pima and Maricopa still enjoyed during the first half of the nineteenth century. There were not even missionaries resident among the Pima and Maricopa at the time.

Sustained Anglo contact began in 1846 as a result of the war between the United States and Mexico. In that year, two United States military expeditions passed along the Gila River on their way to do battle in California. By the 1850s, the Gila River had become a well-traveled route for California gold seekers and other emigrants. These parties relied on the Pima and Maricopa villages as a place to rest in relative safety from Apache attack and replenish their supplies before the final stage to California. Consequently, even as late as the mid-nineteenth century, Pima-Maricopa territory was still a place to pass through for Anglos, and was not an objective in itself. Although the United States had acquired most of what became Arizona through the Treaty of Guadalupe Hidalgo of 1848, the main area of Pima-Maricopa settlement, the left or south bank of the Gila River, did not become part of the United States until 1853-54 as part of the Gadsden Purchase. Even so, Indian agents were not stationed among the Pima and Maricopa until 1858 (Hill 1972:79). From 1858 to 1869, a continual stream of special and regular Indian agents visited the Pima and Maricopa, few of them remaining there for any significant length of time. These early Indian agents were either in the United States Army or connected with private interests, such as mining or the Overland Mail, which began in 1858 and ran through Pima and Maricopa territory.

In 1859, a reservation along the Gila River was authorized and surveyed (Act of February 28, 1859, 11 Stat. 401; Mowry 1859a:357-59). The area reserved included Pima-Maricopa farmland, but did not recognize their use of the area surrounding the reservation for hunting and gathering. In 1861, federal officals and troops were withdrawn from what became Arizona because of the Civil War. Although in 1862 Union troops from California drove out Confederate forces from what became Arizona and established military posts (Lamar 1970:429), it was not until the establishment of the Territory of Arizona (from the Territory of New Mexico) in 1863 that Indian affairs were given much attention. The office of Superintendent of Indian Affairs for Arizona was created, under which served several Indian agents. An agent for the Pima and Maricopa was appointed 1 January 1864 (Poston 1864:158). Nevertheless, the tenure of agents continued to be brief, and the Pima and Maricopa were still relatively autonomous. However, by 1870, white settlement near the reservation and expropriation of Pima-Maricopa resources had begun, and with it government intervention to regulate relations between Indians and whites. At this time the Pima and Maricopa became integrated into the reservation system and lost their autonomy. The implications of these events on population will be shown in the chapters to follow.

Pima and Maricopa Culture as Related to Population

By the time that ethnographers first described the Pima (Russell 1908) and Maricopa (Spier 1933), over 200 years of Euro-American contact had already occurred. Thus it is difficult to determine how "aboriginal" certain traits are, or what they may have been like during precontact times. Even so, by using Spanish and Mexican documents, Ezell (1961) was able to trace changes in settlement pattern, agriculture, technology, and intergroup relations for the Pima during the Hispanic period.

Settlement Pattern

In precontact times, the Pima presumably lived in dispersed villages of houses 40-50 yards (37-46 m) apart, containing at most an extended family (Ezell 1961:

49). From 1700-1850, there was a trend toward more villages closer together, and thus a denser population (Ezell 1961:134). Houses were dome-shaped, and originally covered with reed mats. After the introduction of wheat during Spanish contact, houses were thatched with wheat straw and then covered with mud (Ezell 1961:49). The Pima settlement pattern contrasts with that of the Pueblo Indians, who live in multistory dwellings with little space between, producing a denser population.

The precontact Maricopa house, even at Gila River, was originally the large, multifamily dwelling characteristic of Yuman-speakers (Ezell 1961:113). Some time after moving adjacent to the Pima, the Maricopa adopted houses like the Pima, spaced about 50-70 yards (46-64 m) apart (Spier 1933:82). Both the Pima and Maricopa burned the house either after the death of its owner or whenever a death had occurred in it (Ezell 1961:110; Russell 1908:194; Spier 1933:304).

Food Supply

Both the Pima and Maricopa relied on domesticated and wild food sources.

Domesticated food sources

Domesticated plants comprised at least 50%-60% of the Pima diet in precontact times (Castetter and Bell 1942:56). Living in an arid climate, farming was made possible by irrigation, which was practiced by the Pima before

Spanish contact (although Winter 1973:69 disputes this, not very convincingly). The staple crops grown by the Pima were originally domesticated in Mexico, and included maize (Zea mays), tepary beans (Phaseolus acutifolius), squash (Cucurbita pepo and C. moschata), and cotton (Gossypium hopi), of which the seed was used for food and the fiber for cloth (Castetter and Bell 1942:56, 74, 98, 102, 103; Ezell 1961:32). The tepary bean is adapted to drought, and produces four times the yield of kidney beans (Phaseolus vulgaris) (Castetter and Bell 1942:193). Both kidney beans and lima beans (Phaseolus lunatus) were apparently introduced to the Pima by the Spanish (Castetter and Bell 1942:98).

Before Spanish contact, the Pima obtained two crops annually of maize, beans, and squash, and one of cotton (Castetter and Bell 1942:148, 179). The first crop was planted in March and April and harvested in late June, while the second crop was planted in July and harvested in October. Planting was done with digging sticks, the seed being deposited in a hill. Ideally, three to five irrigations should have been made, but often it was only possible to irrigate heavily before planting because of the unpredictability of river water during some years. The river was at its maximum flow in January to March and in August, but could fail in winter, and less often in summer, delaying or even eliminating planting (Castetter and Bell 1942:146, 151-52, 170). However, Ezell (1961:10) questions whether drought was ever a problem for the Pima, at least in the Hispanic period, having found no mention of drought in the Spanish and Mexican historical documents which refer to the Pima. He feels that reports of a dry river resulted from observing the river at areas of underground flow, while at the same time, farther downstream or upstream, the river was flowing above ground.

Crop pests apparently caused little trouble for the Pima in precontact times. The most serious problems appear to have been grasshoppers, rabbits, doves, gophers, ants, aphis, and corn smut (Castetter and Bell 1942:176).

The Maricopa grew the same crops as the Pima, but did not practice irrigation until 1850-55 (Spier 1933:58). They relied instead on seasonal floods from the Gila, after which crops were planted in the floodplain. As with the Pima, two crops were obtained: the first was planted and harvested about one month earlier than among the Pima, while the second was planted and harvested about the same times (Spier 1933:61). The digging stick was the main farm implement before Spanish contact (Spier 1933:62). According to Spier (1933:58), the Maricopa relied less on agriculture than the Colorado River Yuman-speakers, and hence less than the Pima as well. Even in 1850, Spier feels that wild plants were the bulk of the Maricopa diet.

As a result of European and Euro-American contact, several important Old World domesticates were introduced to the Pima and Maricopa. The most significant of these crops were introduced during the earlier period of Spanish contact. Wheat (<u>Triticum compactum</u>, <u>T. vulgare</u>) was the most important acquisition for both the Pima and Maricopa, and displaced maize as the grain grown for the first crop. Wheat may have arrived before the Spanish (Castetter and Bell 1942:74). By 1770, Ezell (1961:34) feels that wheat rivaled maize in importance, although Winter (1973:70), reading relatively the same sources, does not come to this conclusion. Certainly, by the 1870s wheat had eclipsed maize in importance, and as a result of subsequent events which eliminated the possibility of growing a second crop, wheat became predominant by the twentieth century. Even today, Pima breads and <u>tortillas</u> are made from wheat flour, which surprises persons familiar with Pueblo cuisine.

Wheat was planted any time from late November to early January or even February, depending upon the timing of the winter rains, and was harvested about one month earlier than the former first maize crop, in May or early June (Castetter and Bell 1942:50, 148). The earlier harvest of wheat as compared with maize was considered of great value by Castetter and Bell (1942:114), who report that supplies of maize, beans, and squash were usually exhausted by the time of the wheat harvest, and before the introduction of wheat the Pima had a lean period of about one month before the first maize crop was harvested.

Ezell (1961:135) postulates an increased population and population density resulting from the introduction of wheat. However, even after the introduction of wheat, the Maricopa apparently continued to rely mainly on wild plants until about 1850 (Spier 1933:58).

The other major introduced crop was melons, especially the watermelon (<u>Citrullus vulgaris</u>) (Ezell 1961:32; Spier 1933:58). The muskmelon (<u>Cucumis melo</u>) was introduced at the same time, again possibly before Spanish arrival in the area, but has never been as popular. The watermelon was valued for its keeping qualities, not possessed by the muskmelon, as watermelons could be stored until winter in the sand (Castetter and Bell 1942:118; Spier 1933:64). Watermelons were planted at the same time as squash, in late March or early April (Castetter and Bell 1942:148).

The ox-drawn wooden plow was also introduced during the Hispanic period (Castetter and Bell 1942:138-40), but did not become important until 1850-80 (Russell 1908:98), at which time the Pima and Maricopa began producing more grain to be sold to the increasing number of whites in the area and passing through. A shortage of cattle previously had prevented widespread adoption of the plow (Ezell 1961:47).

The Pima and Maricopa possessed no important domesticated animals which were used as food. It is assumed that the dog (<u>Canis familiaris</u>) was present among the Pima and Maricopa. Certain other animals were captured and kept, especially birds such as eagles (golden eagle, Aquila chrysaëtos; possibly bald eagle, Haliaeetus leucocephalus), red-tailed hawks (Buteo jamaicensis), and "Sonora doves" (probably the Inca dove, Scardafella inca). These birds were not eaten, but were kept for feathers or as pets.

The horse (Equus caballus) was the most important introduced domesticated animal. Horses were present among the Pima in some numbers by 1750, and were highly valued for transport, although they generally were not eaten (Ezell 1961:45). The Pima always felt short of horses, and much of their trade with the Spanish was directed toward obtaining them. Cattle (Bos taurus) however, were not obtained until about 1820-30, during the Mexican period of contact (Ezell 1961:46). They were used almost exclusively for plowing. Although they were too scarce to slaughter regularly for meat, after the death of a household head, any of the cattle which had not been given away were slaughtered and eaten. No use of dairy products was made by the Pima or Maricopa. The Pima kept some poultry, but neither sheep nor swine, although introduced, were readily adopted (Ezell 1961:46). There were a few mules and donkeys, but horses were much preferred (Ezell 1961:45; Russell 1908:86).

Wild food sources

Even though the Pima were irrigation farmers, wild plant foods formed an important part of the diet, and to a lesser degree, so did wild animal foods, especially fish. If Castetter and Bell (1942:56-57) are correct, 40%-50% of the precontact diet was from gathering, fishing, and hunting. Ezell (1961:41) feels that the proportion of wild foods was much lower, but would not deny that wild foods were utilized to a significant degree by the Pima. According to Spier (1933:48), even as late as 1850, the Maricopa still relied largely on wild food sources.

Both the Pima and Maricopa utilized essentially the same wild plants and animals for food. Wild plants appear to have been more important than wild animals. Three plants stand out as the predominant wild plant foods of the Pima and Maricopa. The pods and seeds of the mesquite (Prosopis juliflora) tree were valued as a food, and became a staple whenever crops failed (Castetter and Bell 1942:57; Spier 1933:50). The mesquite beans (which look somewhat like a wax bean) were ground into flour, which could be baked or mixed with liquid and drunk (Russell 1908:74-75). The second major wild plant food is the fruit of the saguaro cactus (Cereus giganteus). These columnar, branching cacti, which attain heights of over 35 feet (10 m), bear luscious, vivid red egg-shaped fruits around the tips of branches, often well above the height of a person. The Pima and Maricopa used long poles made from the woody skeleton of dead saguaros to knock loose the fruit. The fruit flesh can be eaten fresh as well as made into syrup or a wine of low alcohol content. The Pima and Maricopa also used the small seeds, which were ground to make flour (Castetter and Bell 1942:63; Spier 1933:50).

The third major wild plant food also came from a cactus, in this case the flower buds of several species of cholla cactus (<u>Opuntia fulgida</u>, O. acanthocarpa) (Castetter and Bell 1942:57, 63; Spier 1933:53). Besides the mesquite, the seeds and pods of several other leguminous trees were used by the Pima and Maricopa. These include the screwbean mesquite (<u>Prosopis pubescens</u>), ironwood tree (<u>Olneya tesota</u>), both species of palo verde trees (<u>Cercidium microphyllum</u>, C. floridum), and the catclaw acacia (<u>Acacia greggii</u>) (Castetter and Bell 1942:57, 64; Russell 1908:70, 75, 76; Spier 1933:53). Other cacti were also used, but less extensively than saguaro and cholla, such as the fruit of the local variety of prickly pear (<u>Opuntia engelmanni</u> - O. phaeacantha) and the pulp of a barrel cactus (<u>Ferocactus wislizenii</u>), which was boiled.

Several succulents were also highly regarded as food sources, but grew at higher elevations in territory controlled by the Apache and Yavapai, who were enemies of the Pima and Maricopa. Two plants, the agave or mescal (<u>Agave americana</u>) and the banana yucca (<u>Yucca bacatta</u>), became especially important to the Pima and Maricopa when crops were poor (Castetter and Bell 1942:64; Russell 1908: 70, 72; Spier 1933:55). Some agave was obtained from the Papago through trade (Russell 1908:70). The Pima also obtained acorns (<u>Quercus oblongifolia</u>, <u>Q. emoryi</u>) from the Papago (Castetter and Bell 1942:61; Russell 1908:77). Besides these, the Pima and Maricopa utilized a variety of seasonal greens and grass seeds (Ezell 1961:41), especially various species of saltbush (<u>Atriplex</u> spp.) and lambsquarter (<u>Chenopodium</u> sp.) (Russell 1908:69-78). It is interesting to note that neither the Pima nor Maricopa were reported to consume sunflower (<u>Helianthus annuus</u>) seeds (Castetter and Bell 1942:42; Spier 1933:56).

Wild animal foods were much less important than wild plant foods. However, fish perhaps were formerly a staple, especially two species or subspecies of chub (<u>Gila robusta</u>, <u>G. elegans</u> = <u>G. robusta elegans</u>) (Castetter and Bell 1942:57, 71; Ezell 1961:43; Spier 1933:48, 74, 75). Jackrabbits (<u>Lepus alleni</u>, <u>L. californicus</u>) and desert cottontail (<u>Sylvilagus audubonii</u>) were also hunted and eaten with some regularity (Castetter and Bell 1942:57; Ezell 1961:43; Russell 1908:82; Spier 1933:48, 65, 66). A seasonal delicacy were the larvae of the sphinx moth (<u>Celerio lineata</u>) which were boiled and eaten (Castetter and Bell 1942:68; Russell 1908:81; Spier 1933:73). Other wild animals were of distinctly minor importance, serving only to add variety to the diet when they were available.

These included an unnamed species of turtle eaten by the Maricopa (Spier 1933:65), Gambel quail (Lophortyx gambelii), including the eggs for the Pima but not the Maricopa (Castetter and Bell 1942:69; Russell 1908:80; Spier 1933: 65), white-winged doves (Zenadia asiatica), mourning doves (Zenaidura macroura), and an occasional turkey (Meleagris gallopavo) (Castetter and Bell 1942:68, 69; Spier 1933:65).

Other than rabbits, both the mule deer (Odocoileus hemionus) and white-tailed deer (Odocoileus virginianus) were the most important mammals taken (Castetter and Bell 1942:57, 64; Spier 1933:65). Bighorn sheep (Ovis canadensis) may have been an important precontact food, but this matter is in dispute (Castetter and Bell 1942: 57, 64; Ezell 1961:42; Spier 1933:65; Winter 1973:69). Briefly, other mammals taken in very small numbers included javelina or peccary (Pecari tajacu), beaver (Castor canadensis), pronghorn antelope (Antilocapra americana), and for the Pima but not the Maricopa, ground squirrels (Citellus spp.) and gophers (Thomomys bottae) (Castetter and Bell 1942:57, 64, 68; Russell 1908:80, 88; Spier 1933:57, 65, 71, 72). The Pima professed not to eat snakes or lizards (Russell 1908:88). The important point to observe is that the Pima and Maricopa were never so committed to agriculture that they ignored wild food sources nor forgot how to find and utilize them.

Space does not permit any detailed description of food preparation, but broiling, roasting, boiling, baking, and parching were all done, depending upon the type of food (Ezell 1961:40; Russell 1908:65, 68; Spier 1933:63, 64, 72, 77-80). Grain, flour, and some other foods were stored, such as squash and saguaro syrup. Ceremonial redistribution of food also occurred in order to equalize supplies among the various communities. A village short of food camped near a village with a surplus. The visitors learned the names of the inhabitants of the host village, and each visitor took the name of a host villager during the ceremony. Each visitor sang part of a song, mentioning his namesake, who then became the benefactor of the visitor, rewarding him or her with food. Within a year, the visitors were expected to return the favor (Russell 1908: 98). The Papago occasionally came to the Pima to carry out this ceremony, but the Pima claim that they seldom went to the less agricultural Papago for food. The Maricopa, apparently as a group, also maintained this relationship with the Pima, and after receiving food from the Pima, further redistributed what they had received until they were satisfied among themselves (Spier 1933: 229, 231).

Social Relations

Although all writers on the Pima and Maricopa stress their distinctiveness, even to the point of having known little of the culture of each other, nevertheless contact occurred between the two peoples (Ezell 1961:22;

Spier 1933:42). The food redistribution ceremony has been described above. Trade, warfare (as allies against common foes), games, and intermarriage also brought Pima and Maricopa together (Ezell 1961:22). However, Spier (1933: 44) feels that there were few marriages between Maricopa and other ethnic groups, including the Pima, until the twentieth century.

It is difficult to determine what precontact Pima social organization may have been like. The Pima could name five patrilineal clans grouped into moieties, but the clans and moieties appeared to have no function. Marriage could occur within or without the clan or moiety (Ezell 1961:102; Russell 1908:197); it was neither endogamous nor exogamous, but rather hologamous. The only proscribed marriages were between "uncles" and "nieces" and between "cousins" (Russell 1908:184). The household consisted at most of an extended family (Ezell 1961:99; Grossmann 1871a:415).

Maricopa social organization was somewhat more complex and operative, perhaps in part so that the smaller number of Maricopa could restrict access to their resources. The Maricopa had a number of patrilineal, named, exogamous, nonlocalized, totemic clans (Spier 1933:186). Other than clan exogamy, there were no prescribed or preferred marriage patterns. Other marriage proscriptions included known blood relatives of either parent in any clan, and probably parallel and cross-cousins. The Maricopa attempted to prevent women from marrying into clanless or matrilineal tribes, as the children would have no clan affiliation (Spier 1933:44).

Among the Pima and Maricopa, marriage occurred with little private and no public ceremony (Ezell 1961: 100; Grossmann 1871a:415; Spier 1933:219). Pima married shortly after puberty, and an unmarried adult was considered unusual or suspect (Ezell 1961:100; Russell 1908:184). Residence was virilocal, and uxorilocal residence was disparaged (Ezell 1961:100). Polygyny occurred, but was uncommon (Ezell 1961:99). The sororate, in which a widower marries the sister of his deceased wife, occurred (Russell 1908:184), but not the levirate, in which a widow marries the brother of her deceased husband. Widows were not supposed to remarry for a year (Grossmann 1871a:415).

Maricopa women married a few months after puberty, but apparently some held out for several years; Spier (1933:220) called males "youths" at their normal age of marriage. The Maricopa were also virilocal, living in patrilineal extended families, but following the birth of a second child, a man's son might move into a separate house. Uxorilocal residence was considered unusual (Spier 1933:222). Although uncommon, polygyny was permissible (Spier 1933:223). The sororate was common, and the levirate compulsory, but a year or two was expected before widows or widowers remarried (Spier 1933:223). As with the Pima, divorce was permitted with little ceremony, and occurred fairly frequently (Spier 1933:224). Finally, among the Maricopa, transvestism occurred, but was rare. The transvestite married a person of the same sex (Spier 1933:242).

The importance of social organization to demography is that marriage practices and other social traits can have an effect on population size through the birth rate, which may be regulated by factors such as age at marriage, the degree of polygynous marriages, enforced widowhood, and other factors which can reduce the potential reproductive span of a woman, or less importantly, a man.

Sex, Pregnancy, and Birth

Sexual practices can also affect the birth rate, depending upon at what ages and times sex is considered appropriate. Birth practices can affect both infant mortality rates and maternal mortality rates, and are thus discussed here. For the Pima, premarital sex was not permitted (Russell 1908:182). However, if marriage occurred shortly after puberty, this appears to be no real disadvantage to the birth rate. I could find no such information for the Maricopa. However, the Maricopa had a belief concerning sex and conception which could have had some influence on the birth rate. The Maricopa believed that if a person had an appropriate dream before coitus, conception was certain, but that if there was no such dream, then conception could not take place as a result of sexual intercourse (Spier 1933:238, 243). It is difficult to determine in which direction (perhaps both) this belief may have affected the birth rate. Assuming the Maricopa wanted children, which there is no reason to doubt, persons not having a proper dream for conception to take place might not engage in sexual intercourse, figuring that the effort was not worth it if conception could not occur. On the other hand, if a Maricopa woman did not want to be constantly pregnant, she might feel that she could engage in coitus when she did not have a dream favoring conception, and thus escape the consequences, when in fact she would not.

Apparently there were no periods or situations, other than menstrual periods, when sexual intercourse was prohibited among married Pima. The Maricopa prohibited coitus before mountain sheep hunting, but not before any other kind of hunting, nor apparently in any other situation, again save menstruation (Spier 1933:70).

Both the Pima and Maricopa preferred male children (Russell 1908:185; Spier 1933:70). A Maricopa wife could be divorced if the first child was a girl. Russell (1908: 185) reports that the Pima generally welcomed children, but Grossmann (1871a:415) claimed that Pima women did not desire children, since as widows they would have little chance of remarriage, and their husband's possessions would be destroyed at his death. However, this report is from a period of tremendous social and economic pressure on the Pima, and probably does not represent the usual situation.

Russell (1908:186) reports that death in childbirth occurred with some frequency among the Pima, and Spier (1933:311) felt that it was quite common among the Maricopa. Both the Pima and Maricopa practiced abortion under certain circumstances. Among the Pima, abortion occurred if a previous child had not yet been weaned, as well as in the case of illegitimate products of conception. These were aborted at 3 to 4 months. The process was mechanical, in which pressure was applied to the abdomen (Russell 1908:186). Abortions were reportedly successful, with but a few deaths remembered. Spier (1933:314) did not speculate on the frequency of abortion among the Maricopa before contact, but stated that it was "common enough" in 1929-32, when he carried out his study. A cloth was tied around the abdomen, an infusion taken, and the cloth was repeatedly tightened until the operation was successful. The reasons for Maricopa abortion were not given.

I could find no information on whether the Maricopa practiced infanticide, but the Pima did so under certain circumstances. Deformed children and children of white fathers were killed (Grossmann 1871a: 415; Russell 1908:185). Breastfeeding practices were poorly described. The Pima would suckle children up to 6 or 7 years (Russell 1908:186), but I am sure this represents the exception rather than the rule. Among the Maricopa, children began nursing on the fifth day after birth, consuming warm water the first four days (Spier 1933:312). Thus, the Pima and Maricopa did have some techniques for regulating the number of births, such as abortion, infanticide, and prolonged breastfeeding. At the same time, there were few restrictions on sexual relations within marriage, and hence we would expect a high precontact birth rate among the Pima and Maricopa. However, as there is little information on the intimate sexual practices of the Pima and Maricopa, such as whether they practiced coitus interruptus, fellatio, cunnilingus, and mutual oragenitalism, we do not know to what extent these practices may have affected the birth rate.

Sickness and Its Treatment

The Pima believed that other than physical injuries, sickness had a supernatural origin. Agents such as animals, the Apache, the sun, and mythological beings magically introduced foreign objects into the body, causing sickness. Symptoms were associated with specific sources, especially animals (Ezell 1961:80; Russell 1908: 260-61). Russell (1908:263) gives a list of symptoms and the animal believed responsible for causing them. The

Maricopa theory of disease was somewhat different. Sickness could occur from a number of causes, such as violence, natural causes, witchcraft, in which witches sent objects to enter a healthy body, and soul loss from dreaming of the dead and other bad omens (Spier 1933:280).

The Pima possessed three types of curers, two for personal illness and one for social illness. The "magicians" (Russell 1908:256) had power over crops, weather, and war, and did not treat individuals. "Medicine men" (Russell 1908:256) and women treated disease with plant remedies. Although the "medicine men" were held in low esteem, they claimed remedies for diabetes, impetigo, tuberculosis, stomach aches, rheumatism, hemorrhoids, ulcers, menstrual troubles, constipation, and headache (Curtin 1949:55, 62, 86, 96, 101). Russell (1908:79) lists twenty plants used for medicinal purposes by the Pima. "Examining physicians" (Russell 1908:256, 260) (i.e., shamans) cured illness by magical means, such as sucking wounds, singing songs, blowing smoke over the patient, or brushing the afflicted with the feather or tail of the animal causing the illness. Shamans were sometimes witches and could be killed when people agreed they had caused an epidemic (Ezell 1961:82).

Shamans were the only recognized class of medical practitioner among the Maricopa, while plant remedies were administered by the afflicted (Spier 1933:

289-90). The shaman gained curing power through a dream in which animal spirits taught how to cure (Spier 1933: 250). Treatment consisted of blowing, breathing, and sucking on the patient, and brushing with the hand to allay fever and pain and draw the illness from the body. However, no object was removed from the body as among the Pima (Spier 1933:280). The shaman did not ask for symptoms of the illness, and had up to four nights to effect a cure. As among the Pima, some shamans were bad and caused illness; they were killed when it was discovered. One of Spier's (1933:287) informants felt that since the federal government prevented the Maricopa from killing evil shamans, the Maricopa were declining in population. The importance of the killing of shamans by both the Pima and Maricopa is that if a source does not report an epidemic but mentions that shamans were killed, there probably was an epidemic.

As was the case with other American Indians, contact with Europeans introduced a number of diseases to which the Pima and Maricopa had little immunity. Among these were measles, smallpox, tuberculosis, certain other childhood diseases, and possibly syphilis (Ezell 1961:20). The initial epidemics of these diseases were devastating to all American Indian populations.

All sources praise the Pima and Maricopa for their sanitation practices. As described above, houses were located some distance from each other, thus dispersing areas of waste accumulation. Both the Pima and Maricopa burned a house where a death had occurred. Russell (1908: 199) praised Pima housekeeping practices, and Whittemore (1893:59) stated that houses were "kept so neatly as to astonish one." Russell (1908:199) reported that the Pima bathed daily. Thus, although there is no information on water sources and waste disposal, it would appear that sanitation was quite good among the Pima by the standards of the time.

Warfare

This subject is mostly covered in the following chapters, in which factors affecting population are considered in more detail and in relation to quantitative data. From precontact times until about 1740 or 1765, the Pima were subject to raids by the Apache and Yavapai, and reportedly carried out only defensive actions against them (Ezell 1961:117-18). After 1765, the Pima began to take the initiative against the Apache and Yavapai, so that eventually the Pima raided the Apache and Yavapai for captives which could be traded to the Spaniards for use as household servants. Spanish bounties on Apache scalps also encouraged intensification of Pima militarism. By 1850, the Pima had a standing army, with some men always in the field (Ezell 1961:118, 136). The Pima traded Apache and Yavapai captives for horses and material goods, while the Apache raided the Pima for horses.

Once the Maricopa coalesced on the middle Gila River adjacent to the Pima, they also faced Apache and Yavapai raids. However, a greater problem for the Maricopa was warfare with the Quechan and Mohave. This warfare also increased in intensity during the Hispanic period, and for the same reasons as among the Pima. In this case, each side raided the other for captives for trade with the Spanish (Dobyns et al. 1957; Spier 1933:188).

Neighboring Peoples

Figure 1 shows the approximate locations of ethnic groups bordering the Pima and Maricopa. To the south were the Papago, who also lived in a desert environment. The Pima and Papago are closely related, with many cultural similarities. Both peoples speak dialects of the same language. The main difference between the Pima and Papago was that the Papago did not practice irrigation agriculture, relying mainly on wild plants and animals, supplemented by some floodwater (ak chin) farming (Castetter and Bell 1942). The Papago traded salt, agave, and acorns to the Pima and also provided labor during the Pima grain harvest. In return they received grain. Pima-Papago intermarriage apparently occurred with some frequency.

To the east and northeast of the Pima and Maricopa were the Western Apache. The Apache occupied areas of higher elevation than the Pima and Maricopa, and relied primarily on hunting and gathering, but also engaged in some farming. In relation to the Pima, the Apache entered the Southwest quite late, perhaps even the fifteenth century A.D.

To the north of the Pima and Maricopa, in the mountains, were the Yavapai. The Yavapai are also speakers of a Yuman language, but were quite different from the River Yumans. They relied mainly on hunting and gathering. On their eastern boundary, they intermingled with the westernmost Western Apache (the Tonto Apache). Since the Yavapai were Yuman language speakers but in many ways resembled the Apache in terms of economy, they were often called Mohave-Apache or Yuma-Apache (or Apache-Mohave and Apache-Yuma) in the nineteenth century.

The River Yumans, as referred to in this study, consisted of the Mohave, Quechan or Yuma, Cocopa or Cocopah, and Maricopa. The Mohave and Quechan were enemies of the Maricopa, while the Cocopa were allies. North and south of the confluence of the Bill Williams River with the Colorado River lived the Mohave. The Quechan lived above and below the Gila-Colorado confluence and also upstream on the Gila for a short distance. The Cocopa lived on the delta of the Colorado River. All these groups relied on floodwater farming, as well as fish and mesquite beans. Before the nineteenth century, the Halchidhoma, Kohuana, and Halyikwamai also lived along the Colorado River, but they joined the Opa-Cocomaricopa on the Gila River as described above.

This sketch of the neighbors of the Pima and Maricopa has been much too brief, but other characteristics of these groups are described in following chapters as they are necessary.

Data Sources

Calendar Sticks

We are fortunate in that both the Pima and Maricopa possessed a formalized oral history, preserved by a few persons. These oral historians used long wooden rods as mnemonic devices to assist them in recounting history. Notches and other signs, without conventional meaning, were incised on the sticks. Each notch represented a year, while the other signs served to remind the reciter of other events. Some of these histories were recorded in the early twentieth century. For the Pima, the year began in June, with the saguaro fruit harvest. Thus the Pima year corresponds quite closely with the federal government fiscal year. This is fortunate, because many of the government reports on the Pima were written on a fiscal year basis. In this study, I have used hyphenated years (e.g., 1866-67) to refer to the fiscal year or calendar stick year; this means the last six months of 1866 and the first six months of 1867. When I am referring to two calendar years (such as 1866-67 for 1866 and 1867), it should be clear from the context.

Russell (1908:35) learned of the existence of five Pima calendar sticks, of which three were transcribed and appear in his monograph on the Pima (Russell 1908:38-66). He gives the names of only four of the keepers of the calendar sticks. They are: Ha´hali, or Juan Thomas of Blackwater village, covering 1851-52 to 1899-1900; Tco´kut Nak, or Owl Ear, of the Salt River Reservation, covering 1833-34 to 1900-1; Kâemâ-â, or Rattlesnake Head, or Joseph Head, of Gila Crossing, covering 1833-34 to 1901-2; and Benjamin Thompson of Casa Blanca, whose account was not transcribed. Hall (1907:413) mentions the existence of two Pima calendar sticks of residents at Salt River. No names are given. One was transcribed (Hall 1907:413-23), covering 1833-1901, but there are many lacunae. It is not clear whether the narrator is Tco´kut Nak, Russell's informant at Salt River. The Maricopa also kept calendar sticks, but Spier (1933:xii) found only one, kept by Manyan, a Kaveltcadom-Kohuana. The Maricopa calendar year began in March, so Spier, like Russell, uses hyphenated years to refer to a twelve month period. Manyan's account began in 1873-74, but he had taken over responsibility from an older man. Thus his complete account covers 1838 through 1922-23, but there are many gaps, with no entries from 1889-90 to 1918. Spier (1933:139-142) was only able to obtain accounts of years that had been marked with special symbols.

All told, the calendar sticks reported by Russell

appear to be quite accurate when compared with dates reported by white sources for the same events. The dating could be extended back from the time the calendar sticks were recorded, but the initial date of some of the calendar sticks was established by reference to a large meteor shower in 1833. Unfortunately, the dates in the accounts recorded by Hall and Spier are considerably less accurate, as comparison with the accounts in Russell shows. The accuracy of the calendar stick dates will be further examined in subsequent chapters. As told to Russell, Hall, and Spier, events were briefly described and usually concerned such things as attacks on or by Apache and Yavapai, epidemics, accidents, crops, and unusual weather, among others. This information is of great value in reconstructing the historical demography of the Pima and Maricopa by giving some idea of the population trends that may have been taking place, such as declines from epidemics and the severity of losses from raiding and warfare.

Government Sources

In general, one may say that the major government sources of population and historical data on the Pima and Maricopa are available for all Indian ethnic groups in the United States. The most easily accessible source, for both population data and historical information, is the Report of the Commissioner of Indian Affairs, either published separately or as part of the <u>Report of the Secretary of the Interior</u>. Before 1849, Indian affairs were administered through the War Department, and the report of that department must be consulted.

Until 1907, each annual report of the Commissioner of Indian Affairs contained a long appendix with reports by Indian agents located at or near the reservations or Indians they were to administer. It is these reports that form a continuing account of government relations with specific Indian groups, and often contain much descriptive information on Indians, including population data. These reports have been the major source of qualitative data in this study. Beginning with the 1861 report, Pima and Maricopa were included in a table of population and other social and economic data (such as amount and value of crops raised, acreage cultivated, value of property, and missionary activities). The table did not appear every year, and even when it did, the Pima and Maricopa were not always included or full information was not shown (such as by grouping the Pima and Maricopa together). Moreover, the table was titled in different ways, often within a short time period, usually beginning with "Statement," "Table," or "Statistics." Sometimes there was more than one table. In referring to a specific table from a specific year, I will use the first word of the title in quotation marks, and when referring to the whole series of the tables, I will refer to it as "Table."

More recently, the National Archives has published microfilm copies of documents concerning American Indians. For this study, the two most useful series containing historical information are National Archives Microfilm Publications M234 and M734. For the former, Rolls 3-28 (Arizona Superintendency, 1863-80), 546-51 (New Mexico Superintendency, 1849-63), and 669 (Pima Agency, 1859-61) cover the Pima and Maricopa. This publication contains letters received by the Office of Indian Affairs from 1824-81 from all sources. For publication M734, the entire eight rolls cover Arizona and have some information on the Pima and Maricopa. Similarly, Rolls 1-5 (1849-63) of National Archives Microfilm Publication T21, containing letters received by the New Mexico Superintendent of Indian Affairs, refer sporadically to the Pima.

For demographic purposes, a priceless resource is National Archives Microfilm Publication M595, Indian Census Rolls, 1888-1940. This publication reproduces the original schedules of rolls of Indians by ethnic group or administrative division. It contains individual names, and usually at a minimum, sex, age, and marital status, as well as relation to family head. The importance of individual entries is that the researcher can make tabulations of the data to suit his or her own purposes, rather than rely on a ready-made table which may not include the required cross-tabulations. Moreover, data accuracy can be evaluated in greater detail than when only tabulated data are available. Rolls 15, 344-61, and 460 contain census rolls of the Pima and Maricopa from 1887-1939, although a significant number of years either are without rolls or they are not included if they exist.

As expected, the Bureau (formerly Office) of the Census reports of decennial census enumerations are also valuable to this study. However, the categories and coverage of the Census is quite uneven. While the Pima and Maricopa were included in the 1860 Census, they were excluded from those of 1870 and 1880. What is surprising is not that Pima and Maricopa were excluded in 1870 and 1880, for all reservation Indians were, but that they were included in 1860. In 1890, the Census Bureau finally began including Indians on reservations ("Indians not taxed") and the Pima and Maricopa have been included in every census since then. However, only in 1890, 1910, 1930, and 1970 were Indians enumerated by ethnic group. Nor is it always possible to discover the population of a particular Indian reservation, since Bureau of the Census enumeration boundaries do not always coincide with reservation boundaries. The problems of using Bureau of the Census data on American Indians are explored in more detail in subsequent chapters. In this study, Census, as a proper noun, will always refer to a decennial census undertaken by the Office or Bureau of the Census, while census refers to any sort of census.

Besides the reports of Indian agents and

superintendents and census rolls, other government officials have provided some information about the Pima and Maricopa, including population. The 1846 military expedition under Kearny was chronicled by Emory (1848), Griffin (1943), and A. Johnston (1848), who in various capacities were members of the expedition. The 1846 Mormon Battalion march under Philip St. George Cooke was written up by Cooke (1848, 1849, 1878) as well as by several other expedition members (Bigler 1962; Tyler 1881). Two boundary survey teams spent some time among the Pima and Maricopa. The first, under John R. Bartlett (1854) was to establish the boundary described under the Treaty of Guadalupe Hidalgo, which set the Gila River as the international boundary. The second survey, under William Emory (1857-59) established the Gadsden Purchase boundary, which is the present boundary between the United States and Mexico in Arizona.

Other Sources

Although not listed here, a number of accounts by travelers, emigrants, retired government officials, missionaries, and ethnographers contain information on the Pima and Maricopa. They are mentioned in the text where appropriate.

Pima and Maricopa Population from Precontact Times to 1846

Having set the stage, we are now ready to look at

Pima and Maricopa demographic history. None of the data up to 1846 (or even to 1858) are based on a census as defined above, but are estimates made by non-Indians based on the number of persons seen in particular villages, or the size of the village estimated from the number of houses.

Pima

Several persons have attempted to estimate the precontact population. Sauer's (1935:5, Table I) is the most detailed estimate, with 1000 Pima along the Gila River, 1000 around Tumacacori on the Santa Cruz River, 4500 in the middle Santa Cruz River Valley, and 2500 in the San Pedro River Valley, for a total of 9000 in what became the United States. He also believes there were an additional 11,000 in what is now Mexico. Mooney (1928:22) produced a much lower estimate of 4600 in what became the United States, about half of Sauer's figure. Of this 4600, Mooney wrote that 4000 were Pima and 600 Sobaipuri. Ezell (1961:17) estimates only the precontact population along the Gila River at over 3000, several times higher than Sauer. Dobyns (1966:404) has commented on Sauer and Ezell in the light of his demographic research on the Santa Cruz River Pima. He feels that Sauer's Gila River estimate is too low, because Ezell's figure is higher. He also believes that Sauer's estimate for the Santa Cruz Valley precontact population (5500) is too low, for Dobyns estimates the same population in 1700, at the time of contact. Both Dobyns (1962:23) and Ezell (1961:16) assume that Pima population had been seriously depleted as a result of the transmission of epidemic diseases by populations between the Pima and the Spanish in Mexico. This is why Ezell gives over 3000 as his estimate of precontact Gila River Pima population, 3000 being his estimate for 1700. Although Dobyns (1966) does not comment on Mooney's estimate of 4600, we may assume that if he feels Sauer is too low, Mooney is too low. However, we may question whether Pima population in fact declined before the arrival of the Spanish in the area. Were the settlements between the Pima and the Spanish in Mexico large enough to support epidemics long enough so that epidemics could be transmitted? Visitors from other villages would have to be in a village with an epidemic at the right time in order to carry the disease to their home village, and they in turn would have to be visited by a village closer to the Pima, and so on. Still, with over 150 years from the time the Spanish first entered Mexico to the time of first sustained contact with the Pima, such a situation could have occurred. However, before the arrival of the Spanish in Mexico, trade relations between the Hohokam and Mexico had been broken. The scarcity of Hohokam archaeological sites after A.D. 1400 (Haury 1974:18; Winter 1973:67) suggests that if there was a Pima population decline before 1700, it came before the arrival of the Spanish in Mexico in 1519. Interestingly, Ezell (1963a:65) feels that diseases introduced by the Spanish, but which traveled ahead of them, led to Hohokam decline. As the population became too small to carry on the more elaborate aspects of the culture, such as ball games and luxury trade, only the elements connected with survival were retained and the frills were forgotten. This is asserted to have produced the differences between the Pima and the Hohokam. However, if Hohokam decline occurred by 1400, this would not have been the case. Whenever exotic European diseases may have been first introduced to the Pima, we would expect the maximum decline immediately after their introduction, before the population had gained immunity to them. Later epidemics would not produce as great a degree of depopulation as the population developed immunity (Polgar 1964:202-3). As shown below, Pima losses from disease were considerable in the eighteenth century, and I doubt that the losses would have been so severe had the Pima already been exposed to the introduced diseases. Thus I feel that the greatest losses occurred after Spanish contact, and that the discrepancy between the precontact population and that of 1700 was not nearly as great as Dobyns and Ezell would prefer. However, I make no estimate of precontact population because of the many unknowns involved.

Pima population about 1700

Population figures for about 1700 are from the reports of Jesuit missionaries in the area (Dobyns 1962: 3; Ezell 1961:16). For Gila River, Ezell (1961:17) derives a range of 2230-3050 Pima from several estimates by different observers. He prefers the larger estimate, rounded to 3000 (Ezell 1961:131). Estimates for the Santa Cruz and San Pedro Pima-Sobaipuri have been published by Dobyns (1962, 1963). There were 3100 Pima in the lower Santa Cruz Valley and 1300-2400 in the middle Santa Cruz Valley in 1700 (Dobyns 1962:27, 1963: 180-81). Dobyns prefers the higher estimate for the middle Santa Cruz Pima, making a total of 5500 in the Santa Cruz Valley. This essentially agrees with an estimate of 6000 in 1697 made by the Jesuit priest Kino (Dobyns 1962:27). The Pima population of the San Pedro Valley is less clear. In one place, Dobyns (1962:28) estimates there were 800 Sobaipuri there, while elsewhere (Dobyns 1963:180) he raises the figure to 1930. If we accept Ezell's estimate for the Gila River, Dobyns's for the Santa Cruz, and both of his figures for the San Pedro, we obtain an estimated 9300-10,430 Pima in about 1700, within what became the United States. I will round this figure to 10,000, which hopefully is not as suspiciously round as it looks. It is interesting that a larger population (5500) apparently lived along the Santa Cruz River than the Gila River (3000). The Gila is a larger river, the Santa Cruz being a reluctant tributary of it. It is possible that the Jesuit missionaries obtained more accurate information for the Santa Cruz Pima, since they had missions among them, but not among the Gila River Pima. Thus the Gila River population may have been higher. However, if the estimate for Gila River is fairly accurate, and if the Santa Cruz Valley could support fewer persons, then the Jesuits may have overestimated the number of Pima along the Santa Cruz. Moreover, Dobyns's (1963: 180-81) figure of 2400 for the middle Santa Cruz is not based on Spanish records but rather his inferences about the expected number and size of villages in relation to other Pima areas. Since arguments can be made in both directions, accepting 10,000 as an estimate is about all that can be done at present.

Pima population about 1775

Between 1700 and 1775, population data on the Pima are extremely few and incomplete. Around 1775, a new wave of Spanish contact began, with regular visits to the Gila River Pima, and population figures became more abundant, mainly from Anza, who traveled through Pima and Maricopa territory on his way to California, and the Franciscan priest Gàrcés. Ezell (1961:18) prefers an estimate of 2500 Gila River Pima for 1775, although the Spanish reports support a range from 1500 to 5270, since not every observer estimated the population of every village. It is unclear whether Ezell thinks a population increase or decrease occurred from 1700-75 at Gila River. On one hand, he feels that the estimate of 2500 in 1775 includes all villages, while the estimate of 3000 in 1700 may exclude some villages. Moreover, he feels that an increase from 3000 in 1700 to 5270 in 1775 would be too high a growth rate for the time. However, this is an annual growth rate of 0.75%, which seems possible to me if Gila River were receiving refugees from the Santa Cruz and San Pedro, as occurred at the time. Ezell finally accepts a figure for 1775 that is lower than 5270 because he feels that Pima went from village to village in 1775 and thus were counted more than once, while in 1700 they were encountering the Spanish and horses for the first time and were intimidated, hiding in their villages. Moreover, Garcés, who is responsible for the estimate of 2500, had visited all Pima villages, while Anza, whose figures would be necessary to produce a higher estimate, had not. Based on this reasoning, Ezell (1961:17) states that Pima population declined from 1700-75. Contradicting this, however, Ezell (1961:17) also says that

> During the Hispanic period the size of Gila Pima population increased despite their exposure to new and epidemic diseases. <u>This increase was going on even in the first part of the contact</u> [emphasis mine], although this may be simply a function of more and better reports.

Further on, Ezell (1961:19) also says that "The greater range of estimates in this period [around 1775] than in Jesuit times [around 1700] is less important than the fact that <u>the figures are larger</u> [emphasis mine]." Thus I am not convinced that the Gila River population of 1775 was lower than that of 1700. Ezell's statements are contradictory. However, I feel that the population at Gila River in 1700 did decline somewhat from epidemics, but that there was a net increase at Gila River from refugees from the Santa Cruz and San Pedro. Thus, overall the Pima population decreased from 1700-75, while at Gila River it increased. In order to determine the possibility of this, we must examine the 1775 population data for the Santa Cruz and San Pedro Pima-Sobaipuri. Once again, the figures originate with Spanish priests and other officials, and have been gathered and interpreted by Dobyns (1962, 1963). Unfortunately, no figures are available for 1775, but in 1783, only 356 Indians were living in the lower Santa Cruz Valley, including some refugees from the San Pedro and some Papago (Dobyns 1962:27). In the middle Santa Cruz Valley, there were less than 100 Indians in 1800, again including some Sobaipuri refugees from the San Pedro and some Papago (Dobyns 1963:181). In 1801, only 61 Pima remained in the lower Santa Cruz Valley (Dobyns 1962:28). The upper Santa Cruz Valley, as defined by Dobyns (1963:163) is now in Mexico and does not concern us here.

From 1700-1801, the Pima population of the lower Santa Cruz River Valley experienced a decline from 3100 to

61 persons, or a depopulation ratio of 51:1 (Dobyns 1962: 28). The middle Santa Cruz Valley went from 2400 persons in 1700 to 100 in 1800, the latter figure including some San Pedro Sobaipuri and Papago, for a depopulation ratio of over 24:1 (Dobyns 1963:181). This is a tremendous population loss, but not impossible. However, while Dobyns emphasizes epidemics as the most important factor in the depopulation of the Santa Cruz River Valley, I think that the population also was being depleted by migration to Gila River. Dobyns provides the description of how this occurred, even though he uses it to apply to concentration of settlements in the Santa Cruz Valley and migration from the San Pedro Valley. Before Dobyns, most writers had emphasized Apache raiding as the main factor leading to population decline among Southwestern Indians (Dobyns 1962:23, 1963:164). Dobyns lowers Apache raiding to a factor of lesser importance. There appears to have been a minimum community size which was necessary for successful resistance against Apache attacks, probably 200-300, but certainly above 100 (Dobyns 1962:176-79). As the San Pedro and Santa Cruz Pima villages were decimated through epidemics resulting from Spanish contact, the survivors were congregated in ever fewer villages in order to maintain the minimum number required for defense. The Gila River Pima apparently faced the same situation, for their territory along the Gila contracted from 1700-75 with the abandonment of the area below the Gila-Salt

confluence (Ezell 1961:109). Moreover, raiding was increasing in intensity under Spanish influence, having a direct effect on population decline rather than just forcing the congregation of population into fewer villages. It thus seems very likely that some of the survivors from the San Pedro and Santa Cruz Valleys went to the Gila River Pima villages. This is reported by Ezell (1961:21) who mentioned the San Pedro Sobaipuri moving to the Santa Cruz and Gila in 1762, and by Dobyns (1963:28), who tells of

> . . . the escape of some residents of the lower Santa Cruz River Valley to the Gila River settlements, rather than to the missions. Thus, all the depopulation was not mortality, inasmuch as the Gila River amalgamated populace also managed to survive and increase during the 19th century.

A further factor complicating the population dynamics of the Santa Cruz Valley was the Pima revolt of 1751. This was confined primarily to the Santa Cruz Valley, where the Spanish missions were located. Although casualties were few, the Santa Cruz Pima abandoned the Santa Cruz River Valley, and after they returned 6 months later, there were fewer villages (Dobyns 1962:7, 8, 10). The most likely destination of the Santa Cruz Pima during their absence was the Gila River Pima villages, and some may have remained there after the others returned to the Santa Cruz.

Returning to Ezell's estimates of the 1775 Gila River Pima population, and in the light of events taking place in the Santa Cruz River Valley, I do not consider it unlikely that as many as 5270 persons were residing in Gila River Pima villages. Interpolating for 1775 from the population of the Santa Cruz Valley given by Dobyns for 1700 and 1800, there were perhaps as many as 650 Indians, including San Pedro Sobaipuri refugees and some Papago, residing in the Santa Cruz Valley. However, by 1775, most of the losses from epidemics should have occurred, especially since a severe measles epidemic had broken out in 1770 (Ezell 1961:20). Thus, the Santa Cruz Valley population in 1775 was probably closer to the approximately 450 reported for 1800 than the 650 obtained from my interpolation. I thus feel that 5300 is a fairly good estimate of Pima population, including the Santa Cruz Valley survivors, in 1775. By 1775 all San Pedro Sobaipuri had died out or migrated to the Santa Cruz or Gila. Strictly speaking, 5270 Gila River Pima plus perhaps 500 Santa Cruz Valley Pima would give 5770 Pima altogether, but some of the Santa Cruz Valley population was Papago, so I have reduced the figure to 5300.

Pima population about 1846

According to Ezell (1961:134), there were 4000 Pima around 1850. This is an increase of 1500 over his estimate for 1775, or a 0.6% annual growth rate. If my estimate of 5300 for 1775 is accepted, the Pima would have experienced a population decrease from 1775-1846.

However, as will be shown in the next chapter, by retrojecting from the first census of the Pima, taken in 1858, I estimate a population of 5875 in 1846. Ezell's estimate was based on a later census (1859) which reported fewer Pima. Thus, from 1775-1846 I estimate that Pima population increased from 5300 to 5875, or 0.1% annually, which is less than the growth rate for Ezell's figures, and more credible in a population that was no longer receiving migrants, and subject to high infant, child, maternal, and even general mortality. Ezell attributes the 1775-1846 population growth to increased immunity to disease and the introduction of wheat. He calls this an "uncommon situation" (Ezell 1961:19) in American Indian demography, and it was indeed, but as will be shown in Chapter 8, it was not unique.

To summarize, my best estimates are 10,000 Pima in 1700 in what became the United States and 5300 in 1775, for an annual growth rate of -0.85%. By 1846, there were 5875 Pima, all living on the Gila River, a 0.15% annual growth rate from 1775.

Maricopa

Precontact population and
population about 1700

Mooney (1928:22) estimated the 1680 population of the Maricopa constituent groups at 10,000, consisting of 2000 "Maricopa" (Opa and Cocomaricopa), 3000 Halchidhoma,

3000 Kohuana, and 2000 Halyikwamai. It is difficult to evaluate these figures, and given later Maricopa population the estimate may be high. Nevertheless, the Maricopa were subject to forces not faced by the Pima, and thus 10,000 "Maricopa" in 1680 or 1700 seems not impossible. Mooney does not disclose the source of his estimates, but they are presumably based on early Spanish explorations, and thus would refer to the beginnings of contact, rather than precontact times. Consequently, I will accept the figures as referring to 1700.

Maricopa population about
1775 and 1846

Estimates centering on 1775 are somewhat more numerous. Spier (1933:3) felt that there were 3000-3500 Opa, Cocomaricopa, and Halchidhoma at that time, although Garcés and others felt there may have been as many as 5000-5500 (Spier 1933:3). The figure chosen by Spier represents a middle course, as Anza first estimated less than 3000 Opa and Cocomaricopa, and later reduced this to only 1000 (Spier 1933:3). Kroeber (1925:796, 799, 883) felt that there were only 1000 Halchidhoma at the time. Thus there appear to have been perhaps 3500 "Maricopa" in 1775 (at least 2000 Opa, Cocomaricopa, and Halchidhoma, plus I estimate 1500 Halyikwamai and Kohuana) and perhaps as many as 4500 or at most 5000. For present purposes, I will estimate 4000 in 1775, which I feel is a middle course.

By 1846, again retrojecting from the first census of Maricopa in 1858, there were probably only 1000 Maricopa remaining. Although very short on support, I estimate the Maricopa declined from no more than 10,000 in 1700 to around 4000 in 1775, with an annual growth rate of -1.22%. In 1846, the Maricopa population had further decreased to 1000, for a -1.95% annual growth rate from 1775. Comparing the Pima with the Maricopa, the differences are immediately obvious. The Maricopa suffered a continuous population decline from 1700-1846, while the Pima lost population from 1700-75, but increased from 1775-1846. From 1700-75, the Maricopa decrease appears to have been proportionally greater than the Pima. The Maricopa had to contend with the same epidemics and raids as the Pima, but additionally, the Maricopa were involved in intensive warfare with the Quechan and Mohave. Furthermore, the Maricopa did not adopt wheat as early as the Pima. As with the Pima, Maricopa movement away from the Colorado River and up the Gila River, resulting in a greatly contracted territory, was the result of depopulation through epidemics, and unlike the Pima, warfare and loss of captives. As villages fell below the size necessary for defense against armed attack, coalescence into a smaller number of villages occurred. At the same time, to minimize the effects of armed attack, the Maricopa attempted to increase the distance between themselves and their enemies, and allied themselves with the Pima.

With this account of Pima and Maricopa population history during the Hispanic period, we are ready to enter the Anglo period.

CHAPTER TWO

FROM THE BEGINNINGS OF SUSTAINED ANGLO CONTACT

THROUGH THE FIRST CENSUS (1846-58)

Factors Affecting Pima Population

Epidemics.

There are no reliable direct reports of epidemics among the Pima from 1846-58. For 1846, the calendar stick recorded in Hall (1907:418) reported:

> . . . the Pimas had a vomiting sickness, and half of them died. The villages were deserted on account of this sickness, the Indians flying where they thought the sickness could not find them. . . . If they lived two days of the sickness, there was some hope of their getting well, but not otherwise.
> Part of the Pimas came over to Salt River, where many died.

However, the Hall calendar stick reports a number of distinctive events at dates occurring about two years later than do the calendar sticks reported by Russell (1908: 38-66). In this case, Russell (1908:42-43) reports a similar event for 1844-45:

> A plague swept through all the tribes during this year. Those stricken with it usually died within twenty-four hours, but if they recovered, they were well again in three days. From 4 to 10 died each day. . . . the Gila villagers fled into the desert. The (cholera or) tcoko vihâsik, "black vomit," . . . as it was called, brought all the medicine-men not in the best repute under suspicion.

Because the calendar stick records in Russell are

more complete, I will accept those dates as more accurate. Thus, the epidemics described above from Hall and Russell are assumed to be the same, and occurred before 1846. If the epidemic were raging in 1846, the Kearny and Cooke expeditions should have witnessed or heard of it. On the contrary, all those who went through the Pima and Maricopa villages in 1846 commented on the good health of the Pima and Maricopa (see General Health, below). Perhaps the epidemic even occurred before 1844-45, as the Pima seem not to have mentioned a recently past epidemic to any of the 1846 expeditions.

However, a further complication in establishing the date of this epidemic is the report by Bartlett's Maricopa guide of a sickness among the Maricopa in 1850 very similar to that described above in Russell and Hall (Bartlett 1854(2):241):

> July 3d [1852]. . . . Near by [on the Salt River] we saw the remains of several Indian wigwams, some of which seemed to have been but recently occupied. Francisco [the Maricopa guide] told us they were used by his people and the Pimos [sic] when they came here to fish. He also told us that two years before, when the cholera appeared among them, they abandoned their dwellings on the Gila and came here to escape the pestilence.

Whether this hypothetical 1850 epidemic affected the Pima as well as the Maricopa is ambiguous in the above quotation. The Pima lived adjacent to the Maricopa and joined with them in war alliances, dances, and games (Spier 1933:163, 232, 335). I would assume that any epidemic among the Maricopa would thus have spread to the Pima, but the calendar sticks recorded by Russell do not report an epidemic in or close to 1850. The calendar stick in Hall does not report an epidemic in 1852. Unfortunately, there is no entry for 1850 in Hall (1907:420). Emory, who was in the Pima villages in 1846 and 1855, estimated 3000-10,000 Pima in 1846 and 5000-10,000 in 1855 (Emory 1848:86, 1857-59(1):95), a higher minimum figure after the supposed epidemic of 1850. Had he heard of an epidemic, he probably would have reduced his estimate. Most likely, the epidemic of 1850 mentioned by Bartlett's Maricopa guide was in fact that of 1844-45.

My conclusion, then, is that there was an epidemic, perhaps of cholera or yellow fever,[1] no later than 1844-45. It was over by the time the Kearny expedition went through the Pima and Maricopa villages in October 1846, and hence occurred before the period included in this study. The evidence fails to convincingly support the existence of an epidemic in 1850 among the Maricopa, much less the Pima. From 1846 through 1858 the Pima thus seem to have been free from devastating epidemics.

General Health

All who commented on health mention the excellent physical condition of the Pima. Perhaps the most valid of these assessments was made in 1846 by Griffin (1943:34), an assistant surgeon with the Kearny expedition: " . . . nor have I seen a man, woman, or child who presented the appearance of ill health." Other favorable comments on Pima health can be found in Bigler (1962:37), Cooke (1849: 50, 1878:161), Eccleston (1950:210), and Tyler (1881:234).

Food Supply

The only reference to a food shortage among the Pima was for 1851 by Stratton (1859:59). It reportedly resulted from Apache raiding. However, the next year Bartlett (1854(2):264) mentioned sufficient food for the Pima. This factor can not adequately be assessed for this period, but was apparently not very significant as no records of extended drought or food shortages appear in the calendar sticks. Such a situation surely would have been remembered, as it was for later periods.

Hostile Encounters with Apache and Yavapai

Raiding of Pima settlements by Apache and Yavapai was apparently continual (Gifford 1932:182, 1936:303; Goodwin 1942:87), the main objective being acquisition of horses (Basso 1971:80; Gifford 1932:184). Russell (1908: 200-201) estimated that every three to four days small parties of five to ten Apache stole stock and attacked solitary persons, such as those out in their fields. Larger war parties appeared once or twice a month. Russell did not estimate casualties from these raids. Most encounters were thus carried out by small groups of Apache and Yavapai, and casualties from any one raid were probably few. The calendar sticks, which noted several attacks almost every year, never mention large numbers of persons being killed; at most, a party out gathering plants (Hall 1907:418-20; Russell 1908:43-47). But over a decade, small losses from each incident would add up to a considerable number of deaths.

The Pima, sometimes in sizable groups, went out after the Apache and Yavapai. These parties are mentioned in the calendar sticks (Russell 1908:32-54) and by Apache (Goodwin 1942:87) and Yavapai (Gifford 1936:304, 355-38) informants. Pima deaths were reported by these sources, but it is difficult to determine how frequent the raids were and how many died during them.

Raiding of and by Apache and Yavapai must have been a recurrent cause of death, especially for males, who were more exposed than females to attack by both defending Pima settlements and making up offensive war parties. I propose that this factor, along with assumed high infant, child, and maternal mortality, acted to maintain Pima population at a relatively stable size. The number of deaths from raiding probably was not large enough at this time to result in population decrease among the Pima.

Warfare with River Yumans

The Pima became involved in battles with certain Yuman-speaking peoples of the Colorado River, principally the Quechan, as allies of the Maricopa (Russell 1908:200; Spier 1933:42). When the Maricopa were attacked by the

Quechan and their allies, the Pima came to the assistance of the Maricopa (Hall 1907:418, 420; Russell 1908:44, 46). Apparently the Pima as a group did not participate in journeys to the Colorado River to battle the Quechan and their allies, as no mention of this is made in the calendar stick records. A single Pima accompanied the Maricopa on a war expedition to Quechan territory in 1841-42. The Quechan were surprised to see a Pima there (Russell 1908:41). One of Spier's informants (1933:174) emphatically denied that Pima went to fight the Quechan.

Reported battles with Quechan in Maricopa territory, involving Pima, are:

1846 (2 battles) (Hall 1907:418), as usual, misdated, and corresponding to battles in 1842-44 mentioned in the calendar sticks in Russell (1908:41-42), thus outside the period of this study

1850-51 at what is now known as Gila Crossing (Bartlett 1854(2):221; Hall 1907:420; Russell 1908:44-45; Spier 1933:161) in which Russell reported no Pima were killed, and

1857 at Maricopa Wells (Russell 1908:46; Spier 1933:140) for which Russell reported one Pima death

The 1857 battle ended warfare between the Maricopa and Quechan, and thus the Pima and Quechan as well.

Consequently, as the calendar sticks mention few Pima deaths from battles with the Quechan, it would appear that these battles had little effect on Pima population.

Captives

Most war captives taken by the Pima were Apache and Yavapai women and children, along with a few Quechan. They were usually sold to Mexicans (Russell 1908:197). The Apache took Pima, especially children, as captives (Goodwin 1942:87), but claim not to have sold them to other Indian groups (Goodwin 1942:96), nor to Mexicans, with whom relations were hostile (Goodwin 1942:93-94).

The Yavapai occasionally took a woman or child captive (Corbusier 1886:331), but apparently preferred to kill those they raided. Those taken captive apparently also were often killed (Gifford 1936:304).

The Quechan presumably acquired but a few Pima as captives because their focus of attack was on the Maricopa.

Captives taken by the Pima seem to have been relatively few, and but a few Pima seem to have been taken captive. Lacking any quantitative information, I will assume that Pima population suffered a small and insignificant net loss through taking of captives, since the Pima sold many of their captives.

Intermarriage

Pima sometimes married Apache and Yavapai women taken as captives (Gifford 1932:182; Russell 1908:186). Pima children captured by the Apache sometimes later married among the Apache (Goodwin 1942:87), but the Yavapai claim to have never married Pima (Gifford 1932:182).

Most Pima intermarriage was with the Papago, who often came to help the Pima harvest crops (Russell 1908:185). Some marriage with Maricopa took place, but its extent is unclear. Writing in a later period, Russell (1908:186) and Spier (1933:44-45) speak of Pima-Maricopa intermarriage as uncommon, but Bailey, who was on the scene in 1858, wrote that the Pima and Maricopa had intermarried so much that they were no longer distinct (Bailey 1858:202). This probably reflected more Bailey's inability to distinguish Pima from Maricopa than the actual situation.

Although lacking any figures, I will assume that intermarriage was a source of neither population gain nor loss for the Pima. If other tribes married Pima captives, the Pima married their captives. Intermarriage with Papago was two-way. Pima men may have married more Maricopa women than Maricopa men did Pima women, as will be discussed below, but the number of such marriages was probably not so great as to significantly affect Pima population size.

Taken together, all the above factors lead me to expect a fairly stable population among the Pima for the period 1846-58.

Factors Affecting Maricopa Population

Epidemics

I have already established that no devastating epidemics seem to have occurred during this period among the Pima. Consequently, there were most likely no epidemics among the Maricopa from 1846-58.

General Health

There are no adverse comments on the health of the Maricopa for this period. In fact, Emory (1848:87) felt that compared to the Pima, the Maricopa were "superior in intelligence and personal appearance." Griffin (1943:34) described Maricopa men as larger, more muscular, and taller than the Pima, but he considered Maricopa women fat.

Food Situation

No food shortages were mentioned for the Maricopa during this period. Presumably they also suffered a poor year in 1851 (Stratton 1859:59).

Warfare with River Yumans

Because the Maricopa were involved more deeply than the Pima in warfare with the Quechan and their Mohave allies (Forbes 1965:80; Forde 1931:162-63; Spier 1933:160-61; Stewart 1947:431), as well as because of the nature of Yuman warfare, I feel that Maricopa population loss through warfare was much greater than for the Pima.

When the Quechan and Mohave attacked the Maricopa, the Pima had to be called for assistance. By the time the Pima arrived, the Maricopa already had faced their enemies unaided (Spier 1933:173-74). Thus, compared to the Pima, the Maricopa faced greater risk of death from attacks.

The Pima were only defensive allies of the Maricopa.

In Maricopa-initiated attacks on the Quechan, the Maricopa were on their own or had the aid of only their Cocopah allies (Spier 1933:42). In this case again, the Maricopa faced greater risk of death than the Pima.

As with Apache-Yavapai attacks on the Pima and Maricopa, most hostile encounters between Maricopa and Quechan-Mohave were raids carried out by small parties (Forde 1931:164). For the Mohave, Stewart (1947:439) estimated the size of such groups as ten to twelve persons. Whenever a sufficient number of warriors felt like going on a raid, they went out.

Unlike Apache-Yavapai attacks, the Maricopa and Quechan-Mohave engaged in "massed battles in which a large proportion of their able-bodied men took part" (Spier 1933: 154). For the Mohave, Stewart (1947:439) was told that such large war parties contained forty to fifty persons, but that over one hundred occasionally had been mobilized. For the Quechan, Forde (1931:162) mentions memorable battles of 200-300 persons. By my estimates, these larger groups could well have included all able-bodied (and some not so able-bodied) Maricopa males.

While Stewart (1947:439) reports that these large battles occurred no more than once or twice a year, losses could be considerable, even allowing for exaggeration, and especially considering the small size of the Maricopa population. According to Stewart (1947:441), five to seven persons were killed in an "average" battle, while fifteen dead would be considered a great loss. Battles could go on for as long as 48 hours, and ended only with annihilation of one side (Forde 1931:162; Spier 1933:169; Stewart 1947:439) or mutual exhaustion (Stewart 1947:439). Spier (1933:169) mentions a battle in which "Of the several hundred engaged on each side, not more than a handful of the vanquished . . . were left after the battle."

Although even large war parties attempted to surprise their intended victims, formal battles were sometimes arranged, especially if the enemy had been discovered before attacking. In this case they were met by the defenders in battle formation (Forde 1931:162; Stewart 1947:441). Battles ended in a mêlée fought at close quarters, with clubs, rather than at a distance with bow and arrow. Because of this close combat, casualties were probably greater than if primarily bow and arrow had been used.[2]

Moreover, the Maricopa were at a disadvantage against the Quechan because the Maricopa used only short clubs, while the Quechan used longer clubs and long staves (Spier 1933:171). Again, the Maricopa faced a greater risk of death.

Most Maricopa war casualties seem to have been males, exclusively so in attacks on the Quechan. However, while adult males fought on foot, a cavalry composed of old men and boys backed up the foot soldiers (Spier 1933:171). The mounted males charged through the opposing forces, and some on both sides were usually killed. Consequently, Maricopa males of all ages died in battle, a factor which will be of importance in the analysis of population data below.

According to Spier (1933:169), "It does not seem possible, that . . . this type of warfare could have gone on from time immemorial. All of the nations would sooner or later have been reduced in numbers or wholly exterminated." He goes on to note, however, that the Halchidhoma, Kohuana, and Halyikwamai were largely reduced in numbers while living on the Colorado River, and came to live with the original or "true" Maricopa on the Gila River. The original Maricopa in turn were living lower on the Gila River and moved upstream, closer to the Pima, before the period covered by this study (Ezell 1963; Spier 1933:2).

It seems likely that the Maricopa, like the Halchidhoma, Kohuana, and Halyikwamai, would have been more greatly reduced in numbers except for three distinguishing factors:

1. Their long distance from the Quechan and Mohave, who also fought the nearer Cocopah (and before their move, the Halchidhoma, Kohuana, and Halyikwamai)

2. The accretion to the Maricopa of the remnant Halchidhoma, Kohuana, and Halyikwamai, and most important

3. The protection of the numerically larger Pima, which helped limit the number of Maricopa war casualties.

When battles occurred, Maricopa losses were significant, but not to the extent of the genocide the Halchidhoma, Kohuana, and Halyikwamai experienced. But that the Maricopa alone were at a numerical (and perhaps tactical) advantage facing the Quechan and Mohave seems apparent from both their move up the Gila River to be simultaneously closer to Pima protection while increasing their distance from the Quechan, and the Maricopa use of males of all ages in raids on the Quechan.[3]

Only three major Maricopa-River Yuman battles can be dated as occurring from 1846-58. Hall's (1907:418) calendar stick record of two 1846 battles is similar to Russell's (1908:41-42) entries for 1842-45, in which three battles occurred. I will assume these battles took place before 1846.

For 1848, Couts (1961:69), Spier (1933:140),[4] and Sweeny (1956:63) recorded that the Maricopa went out against the Quechan. Spier (1933:61) believes this is actually an 1851 battle that took place in Maricopa territory, but Couts was among the Maricopa when the surviving warriors returned from the Colorado River. Sweeny obtained his information in 1850 from a Quechan. Thus it would appear that Spier's informant (1933:161, 173) and the Maricopa calendar stick (Spier 1933:140) are correct as to the date and location of this battle, and Spier is incorrect in equating it with an 1851 battle in Maricopa territory.

According to Couts (1961:64), the Maricopa lost

thirty-one in the 1848 battle. Spier's informant (1933: 173) claimed heavy losses, but gave no number. Sweeny's informant (1956:63) claimed to have killed eleven Maricopa by himself.

In 1851, the Quechan came to fight the Maricopa, and the Maricopa lost. Bartlett (1854(2):221), Hall (1907: 420), Russell (1908:44-45), and Whipple (1852:599) all report this battle. The attack was a surprise and several Maricopa were killed immediately. Whipple (1852:599), who was in the Pima and Maricopa villages in 1852, mentioned large Maricopa losses, but no complete count of casualties appears in any of the reports. The calendar stick recorded by Hall (1907:420), as usual, reports the event occurring later, in 1852.

Another large battle in which the Quechan attacked the Maricopa took place in 1857. This battle has been reported by both whites and the Pima and Maricopa calendar sticks. According to the calendar sticks (Russell 1908:46-47; Spier 1933:140), Quechan and Mohave killed some Maricopa women who were gathering mesquite beans, burned a Maricopa village, and then battled the Maricopa and Pima. No statement of battle deaths was made.

Browne (1871:102-4), who visited the Pima and Maricopa villages in 1864, obtained his information from a white who witnessed the battle, but only stated Quechan losses. Mowry (1857:296-305) also wrote about the battle, exaggeratedly claiming 1500 warriors on each side, composed of Quechan, Mohave, Yavapai, Tonto Apache, and one or two Diegueño vs. Maricopa, Pima, and Papago. He did not state the number of Maricopa killed, but also mentioned that the Quechan killed some Maricopa women and children and burned houses. The Quechan were defeated and apparently never again returned to make war on the Maricopa.

All the above factors lead to the conclusion that Maricopa-River Yuman warfare was most likely producing a Maricopa population decline, although the lack of numerical statements impairs the possibility of accurately assessing how great a population loss occurred.

Hostile Encounters with Apache and Yavapai

The Yavapai are mentioned as Quechan allies by Mowry (1857:300) and Spier (1933:160). However, most encounters with Yavapai were probably similar to those with Apache: small groups raided Maricopa settlements, just as they did the Pima (Gifford 1932:182; Spier 1933: 161). Maricopa also went out against the Apache and Yavapai, but the size of war parties was considerably smaller than those which faced the Quechan in big battles (Spier 1933:175). As a cause of Maricopa deaths, Apache and Yavapai raiding and Maricopa actions against them probably had the same effect as among the Pima. However, when combined with deaths from battles with Quechan and Mohave, this further increased the total number of deaths from warfare, and may have somewhat weakened the Maricopa for showdowns with the Quechan-Mohave.

Captives

Sources of information on captives are conflicting. In general, it appears that captives taken by the Maricopa were not a significant source of population growth, but that taking of Maricopa by Quechan and Mohave may have reduced Maricopa population. Spier (1933:182) states that captives were not an objective of warfare because the Maricopa feared contamination by the enemy. Captives were nevertheless taken and sold to Mexicans. Dobyns et al. (1957:48), Forbes (1965:78, 288), and Forde (1931:168-69) believe that captives, to be sold as domestics, were an objective of warfare. Since all seem to agree that captives, whether an objective of war or not, were usually sold, captives should not have been a source of population replenishment or increase for the Maricopa at this time.

The extent to which Quechan and Mohave taking of Maricopa captives reduced Maricopa population cannot adequately be assessed, as there are no figures on captives taken or held. Dobyns et al. (1957:48) and Forbes (1965: 78, 288) mention an annual "fair" during the 1840s in the Pima and Maricopa villages in which captives were sold or traded to Mexicans, apparently from Tucson. How many captives were offered each year is not known; use of the term "fair" makes it sound like a large event. Thus there may have been a considerable trade in captives. If so, I presume that primarily women and children, to serve as domestics, would have been taken. This would have further reduced population size, as the Maricopa reportedly sold most of their captives. The relative influences on the sex ratio of male battle deaths and loss of women and children through capture is discussed below. The taking of children as captives was especially important, as this reduced Maricopa numbers before these persons could reproduce.

Occasionally, Yavapai women were taken as captives by the Maricopa (Gifford 1932:182), and perhaps not all were sold as slaves (Spier 1933:183). The Yavapai claim they took no Maricopa captives, preferring to kill their enemies (Gifford 1932:182), but may have occasionally made an exception regarding children or women (Corbusier 1886:331).

No one mentions Apache captives among the Maricopa, but presumably a few were taken. Maricopa captives were found among the Apache, but were not sold (Goodwin 1942: 96). The Apache were more concerned with the larger Pima population (Goodwin 1942:87-88).

Evaluation and Analysis of Population Data

I would have liked to evaluate the population figures in Tables 1 through 3 for both internal consistency (i.e., whether the trends shown are credible) and whether the figures support my inferences about population based upon the historical factors discussed above. Unfortunately, the figures in Tables 1-3 show no consistent trends, and are difficult to evaluate. Only one census was taken during this period, the other figures being estimates.

An extremely wide range of estimates (2000-20,000) has been made for the combined Pima and Maricopa populations, and all within one year (1846; see Table 3). Most estimators were in the area only a short time and were quite unfamiliar with the peoples they encountered, generally seeing them for the first time. Therefore, I will use the 1858 census as a base, and work backwards from there, using recorded events to suggest Pima and Maricopa population dynamics for the period.

Total Population: Maricopa

For figures and sources in the discussion below, refer to Table 1.

The Pima-Maricopa census of 1858 was reported by G. Bailey, a Special Agent of the Office of Indian Affairs, who spent a short time among the Pima and Maricopa (Bailey 1858:202-8). The census appears to have been taken by a Lieutenant Chapman of the United States Army. The 1858 figure for the Maricopa is 518. However, I would expect some underenumeration; at least 10%, and probably more, judging by later estimates of underenumeration (e.g., 1970; see Chapter 7). Therefore, I will assume 575-750 Maricopa in 1858 (10%-30% underenumeration).

Bancroft (1888:501) shows 500 Maricopa around 1858; he appears to have rounded the 1859 census figure of 472 (St. John 1859:131-36), perhaps assuming underenumeration; but he states neither the source nor the basis for his estimate.

Having established a base figure, let us turn to estimates for 1846. Both Cooke and Tyler (Table 1, column 1) estimated 10,000 Maricopa. This estimate was apparently their own, as neither mentioned receiving a population estimate from the Pima or Maricopa. The figure is much too high, even allowing for three large battles with the Quechan and Mohave and later confusion of Pima and Maricopa because of intermarriage. Perhaps the figure is a misprint of 1000, which is a much more credible estimate. It is also possible that Tyler may have used Cooke's estimate. Neither Cooke nor Tyler, as members of the 1846 Mormon Battalion, spent more than a few days among the Pima and Maricopa. Both were writing more than 30 years after they went through the area. Interestingly, Cooke does not attempt to estimate Maricopa population in his official reports as leader of the Mormon Battalion (Cooke 1848:561, 1849:51). In these reports, he gives only an estimate for the Pima and Maricopa combined. Tyler, who estimated Pima population in 1846 at 4000 (Table 2, column 2), would have us believe that Maricopa outnumbered Pima considerably, while Emory (1848:87), passing through the same area a few months before, stated that Pima outnumbered Maricopa.

Dale (1949:18), writing 100 years after the fact, estimated Maricopa population in 1848 at "a few hundred." This seems too low. It is likely that Dale was projecting a later figure back to 1848 without explaining the basis of his estimate.

For 1849, Hayes estimated 1000 Maricopa. This figure was given to Hayes by a Maricopa interpreter. Hayes (1929:44-45) spent less than a week among the Pima and Maricopa. The figure is a good round one, and is thus suspect, but may not be too far off. It allows for population decrease from deaths in the battles of 1851 and 1857, as well as by raiding for captives. Hayes also estimated 10,000 Pima at this time (Table 2), so that Maricopa make up 9% of his combined Pima-Maricopa population estimate. This percentage (but not the population figures) is quite close to the 1858 census, in which Maricopa are about 11% of the combined population. But Hayes's figure for the Pima is too high, and if the Maricopa lost population while the Pima population remained relatively stable, I would expect Maricopa to constitute more than 10% of the combined population in 1849.

For 1852, Bartlett estimated 667 Maricopa. This is probably a fair estimate, but Bartlett also estimated the Maricopa as one-third of the combined Pima-Maricopa population. This proportion is too high for the Maricopa, even allowing for later Maricopa losses. Bartlett may have had the right number for the wrong reasons. His estimate is from "chiefs, and the Mexican officers in Sonora" (Bartlett 1854(2):261). Thus his estimate is not very credible.

Domenech estimated 3000 Maricopa for around 1855.

His estimate is incorrect for the 1850s, which is the period he intends it to refer to. Domenech did not visit the Pima and Maricopa villages (although apparently he had been through northern Arizona). He did not state his source for the figure, but apparently obtained it from a monograph on Indians in the Pacific Railroad Reports (Whipple, Ewbank, and Turner 1855:123). But this estimate was not made by the survey parties for a railroad route to the Pacific; it is from a previously unpublished 1799 manuscript by José Cortez, extracts of which were published in the Pacific Railroad Reports. I thus reject Domenech's estimate.

Although highly speculative, I estimate that in 1846 there were perhaps as many as 1000 Maricopa. After losses in the battles of 1848 and 1851 and from raids for captives, there were perhaps 650-800 in 1852. With continuing deaths from warfare and raids for captives, perhaps 575-750 remained by 1858.

Total Population: Pima

For figures and sources discussed below, refer to Table 2.

Bailey's report of the 1858 census shows 4117 Pima (Table 2, column 1). As with the Maricopa, I assume 10%-30% underenumeration, giving a base range of 4575-5900. Mowry's 1858 estimate of 6000 (column 3) thus appears to be only slightly too high. He had reduced his estimate from 10,000 in 1850, which he obtained from "Antonio, chief of the Pimas" and felt to be too high (Mowry 1857:296-305). Bancroft (column 2) once again appears to have rounded a census figure, probably from the 1859 census (i.e., 3770 rounded to 4000; see Table 5).

For 1846, Cooke's estimate of more than 2000 (column 1) refers only to the number of Pima in Cooke's camp, not the whole population. Both Tyler and Bigler were with Cooke's expedition. Tyler estimates the entire Pima population at 4000 (column 2), somewhat low. Bigler's estimate of 5000 (column 3) is well within the range I postdicted. How Bigler arrived at his figure is unclear. Presumably he obtained it from a Pima or Maricopa, for he states that he "understood" there were about 5000 Pima (Bigler 1962:36).

Both Hayes for 1849 and Mowry for 1850 estimate 10,000 Pima. Mowry, of course, later felt this figure was too large, and it is. Hayes obtained his information from a Maricopa interpreter.

Bartlett's estimate of 1333 Pima in 1852 is much too low. He relied on estimates of others even though he spent two weeks among the Pima and Maricopa.

Poston's estimate of 7000-10,000 in 1854 (column 1) seems too high. He was in Arizona at the time of the estimate, but first published the figure forty years later.

Ezell's estimate for 1854 of 4000 seems to be too low. Apparently he was not aware of the 1858 census which counted 4117 Pima.

Domenech's estimate of 2500 in the 1850s is again from the 1799 Cortez manuscript and must be ignored.

None of the above figures compellingly refute the assumption of a relatively stable Pima population from 1846-58, as they are inconsistent, often even for the same year.

Total Population: Pima and Maricopa Combined

See Table 3 for the figures and sources in the discussion below.

Combining the 1858 census figures for Pima and Maricopa produces 4635 (column 1). Again allowing for 10%-30% underenumeration, I set 5150-6650 as a base range.

The Bancroft figure for 1858 (column 2) is a combined estimate for Pima and Maricopa, and it is too low. Turning to 1846, estimates are abundant. Griffin's 2000 (column 1) only refers to those persons who came to the camp of the Kearny expedition. Johnston's estimate of over 2000 (column 2) and Connelley's estimate of over 4000 (column 3) are minimum figures and thus provide little information. Connelley was writing many years after the event as well.

Somewhere within the wide range of Emory's estimate of 3000-10,000 (column 4) lies the truth. He felt 3000 was too low, apparently using estimates of others, but does not state his sources of information (Emory 1848:86).

Cooke's estimate of over 12,000 (column 5) is

useless as it consists of over 2000 Pima in the expedition's camp plus 10,000 Maricopa, which is too high. His other estimate of 15,000-20,000 (column 7) is too large, and is in fact the largest made for the combined Pima and Maricopa population. He seems to assume 10,000 Maricopa (Table 1) and 5000-10,000 Pima. While his range for the Pima, at least the lower end, is credible, he estimates too many Maricopa. For similar reasons, Tyler's estimate of 14,000 (column 6) is too high, as it too includes 10,000 Maricopa.

Dale's retrospective estimate for 1848 (column 1) seems about right, allowing for some Maricopa decline to 1858. He does not explain how he arrived at this figure.

Couts (1961:64) obtained as estimate in 1848 3000 Pima warriors from a Pima "chief" (column 2). However, Couts did not mention Maricopa at any time in his journal and identified a war party returning from the Colorado River as Pima. Apparently he was unaware of the existence of the Maricopa even though he saw some. The returning war party must have been Maricopa, since Pima did not go to fight the Quechan. I will assume his estimate thus refers to both Pima and Maricopa. Allowing a ratio of 3-5 total population per warrior produces 9000-15,000 total population, which is too high for Pima alone or Pima and Maricopa combined. Couts was probably given an inflated figure by his informant, who may not have been sure of the intentions of the troops Couts was with.

Hayes's estimate of 11,000 in 1849 is too high,

while Bartlett's estimate for 1852 of 2000 is too low. Emory returned to the Pima and Maricopa in 1855 (column 1) and raised the lower end of his wide estimate for 1846 (column 4). To Emory, no apparent decline in Pima and Maricopa numbers had taken place since 1846. Nevertheless, the wide range of Emory's estimates allows for Pima stability, since Pima made up the vast majority of the combined Pima-Maricopa population.

Domenech's estimates from the 1799 Cortez manuscript combine to give a credible 5500 (column 2), but must be rejected. Tevis gives only an estimate of 1500 warriors in 1856. Again assuming a ratio of 3-5 total population to each warrior produces as estimate of 4500-7500 total population. This is quite close to the range I have estimated (4575-5900) and allows for Maricopa population decline in the 1857 battle with the Quechan and their allies.

My highly speculative conclusion is that there were as many as 5575-6900 Pima and Maricopa in 1846, 5225-6700 by 1855, after the bulk of Maricopa war losses and raids for captives, and 5150-6650 in 1858. None of the figures in Table 3 can convincingly refute my assumptions, but neither do they support them very well. There is no way to rigorously test the accuracy of these estimates, and perhaps they should remain buried in government reports and books published privately or by little-known publishers. McArthur (1970:1097), facing wide-ranging estimates for the Tahitian population at the time of first European contact, felt that each time an estimate was republished it became more acceptable for lack of better data. Yet the estimate was seldom more than an uninformed guess.

It is sad but honest to say we can really know very little about Pima and Maricopa population during this crucial period of initial Anglo contact.

Mobilization Ratio

Figures for this section are shown in Table 4.

There are no figures by sex for this period, even in the 1858 census. However, some sources provide figures for the number of warriors and total population. From these, a ratio of total population to warriors can be obtained (the mobilization ratio; see Appendix A). Non-warriors include women of all ages, children of both sexes, and old men. For the Maricopa, I would expect a higher mobilization ratio than for the Pima, as Maricopa males were much more exposed to risk of death from warfare.

Emory's 1855 estimate of total population is much too broad to calculate a useful mobilization ratio, which is from 2.5 to 5.0 (Table 4). Mowry's 1858 estimate of 6000 total population and 1200 warriors gives a ratio of 5.0, higher than the census of 1858. The 1858 census gives a ratio of 3.4 for the Pima and Maricopa combined. But the Pima alone have a ratio of 3.6 and the Maricopa 2.7, the opposite of what I postdicted. There are a number of factors, some or all of which may have been acting to produce this result.

If proportionally more Maricopa males died in battle than Pima males, there would be more Maricopa widows. In order to remarry, a Maricopa widow might marry a Pima. The children would probably be considered Pima, since both the Pima and Maricopa were virilocal (Russell 1908:184; Spier 1933:222). The loss of women and children through intermarriage would decrease the Maricopa mobilization ratio.

There were probably proportionally fewer old men and young boys (i.e., non-warriors) among the Maricopa than the Pima because these males made up the cavalry in battles with the Quechan and Mohave. There would also be relatively fewer old men among the Maricopa if relatively more males died when younger, as warriors. This would also decrease the mobilization ratio.

If old men and boys were counted as warriors among the Maricopa, but not the Pima, this could account for a lower Maricopa mobilization ratio.

Finally, if Maricopa women and children were captured by the Quechan and Mohave to a greater degree than Pima women and children, and with a smaller population as well, the Maricopa mobilization ratio would be lower.

There is no way to assess the importance of these factors, but some evidence has been marshalled above to suggest that they were at work. Unfortunately, we cannot learn much about the sex ratio from the mobilization ratio.

Non-warriors include persons of both sexes. Even "warrior" is not defined precisely nor, apparently, used consistently.

Age Distribution

Since nearly all the figures from this period are estimates, there are no figures for age distribution, which would in effect be estimates of estimates. All that is available is Griffin's (1943:34) statement that " . . . there were as many or more children than a person would meet with in one of our new States [sic] among the same number of people." But Griffin was there for only 3 days and did not see the total population, so his statement is based on an impression, rather than any sort of sample count. Nevertheless, it is what we would expect.

Geographic Distribution

Very little information is given on the number, names, and locations of specific Pima and Maricopa villages. Hayes (1929:45) mentions eight Pima villages and three Maricopa villages in 1849, but does not name them. The 1858 census lists eight Pima villages and two Maricopa villages, showing considerable consistency in number from 1849 to 1858. Domenech (1860(2):50) names five Pima villages: Atison, San Juan Capistrano, San Serafin de Napgub, Sutaquison, and Tubuscabar. These, of course, are the names found in the 1799 Cortez manuscript, and refer to the Spanish period.

Distribution by village in the 1858 census will

be discussed in the next chapter in order to compare the censuses of 1858, 1859, and 1860, all of which show population by village.

Notes to Chapter Two

1. Whether the epidemic of 1844-45 was in fact cholera is unclear. The symptoms, such as vomiting, short duration of severe illness, and 50% of the cases ending in death follow modern descriptions of the disease (Lyght 1966:820-21). However, it is difficult to determine how cholera could have been transmitted to the Pima villages. A large, dense human population is required to support a cholera epidemic, as the infective organism can live only a short time (at most, several days) in water or sewage (Napier 1950:949-50). Man is the only organism susceptible to cholera.

Thus cholera would have to have been introduced by persons traveling through the Pima villages from Mexico, California, or the eastern United States. But with an incubation period of 6 days at most, it seems unlikely that an infected person could have arrived at the Pima and Maricopa villages before dying on the trail. Transmission to other members of the party of travelers would have been necessary.

Also failing to support cholera as the cause of the 1844-45 epidemic are the dates of cholera pandemics. Cholera occurred in the United States or Mexico in 1833 and 1850-54 (Second through Fourth Pandemics; pandemics also occurred after the period covered by this chapter) (Chambers 1938:134-35, 200-209, 242, 253-55; Pollitzer 1959:22-35). Thus it seems likely that the epidemic of

1844-45 was either misdated in the calendar sticks, or was not cholera, as the reported date seems too late for the 1833 pandemic and too early for the 1850-54 pandemics.

Moreover, in cholera, vomit is generally clear, or occasionally contains erythrocytes, giving it a reddish tint (Pollitzer 1959:695). Yet in the descriptions above, the vomit was described as black. Black vomit (hematemesis) often occurs with yellow fever, and the common name for yellow fever in Spanish and Portuguese translates as 'black vomit' (Lyght 1966:858; Strode 1951:395). Yet hematemesis seldom occurs before the third day of illness. Death seldom occurs before the third day, and usually later (Lyght 1966:858; Strode 1951:416). Although recovery may occur in 3 days (Strode 1951:394), the reports of the unknown epidemic claimed death or recovery within a day.

The means of transmission (vector) of yellow fever, the mosquito Aëdes aegypti, is found in the Gila River Valley (Carpenter and LaCasse 1955:262). From 1800-1900, yellow fever occurred along the west coast of Mexico north to the Colorado River delta (Napier 1950a: 913). Thus it appears that the unknown epidemic could just as well have been yellow fever, and perhaps this was even more likely than cholera as yellow fever could be transmitted by mosquitoes which bit an infected person during the first 3 or 4 days of the illness, or from infected mosquitoes introduced into the area in water barrels of travelers (Lyght 1966:857; Napier 1950a: 914; Strode 1951:264).

This does not exhaust the diseases from which the 1844-45 epidemic could have sprung. Quebbeman (1966:30) feels that typhoid fever was confused with cholera in Arizona during the nineteenth century. Other possibilities include shigellosis, algid malaria, and bacillary dysentery (Lyght 1966:820; Napier 1950:954; Pollitzer 1959:739).

2. Forde (1931:171) feels that the Quechan bow and arrow were poor equipment. The bow was light; the arrows had "limited range and impact." He further states:

> . . . the role of the archers in battle was rather to intimidate and demoralize than seriously to injure the enemy. Hand-to-hand battle was the objective in warfare and arrow wounds are rarely spoken of as fatal.

3. The Quechan used women in defensive actions but apparently not in battles on the Maricopa (Forbes 1965:74-75).

4. The Maricopa calendar stick date for the battle is 1848 (Spier 1933:140); Spier's informant dated it as 1847, 1848, or 1849 (Spier 1933:161, 173).

CHAPTER THREE

ESTABLISHMENT OF THE GILA RIVER INDIAN
RESERVATION TO THE BEGINNING OF
OFF-RESERVATION MIGRATION
(1859-69)

Factors Affecting Pima Population

Epidemics

The 1860s were a period of epidemics of various diseases. Unfortunately, poor documentation prevents accurately identifying the diseases, and there is only one source which reported the number and causes of deaths (for but one year), the 1860 Decennial Census (USOC 1860).

A Pima calendar stick entry for 1860-61 recorded that "A plague which killed its victims in a single day prevailed throughout the villages." This may be another "cholera" epidemic, but the disease is described much too vaguely to be identified with certainty, and this is not a year in which cholera would be expected to occur (see note 1 to Chapter Two). Three shamans were killed for causing this epidemic, which then abated. Unfortunately, no report appeared in 1860-61 from an Indian agent in the area, so corroboration is lacking. Nevertheless, I will assume that an epidemic of some sort occurred in 1860-61.

For 1862-63, a Pima calendar stick entry reported that two shamans were killed, but mentioned no illness (Russell 1908:50). However, Grossmann (1871a:412) reported the occurrence of a smallpox epidemic among the Pima "Eight years ago," i.e., 1862 or 1863, and that many died, especially children. A calendar stick entry for 1862 in Hall (1907:420) reported that "The Pimas killed a powerful medicine-man, thinking he caused a sickness from which several of them died." This may be the equivalent of either the 1860-61 or 1862-63 entries in Russell. The meager information does not permit calibration. Judging by other events, the account in Hall probably refers to 1860-61.

From 1866-69, one epidemic after another occurred. For 1866-67, a calendar stick entry from Russell (1908:52) reported: "Many died this year of a sickness characterized by shooting pains that resembled needle and knife pricks." Three shamans were accused of causing the illness, and two were killed. It is difficult to identify this disease. The most likely causes seem to be pneumonia or typhoid fever, but this is merely speculation. It does seem to have been a serious disease that reached epidemic intensity.

The same " . . . year was marked by a devastating fever at Rso´tûk [one of the Pima villages] and three medicine-men were killed there in hope of stopping it" (Russell 1908:52). This may have been pneumonia, typhoid fever, diphtheria, scarlet fever, or something else, and was severe, but perhaps confined to one village.

A calendar stick reported that during 1867-68, many died from a disease Russell (1908:52) identified as malaria. The calendar stick in Hall (1907:422) reported for 1869 that a shaman was killed; I assume this refers to the same event.

It is quite likely that the 1867-68 epidemic was malaria. Rusling (1874:381), who visited the Pima and Maricopa villages in 1867, reported that in March the Gila River overflowed. As the water receded, pools would have remained in low-lying areas, providing breeding grounds for mosquitoes. Farther from the river, shallow pools would have formed in depressions, also providing mosquito breeding pools. The principal malaria vector of the semiarid western United States, the mosquito <u>Anopheles freeborni</u>, is present in the area (Carpenter and La Casse 1955:41-42).[1]

Indian Agent Ruggles (1869a:209) reported sickness, chills, and fever in autumn 1868. He felt that children were especially affected by this malady, more of them dying than in the previous 2 years. This could have been a continuation of malaria, since a long-remembered period of heavy rain and floods occurred in September 1868 (J. Hayden 1959:10; Russell 1908:52) and perhaps destroyed villages (Bancroft 1888:536). This also could have been at least in part an influenza epidemic which developed into pneumonia for many persons, especially children. Unfortunately, no estimate of the number of deaths was made.

General Health

It is inconsistent that while the Pima calendar stick keepers remembered the 1860s as a time of sickness and death, one Anglo observer wrote that the Pima were healthy. Rusling (1874:369), visiting the area in 1867, described the Pima as ". . . healthy, athletic, vigorous-looking people, . . . decidedly the most well-to-do aborigines we had yet seen." Although this was before the malaria epidemic of 1868, it was almost certainly after or during the "shooting pain" illness and the fever at Rso´tûk. That Ruggles (1869a:209), the Indian Agent, claims more children died from fever in 1868-69 than in the previous 2 years also casts some doubt on the epidemics mentioned in the calendar sticks for 1866-68. The Ruggles report, however, may not be based on permanent residence among the Pima.[2]

As is the case for the previous period (1846-58), it is difficult to assess the effect of maternal, infant, and child mortality, but we can quite safely assume it was high.

Thus, despite the contrary reports of Rusling and Ruggles, it appears that the entire decade 1859-69 was essentially one long epidemic resulting from various diseases.

Food Situation

All sources but one mention constant crop surpluses

for the Pima. Surplus food, mainly grain, was sold to local traders, emigrants, the Overland Mail, and the Army. Browne (1871:110-11) gives the amount of crops sold every year from 1858-63. Others report crop surpluses for 1864 (Poston 1864:152), 1866 (Rusling 1874:370), and 1869 (Jones 1869:219; Ruggles 1869a:209).

However, in 1868, when there was no report by the Indian Agent, the Pima may not have produced a surplus. 1867 and 1868 were years of much rain and flooding which could have adversely affected crops, both in the field and stored in the villages. A Pima woman, remembering the period, said that stored grain rotted, and people "had a difficult time" (J. Hayden 1959:10). It seems doubtful, however, that anyone starved, for there were wild plant foods available, even more so than usual in that it was a rainy year, and the calendar sticks do not mention any starvation. Thus it seems unlikely that by themselves food shortages were a major cause of population decline during this period, but in 1867-68 may have contributed to population decline by increasing susceptibility to disease.

Hostile Encounters with Apache and Yavapai

According to the calendar sticks, with the exception of a short truce in part of 1863-64, raids by or on the Apache and Yavapai occurred every year (Russell 1908:48-53). White observers mentioned such hostilities as well (Mowry 1859a:361; Poston 1863:386; St. John 1859:131-36, 1860:186-

205). At this time Pima and whites started going out together against the Apache and Yavapai. According to the calendar sticks, a white man accompanied the Pima in a raid in 1859-60 (Russell 1908:48). In 1863-64 the Pima claim to have accompanied white ranchers, in which the combined party lured some Apache into camp and then massacred them. However, most of the Indians were more likely Maricopa, as discussed below.[3]

In 1864-65, according to the calendar sticks, the Pima went for the first time against the Apache with United States Army troops (Russell 1908:41).[4] Further sorties with Army troops are noted in the calendar sticks for 1866-67 and 1869-70 (Russell 1908:52-53). Ruggles (1867:165) states that 100 Pima were enlisted in the Army in 1865, but by 1867, 70 had been mustered out. Nevertheless, Jones (1869:219) found that in 1869, while the enlisted contingent had been disbanded, Pima, in capacities as scouts and guides, accompanied Army troops against the Apache east of the Verde River. These Pima groups were larger than 100.

Few casualties from Apache and Yavapai raids are mentioned. The calendar sticks record the following deaths (Russell 1908:48-52): 2 in 1860-61; 1 in 1862-63; 1 in 1863-64; and 4-5 in 1865-66.

However, the 1860 Census (USOC 1860) reports fourteen persons killed in one year by Apaches (eight males and six females). Consequently, the number of deaths from raiding would appear to be understated in the calendar sticks (and may well be in the 1860 Census also).

Based on a count from the calendar sticks, deaths during this period from Apache and Yavapai raids were not any more numerous than during the preceding period (1846-58). But if the 1860 Census is to be believed, during both periods Pima deaths from raiding were five to ten times as numerous as reported by the calendar sticks.

Since the Pima were now periodically going out against the Apache and Yavapai with whites, compared to the preceding period, Pima male risk of death in battle may have decreased. Pima battle deaths may also have decreased because of the acquisition of guns during this period. St. John (1860:51) claimed that in 1860 the Pima lacked rifles and were at a disadvantage facing the Apache, who had guns. By 1864, the Pima appear to have overcome this disadvantage by acquiring firearms (Grossmann 1871a:417; Russell 1908:51). Furthermore, with more white settlements (but only if Apache-Yavapai attacks did not increase) some raids, which formerly would have been on the Pima may have been diverted to areas of white settlement.

However, while risk of death in battle may have decreased somewhat for males, females may have faced increased risk of death from Apache-Yavapai attack. This would occur while women were out collecting firewood. According to Lord (1866:112) and Rusling (1874:372), by 1866, women had to travel 6 to 8 miles (10-13 km) for firewood. This appears to be a result of upstream diversion of Gila River water by white farmers to the extent that it was adversely affecting the Pima.[5] With less water, there would be fewer mesquite trees for firewood. Perhaps heavy cutting of trees by Pima and non-Indians was also depleting the supply of firewood.

The Pima and Papago are mentioned once in the calendar sticks as going out together against the Apache, in 1868-69 (Russell 1908:53). However, they quarreled and separated before attacking their common enemy.

While the short peace of 1863-64 between the Pima and Apache was ineffective, Ruggles (1867:163) felt that Pima population was increasing rapidly because of less fighting with Apache. Given the number of epidemics reported for this period, I do not find any support for assuming an increasing population.

Captives

As before, captives were not a source of population growth for the Pima. Pima taken by Apache similarly had little influence on Pima population loss. If raiding were less frequent than in the preceding period, fewer captives would have been taken.

Intermarriage

Once again, the degree of Pima-Maricopa intermarriage is unclear. The only statements available are from 1859-60. According to Mowry (1859a:361), it was "an honor" for a Maricopa man to take a Pima woman as wife. According to

St. John (1860:198), Maricopa men were marrying Pima women and became classed as Pima because Maricopa women were dying of venereal disease. This is certainly a bit of overstatement. Intermarriage will be discussed in more detail below in relation to the Maricopa. Pima-Maricopa intermarriage would have had a greater influence on the numerically smaller Maricopa, while the influence on Pima population should not have been very noticeable.

Pima Population Dynamics

Based on the factors discussed above, I would expect population figures to show a declining Pima population from 1859-69, mainly as a result of epidemics in 1860-61, 1862-63, and 1866-68, intensified and aggravated by a possible food shortage in 1867-68, constant deaths from raids by and on Apache and Yavapai, as well as high infant, child, and maternal mortality even without epidemics. The population data in Table 5, at least those figures based on censuses, are consistent with the assumption of a declining population. (For evaluation of the accuracy of all figures in Table 5, see Appendix B.) Remembering that in 1858 (Table 2, column 1) 4117 Pima were enumerated, a census taken in 1868 reported only 3878 (Table 5, column 1). The census figures from 1859 and 1860 (both in column 1 in Table 5) also reported fewer persons than 1858 (and surprisingly, 1868). However, because of considerably greater underenumeration in the censuses of 1859 and 1860, I feel that population decline was relatively constant from 1858-69, rather than rapid from 1858-60 with some recovery from 1860-68, as the census figures of 1858, 1859, 1860, and 1868 would imply.

I estimate that in 1868, Pima population numbered 4075-5175, with a figure toward the higher end of the range more likely. This assumes 5%-25% underenumeration in the 1868 census. My estimated range for 1858 was 4575-5900. The wide range of these estimates does not permit calculation of the percent population loss for the period, nor the annual growth rate, without more precise assumptions of the degree of underenumeration in the 1858 and 1868 censuses. For example, if underenumeration were proportionally the same in 1858 and 1868 (regardless of the actual percentage), population loss would be 5.8% over 10 years, or -0.6% annually. Given the number and severity of epidemics from 1859-69, the rate of decline may have been greater, in which case enumeration would be relatively more complete in 1868. Assuming 30% underenumeration in 1858 and 24% in 1868, population loss was 13.2% over 10 years, or about -1.4% annually. Unfortunately, at this time there is no good reason to choose one rate of underenumeration over another, other than assuming probably better enumeration in 1868. We are thus still largely in the realm of hypothesis and speculation rather than proof.

Factors Affecting Maricopa Population

Information about the Maricopa alone is very sparse

for this period. The Maricopa were outnumbered about ten to one by the Pima; hence, most sources only mention the Maricopa briefly (or not at all) or group them with the Pima and assume both groups were largely the same.

Epidemics

I presume epidemics among the Pima also affected the Maricopa, without knowing whether they were of equal frequency and severity. The Maricopa calendar stick is much less complete than that of the Pima, and lacks entries for 1860-62 and 1866-69 (Spier 1933:140-41). These are almost precisely the years of epidemics, according to the Pima calendar sticks. Perhaps this absence of entries is in itself evidence of epidemics.

There is a remote possibility that the Maricopa escaped the worst of the epidemics among the Pima by moving to the Salt River, such as was reported for the epidemic misdated as 1850 (Bartlett 1854(2):241). The evidence is indirect, however, as the Maricopa calendar stick entry for 1869-70 records that in that year the Maricopa left the Salt River (to which they would have moved during the epidemics) to go to the Gila River-Salt River confluence (Spier 1933:140). But none of the agents mention Maricopa living off-reservation before the 1870s.

It appears that the calendar stick account has reversed the situation, in that it was probably in 1869-70 that Maricopa first left the Gila River for the Salt River (because of declining river flow). That the Maricopa might precede the Pima in leaving for the Salt River is understandable, in that the Maricopa were farther downstream, and would be the first to suffer the effects of decreased flow.

I thus assume that the Maricopa suffered epidemics and population decline during the 1860s.

General Health

Overall, there is little evidence that the health of the Maricopa was good during this period. Reports are rather conflicting, but the consensus of agents seems to be that Maricopa women engaged in "prostitution," and because of venereal diseases, Maricopa population was declining. Among those who mentioned this factor were, in 1859, Mowry (1859a:361) and St. John (1860:198), and in 1867, Ruggles (1867:163), who stated: " . . . their numbers are evidently decreasing, caused principally by prostitution and its attendant evils, in which vice they indulge to a great extent among themselves."

All three of these reports of Maricopa population decline come from agents who were either present on the reservation for some time (St. John, Ruggles) or who visited a number of times (Mowry). The two reports of good Maricopa health came from persons passing through on inspection tours.

In 1860, according to McMahon (1860:230), "Both tribes [the Pima and Maricopa] . . . are advancing in civilization, and I cannot learn that either have suffered to any alarming degree by a knowledge of its vices." Rusling (1874:369) described both tribes as healthy and well-to-do. It seems likely that the Indian Agents may have tried to hide the epidemic-ridden condition of the Maricopa (and Pima) from the inspectors. We must recognize the cultural bias in the term "prostitution" when applied by whites to sexual relations among Maricopa. Nevertheless, perhaps venereal diseases were (re-)introduced[6] by Anglos traveling along the Gila River since 1846, and were now reaching epidemic proportions, at least among the Maricopa. As a smaller population than the Pima, the Maricopa could have been infected more rapidly (assuming the Maricopa more frequently chose sexual partners of their own ethnic group). Perhaps there was also some contact with soldiers from Camp McDowell (not established until 1865, however) (Spicer 1962:248), located on the Verde River, near its confluence with the Salt. This is 40 miles (64 km) straightline distance from the Gila River Pima and Maricopa villages.

If venereal diseases were rampant among the Maricopa, the main effect would be on fertility rather than mortality.[7] Some data from the 1860 Census (USOC 1860) do support the hypothesis of lower fertility among the Maricopa as compared with the Pima (but not necessarily the assumption that it resulted from a higher frequency of venereal diseases).

The Pima child-woman ratio is 982.6, quite high; the Maricopa, 567.3 (Table 6). It we observe the child-woman ratio by village for both Pima and Maricopa, it is seen that the child-woman ratio for the Maricopa village of Sacate ("Sacaton") is 833.3, within the range of child-woman ratios for the individual Pima villages, but Hueso Parrado is considerably lower (459.5). As seen in Table 7, in Hueso Parrado there is a considerable excess of male children aged 0-4, especially age 2. There is no such large excess in Sacate ("Sacaton"). Thus it seems possible that female children were either more greatly underenumerated or erroneously recorded as male in Hueso Parrado. Either case is likely. Greater underenumeration of females than males means there should be more females in the 0-4 age group, which would increase the child-woman ratio. Misclassification of females as males would leave the child-woman ratio the same whether females were classified correctly by sex or not. Because in Hueso Parrado the number of persons 0-4 is less than twice the number aged 5-9, about six persons could be added to the 0-4 age group without violating the assumption of no more than twice the number of persons at 5-9 in the 0-4 age group (the basis of which is discussed below). But if the number of Maricopa females 0-4, enumerated as 18, were raised to equal the enumerated number of males at 0-4 (41; Table 7), the assumption of the 0-4 age group containing no more than twice the number of persons in the 5-9 age group would be violated. At the same time the child-woman ratio would still be lower than for the Pima, at 788.5 (compared to the Pima 982.6). Thus, regardless of whether it was missclassification by sex or underenumeration (or even female infanticide) that led to the deficit of Maricopa females at ages 0-4, the Maricopa child-woman ratio would still be lower than that of the Pima, and except in the case of infanticide, implying lower Maricopa fertility and the possibility that venereal disease was a greater problem for the Maricopa than the Pima. The evidence for infanticide is very weak, as seen in the relatively equal number of persons by sex in the 5-9 age group.

Examination of family size further supports this reasoning (Table 6). Mean family size for the Pima is 4.0 persons; for the Maricopa, 3.5 persons. There are no large variations by village for either the Pima or Maricopa, but with one exception Maricopa family size is smaller than Pima, regardless of village.

A similar situation appears with persons per occupied dwelling (Table 6). For the Pima, the mean is 5.0; for the Maricopa, 4.5, again a difference of 0.5 persons in the predicted direction.

Finally, while not significant in itself, but in conjunction with the above data, the median age for the Maricopa is 5 years higher than the Pima (Table 8) suggesting the Maricopa were a slightly older population with proportionally fewer children.

There is thus fair likelihood of lower fertility among Maricopa women, but in general, fertility, to the extent that it is measured by the child-woman ratio, was quite high for both the Pima and Maricopa.

Food Situation

The effect of this factor was probably similar to the Pima situation. Ruggles (1867:163) is the only observer who comments specifically on the Maricopa, saying that they generally had sufficient crops, but when they had a poor year, relied on mesquite beans.

The Maricopa may have utilized wild plant foods to a greater extent than the Pima. Spier (1933:48) considered Maricopa staples to be primarily mesquite beans, jackrabbits, and fish. Thus the Maricopa may not have suffered as severely as the Pima during the rains and floods of 1867-68. However, it is unclear whether Spier is referring to the pre-Spanish period, or after the Spanish introduction of barley and wheat.

Overall, food does not seem to have been short among the Maricopa during this period, at least no more so than among the Pima, and perhaps less.

Hostile Encounters with Apache and Yavapai

Compared to the Pima, Maricopa encounters with their enemies are poorly documented. Nevertheless, raids by and on the Apache and Yavapai were probably as frequent as for the Pima.

Several observers specifically mention the Maricopa in battle with Yavapai or Apache. Poston (1864:153) felt Maricopa were more "warlike" than the Pima. Perhaps since they were no longer fighting the Quechan and Mohave, the Maricopa increased their attacks on the Yavapai and Apache.

Although the Pima calendar sticks claim Pima accompanied the white war party which massacred some Apaches in 1864, the whites in the party claim that the Indians were Maricopa--perhaps fourteen in number (Browne 1871: 121-24; Poston 1894:405). These reports mentioned one of the Indians named Juan Chivaria. He is also listed in the 1858, 1859, and 1860 censuses as the "head chief" or "captain" of a Maricopa village (Bailey 1858:559; St. John 1859:136; USOC 1860). Thus at least some of the Indians in this event were Maricopa.

However, except for the Apache no other Indians were killed. Thus it really does not matter in terms of Pima or Maricopa population dynamics whether the Indians which accompanied the whites were Pima, Maricopa, or both.

The Maricopa calendar stick entry for 1863-64 (Spier 1933:140) mentions a period of peace with the Yavapai, at the time of the Pima-Apache peace (Russell 1908:50). The Pima claim that the Maricopa-Yavapai truce ended when the Maricopa killed two men and captured a boy from an "Apache" party visiting the Maricopa, presumably peacefully. The Maricopa claim that the truce with the Yavapai ended in 1864-65 when Yavapai stole some Maricopa horses (Spier 1933:

140). In the same year, the Pima calendar sticks record that Pima and Maricopa went out against the Apache (Russell 1908:51). Thus the truce was short-lived.

In 1865-66, Maricopa were riding with the United States Army against the Apache (and presumably Yavapai). Ruggles (1867:163) stated that the Maricopa "furnished" a company of troops for the Army, while the Maricopa calendar stick said that some men were taken to Camp McDowell to act as scouts (Spier 1933:140). How voluntary their service was is thus open to question. To some degree, as for the Pima, joining white war parties may have somewhat reduced Maricopa male risk of death in battle.

As with the Pima, perhaps women had to walk farther for firewood, increasing their risk of death from Apache and Yavapai raids. But women and children were no longer subject to capture by Quechan and Mohave, so overall perhaps the danger of capture or death faced by women decreased.

In general, the Maricopa suffered deaths from Apache and Yavapai hostilities, but compared to the previous period, when they fought the Quechan and Mohave, deaths from battle were much less significant. This cause of death was now presumably at about the level experienced by the Pima.

Captives

With the end of warfare with the Quechan and Mohave,

captives were no longer being taken by and from the Maricopa in such large numbers. Presumably a few Yavapai or Apache were captured, as the Pima calendar stick notes that an "Apache" boy was taken by the Maricopa when a party visited a Maricopa village in 1863-64 (Russell 1908:50). However, the boy was sold to a local white. The pattern of selling some captives seems to have continued. At this time, captives taken by the Maricopa should have had little influence on population size. Maricopa taken captive were few in number and presumably were not depleting the population. However, captives taken during the time of war with the Quechan and Mohave and not sold remained in the population, and Maricopa taken captive were apparently not repatriated.

Remaining captives appear to have comprised a considerable part of the Maricopa population. Assuming that all "Cocopah" (really Quechan; see Appendix B) and Mohave enumerated among the Pima and Maricopa in 1868 (Andrews 1870b:481) were living with the Maricopa and not the Pima (see Appendix B for the basis of this assumption), 36 of 339 persons living in Maricopa villages were Quechan or Mohave, or 9% of the Maricopa villages population. This is a considerable proportion. It appears that more captives taken by the Maricopa may have been kept than several writers have assumed (Dobyns et al. 1957:48; Forbes 1965:78, 288; Forde 1931:168-69).

Maricopa Population Dynamics

Based on the above factors, I assume Maricopa population continued to decline from 1859-69. Unlike 1846-58, when I assumed that most of the decline resulted from deaths in battle with and loss of captives to the Quechan and Mohave, the population decline in 1859-69 presumably resulted from a series of epidemics. Factors aggravating this decline included raids by and on the Apache and Yavapai and a possible food shortage in 1867-68. It is assumed that maternal mortality was high and constant in both periods, as well as infant and child mortality even when epidemics were not occurring.

Again, the population figures are consistent with my assumption. In 1858, 518 Maricopa were enumerated (Table 1, column 1). As seen in Table 9, all census figures for 1859-69 are lower: 399 in 1868 (column 2), 472 in 1859, and 394 in 1860 (column 1). (All other figures in Table 9 are estimates or erroneous reports of census figures; see Appendix B for an evaluation of all figures in Table 9.) Again, as for the Pima, as a result of evaluating the population figures, I believe that Maricopa population decline was relatively constant from 1859-69, rather than rapidly declining from 1858-60, then remaining relatively stable from 1860-68, as the census figures imply. The 1859 and 1860 census figures appear to reflect greater under-enumeration than those of 1858 or 1868.

For 1868, I estimate there were 420-570 Maricopa, assuming 5%-30% underenumeration in the 1868 census. For 1858, I estimated 575-750. Once again I do not know the degree of underenumeration that occurred in the 1858 and 1868 censuses, but can produce figures based on assumed rates. If underenumeration, regardless of degree, were equally great in 1858 and 1868, Maricopa population loss was 23.0% in 10 years, or -2.6% annually. Assuming 30% underenumeration in 1858 and 25% in 1868, population loss was 28.1% over 10 years, or -3.3% annually.

Regardless of the amount of underenumeration assumed, Maricopa population loss from 1858-68 was proportionally greater than Pima. For the unadjusted 1858 and 1868 census figures, Pima population loss was 5.8%, while Maricopa was 23.0%. The most likely reasons for this appear to be lower Maricopa fertility (as expressed by the child-woman ratio) combined with possible greater mortality by chance from epidemics for the Maricopa.

Another possible factor in greater Maricopa population loss from 1858-68 could be disposal of captives (either through sale or repatriation) who may have comprised a greater proportion of Maricopa population in 1858 than 1868. I have found no data to test the validity of this statement.

Infant Mortality

Age data from 1860 for the Pima (Table 10) and

Maricopa (Table 11) support my assumption of high infant mortality for this period. As seen in Table 10, for the Pima, the number of children 0-4 is 2.0 times the number of children 5-9. For the Maricopa (Table 11) this ratio is 1.9. Assuming relatively constant fertility and mortality from 1850-60 (which seems credible in that no epidemics were reported for that period), the data imply that half the children born from 1850-55 died within five years.

This seems an incredible number, but age-specific mortality figures from other populations provide support for this assumption. Aberle (1932:345) found that from 1855-1930 in the Pueblos of San Juan and Santa Clara, over 40% of the children died before age five. Surprisingly, the death rate for children 1-4 (206.5 per thousand) was fairly close to that for infants (246.7 per thousand). Wissler's (1936:230) report of data for both Arizona and New Mexico Indians show similarly high rates (Table 12). His data for the Dakota in 1910-15 report an almost incredibly high death rate of 532 per thousand in the 0-4 age group--over half of all children born dying within five years after birth.

While less useful, data on the percentage of deaths at all ages occurring among infants and children aged 0-4 are available from additional comparable populations (Table 13). Clements (1931:398) found that about 30% of all Mohave-Chemehuevi deaths from 1910-30 occurred at ages 0-4, and about 9% of all deaths at ages 1-4. For the rural

United States American Indian population in 1924-26, Clements reported that about 35% of all deaths occurred from 0-4, and about 14% from 1-4. Wissler (1936:224), in his data from the Dakota, as well as the United Nations (1954:36), which reports data for a number of countries, found even higher percentages of all deaths at ages 0-4. These figures are shown in Table 13.

The data in Tables 12 and 13 are certainly inaccurate to some degree because of underreporting of infant and early childhood deaths. But if the figures reflect greater underreporting of deaths at ages 0-4 than other ages, as often occurs, then the percentages of deaths at ages 0-4 shown in Table 13 should be even higher, which still supports extreme mortality at ages 0-4 in these populations.

In Table 12, death rates were calculated by using the population at ages 0-4. Since these ages, especially 0, are usually underenumerated, some inaccuracy results. But since the number of deaths at ages 0-4 is also generally underreported, the errors are both in the same direction, and the death rates are not as inaccurate as might be thought, depending on the relative difference in underreporting of population and deaths at ages 0-4.

Sex Ratio

Pima

Compared to the previous period, fewer males and more females should have been dying from Apache and Yavapai raids, but the population figures by sex (which are very few and difficult to evaluate; see Appendix B) do not support this assumption. As seen in Table 14, the Pima sex ratio declined from a considerable excess of males in 1859 to relative numerical equality by sex in 1868.

I believe that to some degree, because of greater inaccuracy in the 1859 and 1860 censuses as compared with 1868, the sex ratios in 1859 and 1860 should in fact be closer to that of 1868, and the 1868 sex ratio is thus not aberrant. (It is one of the few below 100 for the Pima for the whole period 1846-1974.) But it still is necessary to account for a probable trend toward relative equality of numbers by sex from 1859-68.

The most likely reason is the large number of epidemics occurring between 1860 and 1868. With epidemics, more persons than usual would be dying. A large number, perhaps a majority, would be infants and young children. It is true that in most populations there are more males at birth than females; but males are also more likely to die in infancy and early childhood. Thus, during a period of epidemics, even though the number of males might exceed the number of females at birth, more male deaths would occur, absolutely and relatively. In time, this could have essentially equalized the sex ratio, since children made up a large proportion of the total population.

Other factors suggest themselves as well. If the Pima practiced female infanticide in 1860, then abandoned it shortly thereafter, the proportion of females would increase by 1868. Admittedly, there is no definite report of this among the Pima. Russell (1908:184) says that the Pima preferred male children because they would grow up to be warriors, but he does not mention female infanticide. Thus this factor is extremely unlikely.

Another factor for which there is no good evidence is that Maricopa women married Pima men and became classed as Pima. The only statements regarding intermarriage are in opposition to this assumption, claiming that Maricopa males married Pima females and were then classified as Pima (Mowry 1859a:361; St. John 1859:198). If this were the case, the Pima sex ratio might increase, or stay the same from 1860-68, but the effect of Maricopa on the Pima sex ratio would be small because of the small size of the Maricopa population.

Unless females were underenumerated to a much greater degree in 1860 than 1868, the Pima sex ratio decreased toward equality in eight years, the main reason being proportionally greater male (mainly infant and child) deaths from a series of epidemics. It seems unlikely that maternal mortality could have decreased, or that females were dying to a lesser degree from Apache and Yavapai raids than previously, at least to the extent of affecting the sex ratio.

Maricopa

As with the Pima, the Maricopa sex ratio declined from 1859-68, possibly to a greater degree (see Table 14). The 1859 figures are too low because of extreme underenumeration of males; 1860 is probably more accurate, but females may have been more greatly underenumerated, while for 1868 the sex ratio which assumes Quechan and Mohave were female seems most justified (i.e., 92.8; see Appendix B for further information on evaluation of the data). Thus the Maricopa sex ratio appears to have been higher than that of the Pima in 1860, and lower in 1868.

A large part of the difference between the Pima and Maricopa sex ratios is probably the inaccuracy of the data, but to the extent that there was a higher sex ratio in 1860 and a greater decline in sex ratio from 1860-68 among the Maricopa than the Pima, the following factors may have been at work:

1. Since the Maricopa population is about one-tenth the size of the Pima, the Maricopa sex ratio could fluctuate more widely than that of the Pima because of random variation. This would result from the chance occurrence of a large number of female births from 1861-68.

2. The same epidemics which affected the Pima presumably affected the Maricopa. As for the Pima, a

greater proportion of male deaths could have occurred compared to the proportion expected without epidemics.

3. The Maricopa may have been practicing female infanticide in 1860, or shortly before, but after the end of warfare with the Quechan and Mohave, gave it up. Thus, the proportion of females increased.

4. The 1860 Census may underenumerate females in the 0-4 age group to a greater degree than males, either by classifying them as males, or by not reporting them. If female underenumeration occurred in 1860, however, the sex ratio would have been lower, and the decline to 1868 would not have been as great.

5. Maricopa men may have been marrying Pima women and became classified as Pima. However, since this factor was already mentioned in 1860, this type of intermarriage would have had to increase by 1868 to reduce the Maricopa sex ratio. If Maricopa males were marrying into the Pima and became so classified, they would act to increase the Pima sex ratio, which was reported to decline from 1860-68. However, since the number of such males would be small, their influence on the Pima sex ratio would probably not be significant. I doubt this factor is of much importance.

The Sex Ratio and Maternal Mortality

That the Pima and Maricopa sex ratios were reported above 100 in 1860 to a degree unexpected by chance alone (Table 14) is probably a result of high maternal mortality

and minimal loss of males through raiding for the Pima.
For the Maricopa, high maternal mortality and inmarriage
by Pima males appear to produce an excess of males, while
considerable past loss of males from Mohave-Quechan warfare
is balanced by past loss of females through capture and
inmarriage by Pima males. The data discussed below provide
some support for these assumptions.

Sex ratios for five-year age groups are shown for
the Pima and Maricopa in Tables 10 and 11. As discussed
in Appendix B, extreme age misstatement prevents using
grouped age data in five-year or even ten-year intervals.
The fluctuations of Pima age-specific sex ratios (Table 10)
illustrate this problem. (For the Maricopa, even if there
were no age misstatement, because of the small numbers
involved, the sex ratios for five-year age groups should be
ignored and are not shown in Table 11.) For example, the
Pima sex ratio for persons 20-24 is an astoundingly low
70.2, while the sex ratio at 10-14 is 145.2. Because of
the nature of age misstatement in this census, the sex
ratios for these two age groups would probably be much less
divergent if the true ages of all persons were known.

For the Pima, there appear to be too many persons
(especially females) in the 20-24 age interval and too few
females at 10-14, besides a gap for both sexes at 15-19.
In order to determine the level of maternal mortality and
its contribution to the sex ratio, rather than attempt to
redistribute persons across age groups, let us compare the

sex ratio at 10-34 with that at 35-64. As expected, at 10-34 the sex ratio is not especially high, 103.2, while at 35-64 it is higher, 116.3. There are 48 excess males at 0-34, 52 at ages 35-64, and 7 at ages 65 and over, for a total of 110.

This suggests the possibility of considerable maternal mortality. It may further be assumed that warfare was not intense enough to cause great loss of males, because the sex ratio at 35-64 would be lower if this were the case.

As a small population (Table 11) chance factors may affect the Maricopa data to a considerable degree. Nevertheless, there appear to be too many males in the 25-29 and 30-34 age groups and too many females in the 20-24 and 25-29 age groups. The sex ratio for persons 10-34 is 90.0; for persons 35-64, 127.3. It thus appears that maternal mortality may have been quite high among the Maricopa. Males exceed females in number in all age groups from 30-64.

At younger ages, 10-34, there is a deficit of males. This may in part be the result of chance, but it is possible that this group experienced the majority of battle deaths. By age 30, maternal mortality presumably tended to reverse the sex ratio. However, in order to arrive at such a high sex ratio for ages 35-64, maternal mortality would have to be very high. Thus, it is possible that Pima males, who exceeded Pima females in number at probably all ages (Table 10), married Maricopa women, who at younger ages were in excess. These Pima males then were classified as Maricopa by incorporation into the Maricopa clan system (Spier 1933:188), increasing the Maricopa sex ratio, and, perhaps with age misstatement, producing a bulge in absolute numbers at some ages (especially 25-34).

The two largest Maricopa clans in 1915, and probably 1860, were the only two clans into which the Pima were "invariably" assimilated (Spier 1933:194), supporting the assumption of intermarriage.[8] Nevertheless, in spite of considerable excess of males above 35 and deficit at 10-34, the greater part of the excess of Maricopa males is at ages 0-9 (twenty-six), compared to a deficit of ten at 10-34, and an excess of twelve at 35 and over, for a total excess of twenty-eight. As the high sex ratio at ages 0-4 is attributed to either infanticide, misclassification of females or underenumeration of females, the Maricopa sex ratio at ages 0-4 may in fact be lower if either of the latter two cases is true. This, however, while lowering the sex ratio for the total population, would increase the importance of excess of males at ages 35 and over, and hence the probability of high maternal mortality producing the Maricopa excess of males.

Warfare with Quechan and Mohave seems to have taken a heavy toll of young Maricopa males (i.e., a deficit of males at ages 10-29), being greater in importance than maternal mortality and capture of women. However, as women grew older, perhaps maternal mortality began to overtake in frequency deaths from battle, and females became fewer than males. Knowing, perhaps, that many males would die at less than 30 or 35, perhaps the Maricopa practiced female infanticide in an attempt to regulate the number of females for the expected reduced number of males, as well as to keep women from becoming Quechan and Mohave captives. This could account for the extreme excess of males at 0-4. Perhaps even female infanticide was not enough to equalize the sex ratio by marriage age, and Pima men were taken as husbands by excess Maricopa women.

However, all this is extremely speculative, and can not be asserted with any certainty for a population as small as the Maricopa, which is subject to considerable variation in numbers by chance alone.

In conclusion, and as a general warning, much of the detailed analysis of Pima and Maricopa population for this period is based on the 1860 Census, which is the most detailed data source for the period, being the only one with age data. Age misstatement is extreme in this census, and there is an unknown and significant degree of under-enumeration (as well as in the other, less completely reported censuses for this period).

Consequently, we are still mainly in the realm of speculation. Hypotheses cannot be rigorously tested by any formal method of verification. Any statements in this chapter must be evaluated with that in mind.

Notes to Chapter Three

1. Malaria was noted as a seasonal health problem among whites in nineteenth century Arizona, especially in the south (Quebbeman 1966:170).

2. Ruggles was accused by R. Jones (1869: 220) and Grossmann (1870:119) of living 15 or 30 miles (24 or 48 km) off-reservation. Thus Ruggles may have had no basis for comparison with 1866 and 1867. However, at this time the army and Indian agents were contending for control of Indian affairs (Spicer 1962:148, 358-59). In that Jones was an assistant inspector general for the army, and Grossman was an army captain who soon became the agent for the Pima and Maricopa, they are perhaps not without prejudice in evaluating Ruggles, who was not in the army faction (Ruggles 1869a:211-12).

3. This was the infamous "pinole treaty" which is described in more detail in Browne (1871:120-24). The calendar stick date for this event in Hall (1907: 420), once again showing its unreliability, is 1853, 10 years earlier!

4. This is an example of the federal government Indian policy of divide and conquer. Using the already existing enmity between the Pima-Maricopa and Apache-Yavapai, the Apache and Yavapai were brought under federal control at a considerably cheaper cost in white money and lives than if the government had subjugated the Apache-Yavapai alone. With the Apache and Yavapai under strict

government supervision on reservations, attention turned to divesting the Pima-Maricopa of their water, land, and culture (see Chapters 4-6).

5. In 1866, Lord (1866:112) mentioned that sometimes there was not enough water for farming, and the Pima went upstream, off the reservation, to farm. Ruggles (1869a:208-9) also remarked that as early as 1866, American and Mexican citizens occupied lands within a contemplated extension to the Gila River Indian Reservation and constructed irrigation canals. By 1869, according to Jones (1869:219-20), whites above the reservation were not returning irrigation waste water from their fields to the Gila River, allowing it to run off elsewhere, diminishing the flow of the river.

6. It is not clear when venereal disease first appeared among the Pima and Maricopa, or if it was in fact endemic. No mention of this is made in Ezell (1961).

7. Most children with congenital syphilis are fetal deaths (Benenson 1970:244) and gonorrhea produces few deaths, even in women (Benenson 1970:97).

8. The Pima had moieties named Vulture and Coyote (also referred to as Red Ants and White Ants) (Russell 1908:197). The Maricopa had a number of totemic clans, some with multiple totems. Spier (1933: 194) states that Pima who married into the Maricopa invariably were assigned to the Maricopa $l_y$ew´c clan if they were in the Pima Vulture moiety, and to the

Maricopa x̣ipaˊ clan if they were in the Pima Coyote moiety. Among the totems of the lyewˊc clan was the vulture; among the x̣ipaˊ clan totems was the coyote (Spier 1933:191). Using a BIA roll for 1915, Spier found that the two largest Maricopa clans were x̣ipaˊ, eighty-three members, and lyewˊc, fifty-five members. The third largest clan was cĭkåmaˊ, with twenty-one members.

    Maricopa personal names sometimes reflect directly or indirectly the clan membership of a person, especially for women. Quite often, a girl received a name which referred in some way to one of the totems of her clan (Spier 1933:196). A woman's in-laws customarily referred to her by the name of her clan (Spier 1933:197). Knowing that clan membership could be ascertained in some cases from personal names, I went through the 1860 Census schedules for the villages of Hueso Parrado and Sacate ("Sacaton") (the Maricopa villages) and recorded the frequency of clan names used as personal names. I was not able to determine clan membership from names referring indirectly to clan totems.

    The results are consistent with Spier. X̣ipaˊ and lyewˊc, with about thirty occurrences each, vastly outnumber the rest of the clan names, which included: pakĭˊt, eight occurrences; xavåtcaˊc, six occurrences, xamituˊtc, three occurrences, and cŭkåpaˊs, one occurrence.

While there are other reasons why x̣ipa´ and l$_y$ew´c could be the largest Maricopa clans, these were the clans the Pima were assimilated into, there was an excess of Pima males at all ages and a deficit of Maricopa females at younger, marriageable ages, but not at older ages. A good case can be made for the existence of marriage of some Pima males with Maricopa females to a greater extent than other tribe-sex combinations of intermarriage.

CHAPTER FOUR

THE BEGINNINGS OF OFF-RESERVATION MIGRATION
TO THE END OF SELF-SUFFICIENCY (1869-89)

Factors Affecting Pima and Maricopa Population

Because most sources for this period do not usually distinguish Pima from Maricopa, both groups will be considered together in this section. Many of the reports refer primarily to the Pima, the commentators assuming that conditions were relatively similar with the Maricopa (who were primarily off-reservation during this period and hence not as accessible). That this is not always a valid assumption shall be seen from the few sources that attempt to distinguish the two groups.

When it is unclear whether a report refers to Pima only, Maricopa only, or both, the people will be referred to as "the Indians." "Period," as used in this chapter, always means 1869-89.

The Food Situation and Related Factors

From 1869-80, the Pima and Maricopa had to contend with an increasing scarcity of river water for irrigation, primarily during the summer. This resulted from two factors. Since the end of the Civil War, whites had been settling and

farming in increasing numbers along the Gila River above
the reservation.¹

Intensifying the effect of taking of water by
whites were periods of drought from 1869-73 and 1876-80
(Ferris 1873:180; Fisk 1879:54; Ludlam 1880:3; Stout 1874:
292, 1877:32, 1878:3). With little or no water in the Gila
River in the summer, the Pima and Maricopa could no longer
grow the summer crop of maize, beans, and squash.
Fortunately, because of greater river flow in the winter
and spring, some water reached the reservation, and the
winter wheat crop was affected to a much lesser degree.²

The loss of the maize-bean-squash crop caught the
Pima by surprise, and in 1869-71 it was necessary at times
for them to take crops from the fields of whites (Grossmann
1870:120, 1871b:360). This naturally brought forth an
outcry from the whites about "stealing." The whites, of
course, did not consider themselves thieves by taking
water that the Pima and Maricopa had been accustomed to
using, and to which the Indians had prior rights, even
under the laws of whites.³

By 1871-72, the Pima and Maricopa had apparently
become resigned to the new situation in which they would
have to endure a summer water shortage unless they moved
to an area of more abundant water. (This did not mean,
however, that they had relinquished their claim to the
Gila River water.) Some Pima migrated seasonally, then
permanently, to the Salt River to farm. A group of

Maricopa also went to the Salt River, apparently settling there permanently from the first (Azul in Howard 1872:167; Bendell 1872:313; Hudson 1876:7; Walker 1872:57).

Expansion of Pima settlement in the Blackwater area (see Figure 2) above the reservation, begun in 1866, also continued at this time (Stout 1872:316). In this area the Gila River channel narrows somewhat, and underground flow of water rises to the riverbed when the river is dry in other places (Lee 1904:26). A similar situation occurs at Gila Crossing (Lee 1904:24-26), which settlement was established west of the reservation boundary during this period (Russell 1908:54).[4]

The period also saw a change in Pima-Maricopa economic relations with whites. During the 1860s, the Pima and Maricopa raised a surplus of grain, mainly wheat, and sold it to whites. But with the loss of water in the 1870s, while the Pima and Maricopa could still grow a wheat crop, some of it, if not all, had to make up for the loss of maize and beans. Nevertheless, there were still reports of Pima selling wheat to whites (Hodge 1877:161; Hudson 1876:7; Stout 1877:31).

Rather than representing a surplus, it appears that these sales of wheat show the beginnings of Pima-Maricopa integration into the national, and ultimately, world economy as suppliers of raw materials (e.g., grain and labor) and as consumers of manufactured products (e.g., clothing, cooking utensils, flour made from grain supplied by them). The overwhelming effects of such economic involvement on the economy, social organization, and demography of American Indians in general and the Ute in particular have been presented in Jorgensen (1971). To the Pima and Maricopa, at this point it meant that food necessary for survival was traded for material goods that had come to be seen as necessities no less than food.

However, as will be seen in the following chapters, eventually the Pima and Maricopa could raise little wheat, and had to give up agriculture. A more significant feature, which began in 1872, is migration off-reservation to seek employment from whites (Stout 1872:318). With few skills, other than agricultural, valued by whites, the Pima who sought work off-reservation were further integrated into the national economy at its lowest-paying level, that of unskilled workers. It is obvious that off-reservation employment was sought from necessity, not choice. When conditions improved, as in 1873-76, the off-reservation migrants, mainly young men, returned to the reservation to farm (Stout 1873a:283).

During 1873-76, as a result of good rains, the Pima and Maricopa enjoyed a brief respite from large-scale want. Soon afterwards summer droughts returned and conditions rapidly deteriorated. In 1877, further settlement took place along the Salt River. Perhaps the majority was on the left (south) bank of the river, at a community which came to be known as Lehi, established by a group of Mormons from Utah in March 1877 (D. Jones 1960:295). In return for digging an irrigation canal for the settlement, the Indians were encouraged to farm there (D. Jones 1960:300-01). The Indian settlers included both Pima and Maricopa.

Heavy reliance was placed on wild plant foods from 1875-80, but while in 1876-77 the agent (Stout 1877:32) felt that mesquite beans were abundant enough to prevent starvation, the next year even the mesquite bean crop was poor (Stout 1878:2). During the year the agent (Stout 1878:3) reported that half the population of Pima and Maricopa were off-reservation cultivating small plots of land, wherever they could be found, not desired by whites. This is the highest number ever reported living off Gila River Reservation. The occurrence of deaths from starvation at this time seems certain.

The severity of the food situation was finally recognized by the government in 1879-80, when wheat was issued as rations to the destitute (Ludlam 1880:3). In this year apparently even the wheat crop was poor, perhaps because of an abnormally cold period in winter when snow was reported on the ground (Hall 1907:423; Russell 1908:58).

Throughout 1869-80, no reports of starvation were made by the Indian agents, and the Pima and Maricopa were almost constantly referred to as "self-sustaining" (Stout 1872:316, 1877:31) or "self-supporting" (Stout 1878:2). However, in 1879 Ludlam (1879:6) let the truth out by remarking that the Pima and Maricopa were self-supporting only in the sense that the government did not provide them with rations or annuities (in spite of their great need).

Between 1880 and 1889, the Pima and Maricopa were in limbo between permanent loss of the maize-bean-squash crop, which took place during the 1870s, and permanent loss of the wheat crop, at least at Gila River, which began in the 1890s. During the 1880s, a precarious equilibrium seems to have been established between food needs on the one hand and crops produced and wild plants gathered on the other.

No cases of starvation were mentioned, but the summer water supply was almost always too low to permit planting, much less maturing, a corn-bean-squash crop (Jackson 1883:6; Wheeler 1882:6, 1885:3). Nevertheless, compared to the 1870s, the 1880s in general were a time of good spring runoff, and the wheat crop was usually reported as good (Jackson 1883:6, 1884:5; Johnson 1889:120; Wheeler 1881:5, 1885:3, 1886:38), with some sold off-reservation (Johnson 1889:120; Wheeler 1882:9; Whittlesey and Smiley 1884:19).[5]

The situation fluctuated somewhat throughout the 1880s, with 1881-82 perhaps the poorest year (Cruse 1941: 156-57), while 1888-89 seems to have been exceptionally good (Johnson 1889:120).[6]

A false impression of increasingly better conditions is given by Indian Agents Jackson (1883:6, 1884:5) and

Wheeler (1885:3, 1886:38) from 1883-86. In 1885-86, for example, Wheeler (1886:38) optimistically stated:

> I have to report an increased interest in farming. New lands are being cleared, fields enlarged, irrigating ditches improved, and the general outlook is encouraging, each year showing a noticeable improvement.

The next year, however, the new agent (E. Howard 1887a:4) effectively demolished the impression of "progress" built up during the previous 4 years.[7]

Although good crops of wheat were one reason that the Pima and Maricopa were free from dire want during the 1880s, wild plant foods must also have been widely used. In past crop failures, the Pima and Maricopa always relied on mesquite beans and certain other wild plants (Russell 1908:66-78: Spier 1933:48-58). However, since the beginning of intensive raiding between the Pima-Maricopa and Apache-Yavapai in the early or mid-eighteenth century (Ezell 1961:118-20, 136, 144: Winter 1973:69, 71), for the Pima and Maricopa, gathering of wild plant food, even near the Pima and Maricopa villages, had always carried the risk of death by Apache-Yavapai attack. But in the late 1870s and 1880s, with the Apache and Yavapai confined to reservations, the Pima and Maricopa could safely exploit plant resources, such as mesquite, not only near their villages, but also at some distance away. Thus mesquite growing off-reservation along the Gila and Salt could be used, increasing the area, and presumably, quantity of wild plant food gathered.

By going farther from the reservations to collect plant food, the Pima and Maricopa now could also go regularly and in safety to areas of higher elevation where different plants grow. In 1883, Bandelier (1970:121) met several Pima near Sunflower, about 55 miles (90 km) northeast of Sacaton. They were cooking the heart of the agave, reporting that they did so regularly. In order to obtain agave, the Pima and Maricopa generally had to enter Apache or Yavapai territory, as the plant grows at a higher elevation than the Gila River Reservation. This was done even during the period of hostilities with the Apache and Yavapai. Now that there was no threat from the Apache and Yavapai by entering their territory, the agave, of small use to whites, could be freely exploited, and must have kept at least some Pima and Maricopa from starvation. The "banana" yucca (<u>Yucca baccata</u>) also grows at higher elevations (over 3000 feet) (Kearney and Peebles 1960:187) and the Pima and Maricopa also must have gathered its fruit at this time.

Overall, then, because of a series of wet years during the 1880s, and the ability to safely exploit the food resources of a wider area than previously because of the absence of Apache and Yavapai, the Pima and Maricopa were able to obtain enough to eat.

Other than a continuing shortage of water, only one catastrophe is reported for this period, an earthquake in 1887-88 (Russell 1908:60; Spier 1933:141). No casualties were mentioned as a result of it, and I assume that it had no influence on population.

Epidemics

As a result of the food situation, the Pima and Maricopa, weakened physically by insufficient food, were ripe for epidemics. However, the epidemics were perhaps not as common as they could have been and seem to have been confined chiefly to children. The main epidemics of 1869-80 were smallpox, which occurred twice, and measles, which occurred twice. Smallpox broke out throughout Arizona in 1869-70 (Grossmann 1870:122; Quebbeman 1966:65). Despite this, the agent at Gila River reported not only no deaths on the reservation, but also no cases of smallpox during the epidemic (Grossmann 1870:122). He attributes this to vaccination of over 1800 persons who had never had smallpox (those who had had smallpox and infants less than 4 months old were not vaccinated).

This is a rather surprising claim, and could immediately be dismissed as an attempt to make conditions seem better than they were except for the absence of any report of a smallpox epidemic at this time in the calendar sticks (Russell 1908:53). Nevertheless, with smallpox occurring so near to the Pima and Maricopa, it seems likely that some cases and deaths occurred, although probably not as many as in previous smallpox epidemics for two reasons: the population was probably becoming more immune to its effects, and the vaccination program may have been effective in reducing the incidence of the disease.

This represents the first reported mass smallpox vaccination for the Pima and Maricopa. After the epidemic subsided, however, vaccination seems to have ceased. The next mention of it is in 1875-76, when some children were vaccinated (Hudson 1876:7).

Smallpox broke out again in many of the white settlements in Arizona in 1876-77 (Quebbeman 1966:114, 157, 159; Stout 1877:33). This time the agent at Gila River (Stout 1877:32) reported both on-reservation cases and less than 100 deaths from the disease among the Pima, Maricopa, and Papago. For this epidemic the Pima calendar sticks report its occurrence in all Pima and Maricopa villages (Russell 1908:55).

Several factors appear to have promoted the appearance of smallpox at this time. Among both whites and Indians there seems to have been no continuing immunization program when the disease was not occurring. The immunity bestowed by the vaccination wears off in about 5 to 7 years, and a person must be reimmunized (Lyght 1966: 1716). Thus, the epidemic occurred when the vaccinations of those who had been immunized in 1869-70 were expiring. Confirmingly, another smallpox epidemic occurred among the Pima and Maricopa in 1883-84 (Jackson 1884:5), when the effect of vaccination received during the epidemic of 1876-77 would have worn off.

Besides those whose immunity had lapsed, children who had been born since the previous epidemic were also vulnerable, and like their parents, were living in a time of economic stress, thus increasing their susceptibility to epidemic diseases.

The mortality from this epidemic was probably greater than that of 1869-70. During the earlier epidemic, vaccination was reportedly started before any cases appeared on the reservation. During the 1876-77 epidemic, vaccination began only after cases appeared, and the agent had difficulty finding a doctor to carry out the immunizations, since most physicians were already occupied with treating cases off-reservation. The government had not felt it necessary to constantly provide a doctor for Gila River (although those sent out may have quit soon after arriving in order to set up their own practice).

The agent's estimate of mortality, because of its vagueness (less than 100) is just a guess. If there is any quantitative basis to it, it would reflect almost entirely Pima and Maricopa mortality. Although the agent at Gila River was also in charge of the Papago, there was in fact little government contact with the Papago. Taking the mortality figure at face value, it is possible that 2% of the Pima-Maricopa population died from smallpox in 1876-77.

According to the calendar sticks, measles occurred in 1871-72, and many died (Russell 1908:53). While the agent mentions no epidemic in his annual report for that year (Stout 1872:316-20), Cook (in Ladies' Union Mission School Association 1893:100), a teacher on the reservation, mentions an unspecified sickness in December 1871 which killed four school children, which must have been measles.

Another measles epidemic appears to have occurred in 1878-79. The report comes from the Maricopa calendar stick (Spier 1933:141), which reported that many children died. Jones (1960:309-10), the leader of the Mormon colony at Lehi, also reported some time after 1877 that both the Pima and Maricopa at Salt River killed some shamans who were accused of killing children. (Measles, of course, would primarily kill children.) Consequently, it appears that a measles epidemic occurred among the Pima and Maricopa at Salt River, and may have occurred at Gila River as well.

Reports of other epidemics from 1869-80 are vaguer as to symptoms and degree of mortality. In 1873-74, the agent (Stout 1874:293) reported that "Fevers of various kinds, previously unknown in this section of the country" occurred. As it was a wet year, this could have been malaria or typhoid fever. The Pima calendar sticks for 1875-76 report a recurrence of the "shooting pain" sickness in one village, Rsânûk (Russell 1908:55).

From 1880-89, two epidemics occurred which caused high mortality. A smallpox epidemic broke out in 1883-84 in every village on the reservation (Jackson 1884:6). A vaccination program was established, but the vaccine was not effective (Whittlesey and Smiley 1884:19). Judging from qualitative statements about the three smallpox epidemics, in 1883-84 mortality was greater than in the epidemic of 1869-70, but less than in 1876-77.

The previous year, 1882-83, Pima and Maricopa calendar sticks (Russell 1908:58; Spier 1933:141) and the agent (Jackson 1883:7) reported a measles epidemic. (The Maricopa calendar stick dates the epidemic at 1883-84, a year too late). All sources agree that many died; these were certainly largely infants and children.

During the first wet years after the drought of 1876-80 malaria was a problem (Wheeler 1881:6, 1882:9), but while a significant number may have been affected, few probably died.

An epidemic of considerable but local effect occurred in Blackwater in 1888-89 (Russell 1908:61), during which three prominent men of the community died.

Throughout 1869-89, other epidemic childhood diseases should have been taking a toll, but are not mentioned. Among these would be infant diarrhea, pneumonia, influenza, diphtheria, whooping cough, mumps, chicken pox, and scarlet fever.

General Health

Assessments by agents of general health vary from fair to "good" for 1869-89 (Hudson 1876:7; Jackson 1883:7; Johnson 1888:6; Stout 1875:214, 1877:33, 1878:4; Wheeler

1881:6; Whittlesey and Smiley 1884:19). This is hard to reconcile with the reports above of epidemics; in addition, many agents considered venereal disease (euphemistically referred to as "immorality") and alcoholic intoxication ("intemperance") to be serious health problems. However, both veneral diseases and drinking were considered greater problems in 1869-80 than during the 1880s.

Venereal diseases

Venereal diseases could affect population size in two ways. Persons infected with syphilis would eventually die of complications from the disease. The main effect of venereal diseases, however, would be to reduce fertility, in the case of both gonorrhea and syphilis. Every agent had something to say about venereal diseases from 1869-75 (Grossmann 1870:119, 1871a:412, 1871b:362; Hinton 1878:364; Hodge 1877:163; Stout 1872:318, 1873:282, 1874:293, 1875: 214, 1877:32, 1878:4). It was claimed that venereal diseases occurred with less frequency among the Pima in 1860 (Stout 1872:318) as earlier sources have also reported. Nevertheless, several times one agent stated that only a minority of the Pima population was infected (Stout 1872: 318, 1874:293, 1875:214).

According to Wheeler (1882:9), the opening of the Southern Pacific Railroad line across Arizona in 1881 reduced stage traffic across the reservation, and led to less intercourse (sexual and otherwise) with transient whites, who had been considered the source and perpetuators of venereal diseases among the Pima.[8] Two years later, however, Agent Jackson felt that the railroad had not decreased contact with transient whites, and stated bluntly (Jackson 1884:5): "Syphilitic affections is the prevailing disease." Jackson, of course, is overstating the case, but there is no reason why venereal disease incidence should decrease in the 1880s with less contact with whites. The Pima did not need to be reinfected by whites in order to transmit disease among themselves.

The agents, reflecting the prevailing views of their time, assumed that venereal diseases were the inevitable retribution for the "immorality" and "prostitution" which they considered rampant among the Pima and Maricopa. Thus, they undoubtedly felt justified in reporting venereal diseases regardless of whether they had actually seen any cases. Consequently, in attempting to determine the extent of venereal diseases among the Pima and Maricopa, we must consider any report of "immorality" or "prostitution" among Pima or Maricopa (i.e., not with whites) ethnocentric on the part of the agent. Among the Pima and Maricopa, sexual relations were much less restricted, and the marriage ceremony was much more informal than among whites during the nineteenth century (Russell 1908:182-83; Spier 1933:219, 224-25).

It seems likely however, that true prostitution to whites occurred to some extent among the Pima in 1869-80 when they experienced a severe food shortage. This was one of the few resources the Pima still possessed. The Maricopa had been accused of prostitution since 1859, over 10 years before the Pima. What happened to the Maricopa during 1869-89 is thus uncertain; presumably venereal diseases were at about the same level as in 1859.

It is questionable whether all reported cases of venereal diseases were in fact that. Two of the most obvious visible manifestations of syphilis would be skin lesions and eye conditions, including blindness. However, skin lesions could result from many other causes, such as ringworm, impetigo, pediculosis, scabies, or nutritional deficiencies (such as of B vitamins or protein). Kolmer (1950:242) states that " . . . diagnosis of syphilis in the secondary stage is by no means as easy as commonly surmised, in view of the fact that its cutaneous and mucosal lesions may be mistaken for other diseases, or the reverse." Conditions involving the eyes would much more likely be trachoma than syphilis, and no mention of trachoma was made by any reports from 1869-89. Consequently, the extent of venereal diseases was probably considerably less than reports claim, but still caused somewhat lower fertility than could have otherwise been realized.

Alcoholic intoxication

The effects of drunkenness on population would be several. A very small number of persons would actually drink themselves to death. A larger, but still relatively small number, would die of alcoholic cirrhosis after a number of years of heavy drinking. Most important, intoxicated persons would more often have accidents and engage in violent behavior which could lead to death.

Every agent, as well as Antonio Azul, the Pima leader, considered drinking to be a problem for some Pima, especially young males, from 1869-80 (Grossmann 1870:122; O. Howard 1872:167; Hudson 1876:8; Ludlam 1879:6, 1880:3; Stout 1871:353-54, 1872:317; 1873a:282, 1874:292, 1875:214, 1877:32, 1878:4). During the 1880s, intoxication was reported less often (Bancroft 1888:548; Bandelier 1970:128; Jackson 1884:5). At this time less drunkenness probably occurred because of relatively better economic conditions.

Unlike many, if not most, American Indian groups (Driver 1969:102, Map 12), the Pima made an alcoholic beverage before European contact, a wine from the fruit of the saguaro cactus (Russell 1908:72). However, it seems unlikely that this beverage could have produced to a significant degree any of the effects on population mentioned above. The saguaro fruit ripens once a year. Only part of the harvest was made into wine, and it spoils quickly (Greene 1936:309-12). When the wine was ready, people assembled in large groups and drank as much as they could. This was intended as imitative magic: as they saturated themselves with wine, so, they hoped, the earth would be wet with rain (Underhill 1938:19-20). According to Levy and Kunitz (1971:108), cirrhosis of the liver results from addictive alcoholism, rather than occasional binge drinking. Thus, even though the saguaro wine ceremony may have lost some of its religious significance by the time Russell (1908:170) visited the Pima in 1901-2, it seems unlikely that an annual excess consumption of wine of low alcohol content could have led to a significant number of cirrhosis deaths among the Pima, or even to many accidents, since many participants would probably have been too weary to go anywhere. The Maricopa also had a saguaro wine festival (Spier 1933:57-58, 162-63) whose effects on population are assumed to have been similarly unimportant.

After white settlement near the boundaries of the Gila River Reservation, however, distilled beverages with at least four times the alcoholic content of saguaro wine became readily available to the Pima. Distilled liquor would have had a much greater effect on population than saguaro wine. Probably the greatest influence came from horseback accidents, this assumption based on the present-day analogy of automobile accidents from driving while intoxicated. Murders, drinking to death, and alcoholic cirrhosis were probably less significant factors at this time.

During the 1880s, a new cause of death developed which some have related to heavy drinking. With the completion of the railroad near the southern border of the Gila River Reservation, the Pima and Maricopa were permitted to ride free on Southern Pacific freight trains (Jackson 1883:6; Shaw 1974:128).[9] The calendar sticks (Russell 1908:59) and agent (Jackson 1884:6) both mention a number of persons who were run over after falling off trains. Six such deaths were reported for 1883-84. These deaths appear to represent the high point of this cause of death, and some time after 1902, the government prohibited free riding on trains (Russell 1908:59n; Shaw 1974:128). Thus this cause of death was in itself never significant, but it added to an increasing number of deaths by accident.

Medical services

A number of persons appear to have sporadically occupied the post of agency doctor about half the time from 1869-89 (Andrews 1870a:118; Grossmann 1871b:358; Jackson 1883:7; Ludlam 1879:6, 1880:3; Stout 1873a:282, 1875:214, 1878:4; Wheeler 1882:9; Whittlesey and Smiley 1884:19). At other times the agent administered what medicines were available. Besides the smallpox immunizations of 1869-70 and 1875-77, the agents reported that the doctor was well-patronized (Grossmann 1870:122, Stout 1872:319, 1877:33). Stout (1875:214) mentioned the performance of some operations that required several days convalescence at the agency office, there being no hospital at this time. Given the periodic vacancies in the doctor position, limited medical facilities, and the distance of many persons from the agency office, it seems likely

Abortion and infanticide

Grossmann, the agent at Gila River from 1869-71, is the only source of comments on infanticide and abortion, which he said "prevails to a very great extent" (Grossmann 1871a:415). The reason he gives is that at a man's death, all his possessions, including house and stock, were burned, leaving the widow impoverished. Because of a reputed prejudice against widows, she would find it hard to remarry, and thus was left to support her children. This practice was thus assumed to encourage Pima women to have few children, and hence to practice abortion and infanticide. While some abortion and infanticide certainly occurred, I doubt it was for the reason claimed by Grossmann. The severe economic situation of the Pima and Maricopa was more likely the reason. It also appears that widows did remarry. While Russell (1908) says nothing about the existence or absence of the levirate, Spier records that it was found among the Maricopa, but not the Pima (Spier 1936:19). Since, according to Spier, the Pima had non-exogamous moieties in which all members of a moiety were classed as cross-cousins (Spier 1936:10), the absence of the levirate would not preclude remarriage by a widow. Although widows were supposed to mourn for four years, Russell (1908:195) claims that very few did. This seems to imply that widows did remarry.

Hostile Encounters with Apache and Yavapai

From 1869-75, the old pattern of hostilities between Pima-Maricopa and Apache-Yavapai continued (Bourke 1891:184; Russell 1908:53-55; Stout 1872:319, 1873a:282, 1874:293). As during the late 1860s, the Pima and Maricopa continued to go out against the Apache and Yavapai by themselves and with the United States Army. The Pima calendar sticks reported three Pima killed by "Apaches" in 1870-71, one in 1872-73, and one in 1874-75 (Russell 1908: 53, 55). Bourke (1891:192, 199) reported one Pima killed in a sortie with the army against the Apache, and an unknown number of Pima killed near Florence.

Stout (1874:293) is correct in stating that raiding of Pima and Maricopa was less frequent than formerly. In 1872, a short truce was established under the efforts of General O. O. Howard, sent to Arizona and New Mexico by President Grant to induce the Apache and Yavapai to settle on reservations and make peace with their enemies. In a meeting on 21 May 1872, a number of Apache had been congregated by the government, along with representatives of the Pima, Papago, and whites (including the territorial governor). All present agreed on peace (Howard 1872:155; Stout 1872:319). More significant, however, is that from 1872-75, the Apache and Yavapai had increasingly been induced or coerced into settling on reservations at various points in Arizona and New Mexico. By 1877, almost all Apache and Yavapai had been concentrated on just one reservation, at San Carlos (Spicer 1962:250-53).

Even before Apache and Yavapai concentration at San Carlos, the Indians at Gila River were increasingly protected by the white settlements which were encircling the reservation, especially Adamsville-Florence on the east, and to a lesser degree, the white and Pima-Maricopa settlements in the Salt River Valley to the north. The Pima and Maricopa at Salt River, of course, were most exposed to the Apache and Yavapai, and D. Jones (1960:301) quotes one white settler who admitted that the whites did not oppose Pima and Maricopa settlement in the Salt River Valley because where the Indians were able to take up residence, they would serve as a buffer for whites farther downstream.

From 1869-75, Pima and Maricopa raids against the Apache and Yavapai were probably more frequent than Apache and Yavapai raids on the Pima-Maricopa. Besides concentration on reservations, which limited Apache-Yavapai raiding, the government used the enmity of Pima and Maricopa toward Apache and Yavapai in order to maintain constant pressure on the Apache and Yavapai so as to force them to settle on reservations the government had designated for them.

Although at peace with the Apache and Yavapai since 1875, the Pima were enlisted three times by government agencies (once by Pinal County and twice by the Army) to make up forces against the Apache and Yavapai (Russell 1908:60-61; Wheeler 1882:7). In none of these cases were Pima casualties nor contact with the Apache or Yavapai reported.

Hostile Relations with Whites

From 1869-80, no group actions by whites against Pima-Maricopa occurred that resulted in violence, and with one exception, no Pima-Maricopa group actions resulting in violence were taken against whites. However, the threat of white vigilante actions against the Pima and Maricopa was quite explicit during the early 1870s when Pima found it necessary to gather food in fields planted by whites (Bendell 1871:349; Stout 1871:354). From 1869-75, the Pima and Maricopa became less and less useful to the whites, who no longer experienced as many Apache or Yavapai raids in the Salt and Middle Gila River Valleys. With the Apache and Yavapai essentially overcome, whites no longer needed the help of the Pima and Maricopa, and could devote themselves to obtaining the fertile Pima-Maricopa farm lands.

By 1872, the government proposed moving the Pima to Indian Territory (Stout 1872:317), rather than attempt to protect their water rights where they were living. However, after a visit to Indian Territory and a wetter year in 1873-74, any interest on the part of the Pima for moving vanished (Stout 1874:293-94), frustrating this attempt by whites to obtain the lands of the Pima and Maricopa.

The exception to the absence of group violence during this period occurred when some Pima removed from a trial a white who had been charged with killing a Pima. The accused murderer was executed by a group of several hundred Pima (Stout 1873:281-82).[10]

During the 1880s, tensions were high, with accusations of horse and cattle rustling from both sides (Howard 1887a:4; Jackson 1884:5), a threatened raid of white fields by the Pima (Cruse 1941:156-58), and whites filing homestead claims on public domain lands already occupied by Pima and Maricopa (Howard 1887a:6). No group violence resulted from these conditions, however.

Only one Pima group action against whites occurred, and its effect of Pima population was nonsignificant. Eleven Pima were held for trial, charged with assault with intent to commit murder on two whites near Tempe (Jackson 1883:5).[11]

In violence between individuals, two Indians, one a Pima, were killed by whites in separate incidents (Russell 1908:59, 61). Thus, overall, very few deaths occurred as a result of violence between Pima-Maricopa and whites.

Group Violence Among the Pima and Maricopa

It is interesting to note that from 1869 to 1880,

when there were food shortages, there are no reports of Pima violence against Maricopa or vice versa; all such violence is directed toward a member of the aggressor's own ethnic group. Intra-ethnic violence appears to replace violence directed against the Apache and Yavapai once the Apache and Yavapai were placed on reservations and no longer attacked the Pima and Maricopa. Before 1877, almost every year produced a calendar stick entry regarding attack on or by "Apache" (Russell 1908:43-56). Violence by Pima against Pima is not mentioned, if and when it occurred. In 1877 and after, many years have entries regarding killings at the saguaro wine festivals, by Pima against Pima (Russell 1908:57-66). Spicer (1962:149) was also struck by the increase in fights and murders reported during the 1870s.

This situation appears to be related to the loss of water by the Pima. Even when they were losing water in the early 1870s, they were still fighting the Apache and Yavapai, and violence was directed in this pre-existing channel. The need for defense against the Apache and Yavapai also probably served to unify the Pima and Maricopa, and intratribal differences that arose were probably played down because of the greater threat from the Apache and Yavapai. However, when the Apache and Yavapai were placed on reservations and the Pima and Maricopa no longer fought them, competition for the increasingly scarce water erupted into violence between Pima or Maricopa. Factions developed, and contending groups separated. Some, but relatively little, violence was directed against whites, the source of the difficulties. Certainly the proximity of the whites, who were continually increasing in number, cautioned the Pima and Maricopa against attacking the whites as they did the Apache and Yavapai. Besides ever-increasing numbers, the whites had the army on their side. The army was interested in the Pima and Maricopa only as a supply of scouts and soldiers to be used against the Apache and Yavapai, and by the 1880s, that campaign was nearly over.

With the whites so close, they could attack the Pima at any time, and had a set of punitive institutions not possessed by the Apache; that is to say, they were prepared to assume near-complete economic, political, and social control over the Pima and Maricopa, which the Apache and Yavapai could never dream of doing. Thus this may have discouraged the Pima and Maricopa from attacking the whites, even though they were an easy target by their proximity.

The only group violence among Pima occurred in 1878-79 and saw the culmination of past grievances erupt in a feud between some of the villages, viz., Blackwater, Santan, and Casa Blanca. In February 1879, three persons from Santan were killed by some persons from Blackwater (Russell 1908:56-57). (The calendar stick in Hall (1907: 423) also reports this event in less detail, misdating it as 1880.) According to Spicer (1962:149), the feud resulted from the attempts of three factions to solve water problems by shifts in residence to different parts of the reservation. There is no mention by the agents of internal violence, not even of the 1878-79 feud. It is most likely that this information was suppressed. No further events in the feud were mentioned in the calendar sticks after 1879. Apparently the Pima were so fragmented by that time that they would rather move than organize and fight.

Five Pima were killed by Pima during this period, three of them at saguaro wine festivals (Russell 1908:58-60). The calendar stick keeper thought it significant in 1888-89 that no murders occurred during the saguaro wine festival at Gila Crossing (Russell 1908:61). We can assume that about one intraethnic murder a year occurred among the Pima at this time.

Captives

Until the cessation of hostilities with the Apache and Yavapai around 1875, captives were still taken, at least by the Pima (Grossmann 1871a:417-18; Russell 1908:55; Shaw 1974:239; Stout 1872:318). As before, some were sold, while a smaller number were adopted or married.[12] There are no reports of Pima or Maricopa taken captive by the Apache or Yavapai during this period.

The only information concerning Maricopa taking of captives at this time is an entry from the Maricopa

calendar stick for 1873-74 (and repeated 1874-75), that
"The Yavapai were all captured" (Spier 1933:141). Rather
than referring to Maricopa capture of Yavapai, this must
chronicle the concentration of Yavapai on reservations by
the government. The Maricopa view of the process as the
Yavapai becoming prisoners of war, with the implications of
loss of freedom of movement and life style, is apt, and at
variance with the official government view of what happened
to the Apache and Yavapai when they were put on reservations.

By 1875, captives no longer were taken, although
apparently none were liberated either. Even before
cessation of hostilities, fewer captives were probably
being taken than during 1859-69. Raids were not as frequent
and when the Pima and Maricopa were accompanied by the
Army on raids, any captives taken would have been claimed
by the Army. Thus at this time captives most likely had
an insignificant effect on the size of Pima and Maricopa
population, especially since some were still being sold.

Intermarriage

As usual, there are few comments on this subject,
much less quantitative assessments of degree. Of the four
sources which comment on intermarriage for this period,
Grossmann (1871a:411) mentioned Pima-Maricopa unions, as
well as some Pima women living with white men. He felt
the latter type of union was increasing in frequency.
Regarding female Apache captives, Grossmann (1871a:417-18)

stated that "In rare instances a Pima will even marry an Apache woman after she has resided for two or three years on the reservation. . . . "

Hinton (1878:362), in mentioning the Pima and Maricopa stated that " . . . many of them have intermarried . . . " but retain their distinctness as ethnic groups. Presumably the person marrying into (i.e., changing residence to) the other ethnic group (or at least the children) took on the identity of the ethnic group of residence, although no one discusses this. Bandelier (1890:252, 257) reported Pima-Maricopa intermarriage, and stated that the children of such unions spoke both languages. Hamilton (1884:296) also mentioned Pima-Maricopa intermarriage while retaining cultural distinctiveness.

Pima and Maricopa thus continued to intermarry, Pima (and presumably Maricopa) continued to marry an occasional Apache or Yavapai captive that was not sold, and some Pima women started living with white men. The number of women lost by the Pima as partners of whites was probably not great and should have had very little or no effect on the total population or sex ratio. The marriage of Apache women to Pima and Maricopa similarly should have had little effect, since the number was small, and the Pima and Maricopa also lost women to the Apache and Yavapai. The unknown is how Pima-Maricopa intermarriage may have affected the sex ratios of each other, primarily that of the Maricopa because of their small size.

Intermarriage with Papago, although mentioned by no sources for this period, must have continued. It probably passed unnoticed because of the linguistic and other cultural similarities of the Pima and Papago. The Papago still migrated to the Pima to help them in the wheat harvest (E. Howard 1887a:6). Lacking any statements on the subject, I will assume that Pima-Papago intermarriage was balanced.

Migration

During the entire period, there was no significant permanent migration outside the area of the Gila River and Salt River Reservations and the nearby off-reservation areas. Pima, and presumably Maricopa, made trips to Florence, Phoenix, and Tempe for recreation and shopping, and after the railroad was built, to Tucson and Yuma as well, where some wheat was sold (Bandelier 1970:128; Jackson 1883:6, 1884:5; Webb 1959:52). There are no reports of Pima (or Maricopa) leaving the reservation to seek work among whites during the 1880s.

However, a new type of off-reservation residence developed during the 1880s with the first children leaving the reservation for boarding schools, some of them quite distant. During this period, Pima and Maricopa were reported attending federal Indian boarding schools at Hampton Institute, in Virginia (S. Armstrong 1881:194), and for Pima only, at Albuquerque (Burke 1887:248-52).

Most of the students, if not all, appear to have returned to the reservation after varying periods of school attendance. Consequently, there appears to be no population loss for the Pima by students at distant boarding schools remaining in the area of the boarding school after graduation or attendance at the school ceased. Moreover, in that very few Pima and Maricopa went to the boarding schools, an older age at marriage is unlikely to have resulted at this time.

Consistency of Qualitative and Quantitative Data
Total Population

As described above, 1869-80 was a time of food shortages, starvation, and epidemics. Added to this was an assumed high infant, child, and maternal mortality associated with a population lacking effective medicine. I thus presume that from 1869-80, Pima and Maricopa declined, although probably at an overall rate of less than 1% annually. The decline from 1869-80 is not assumed to be constant because some years were reported as better than others. I believe a lower rate of decline occurred than during 1859-69 because there appear to have been fewer epidemics, and these were confined more to infants and children. Some reduction of mortality from smallpox was achieved through vaccination. Other factors presumably had little influence on population size.

From 1880-89, food generally appears to have been adequate for needs (although some years were exceptions), and there were fewer epidemics: only one each of smallpox and measles compared to two of each in 1869-80. I thus assume that population was stable or increased slightly during the 1880s at a rate of less than 1% annually, although not necessarily constantly. I assume that infant, child, and maternal mortality was still high, preventing much of an increase in population at this time.

Among the numerous estimates and not so numerous census figures for the Pima and Maricopa during this period (Tables 15 through 17), certain figures are more accurate, or at least more useful, than others (Table 18). The reasons why these figures were chosen for the discussion which follows are set forth in Appendix C, but briefly, the figures are all known to be from censuses, whereas the other figures for this period are estimates, or look like census figures, but are not known to be so.

Looking first at the Pima alone (Table 18), the reported population figures confirm my assumptions based on qualitative data. Population declined from 1870-82, while it increased from 1882-90. The population estimates in Table 15 also support my assumptions, in that they are lower and relatively similar for 1870-80, and higher (with a few exceptions) for 1880-89.

However, the annual growth rates for the Pima population figures in Table 18 are not at the assumed levels.

For 1870-82, the rate (-0.1% annually) seems too low (i.e., not enough decline), while for 1882-90 (+1.7% annually), it seems too high for a population still subject to high mortality, epidemics, and near-starvation at times. If the population were already increasing from 1880-82 with the return of better conditions, this could account in part for the low rate of decrease in the population data for 1870-82. Moreover, the census of 1870 may reflect greater underenumeration than that of 1882.

It is not clear whether the census-like figures of 1872 and 1873 (Table 15, column 1 for 1872, column 2 for 1873) are in fact new censuses, or merely the addition of births and subtraction of deaths reported to the agent respectively to and from the 1870 census. Thus we cannot accept them unreservedly.

It seems possible, although there is no way to prove it from the available data, that underenumeration decreased with each census as the population became better known and censuses were taken more often. After the 1884 law requiring the preparation of an annual roll was passed (Act of July 4, 1884 (23 Stat. 98); see Appendix C), an effort may have been made in the 1887 census to improve accuracy. The 1890 Census was carried out in cooperation with the Office of the Census, and this collaboration may have insured more accuracy through the assistance of the Census Office personnel.

The figures in Table 19 are my estimates and assume increasingly better enumeration of Pima in censuses taken from 1870-90. Although the annual rate of decrease still remains somewhat low for 1870-82, the rate of increase from 1882-90 (and especially that of 1887-90) is reduced to my assumed level of less than 1% annually.

For the total population figures for the combined Pima and Maricopa population (Table 18), the annual growth rates are similar to those for the Pima alone (although slightly closer to my assumed values). This is not surprising since the Pima were over 90% of the combined population. But as will be seen in the figures for the Maricopa (Table 18), a different situation is implied for them, causing the differences in growth rates between the Pima and combined Pima-Maricopa populations.

As I assumed for the Maricopa, the figures show a decline for 1870-82, but decline continues until 1887, after which there is a moderate rate of annual increase (but very small absolute increase) to 1890. I would expect some random fluctuation in a population as small as the Maricopa, but factors other than chance appear to be affecting these population figures.

Looking at the data in Table 16, the Maricopa are implied to have experienced a catastrophic decrease from 1871-72 (or at least from 1870-72, since the 1871 figure appears to repeat that of 1870), and excluding estimates, a moderate increase to 1882 (or a fantastic increase to

1883, but as discussed in Appendix C, the 1883 figure must be rejected as including Pima).

The 1870s were a period of migration to new areas for the Maricopa. By 1872, a group was living along the Salt River (Grossmann 1871b:360). By 1877, all Maricopa were living off-reservation (Wheeler 1881:6). Thus, the catastrophic decrease shown for 1870-72 appears to represent decline in the number resident on the Gila River Reservation. When some Maricopa left the reservation, they were no longer reported in the agent's annual report, since they were no longer the concern of the Office of Indian Affairs.

The Maricopa who moved off-reservation to the Lehi area, just south of the Salt River Reservation, were enumerated in the 1887 and 1890 censuses, but in 1887, the number of Maricopa living in other off-reservation areas (200 out of a reported 310) was estimated. This estimate (as well as the enumeration at Lehi) may have been low, so that there probably was not a decline in population from 1882-87. The 1890 figure (Table 18) may also be too low, in this case because some Maricopa were apparently enumerated as Pima (see Appendix D).

Thus, with some Maricopa excluded because of off-reservation residence, and misclassification of Maricopa as Pima (and apparent misclassification of Pima as Maricopa in 1883), it is impossible to unravel the history of Maricopa population from 1869-89. The population estimates in Table 16, but not the census figures, support my assumption of an increase from 1880-89, but what occurred from 1870-80 is unknown, as could be expected during a period of migration of an entire people.

In making estimates of the combined Pima-Maricopa population (Table 19) I will thus proportionally increase the figures for the Pima alone. Using this method, it is necessary to determine the proportion the Maricopa were of the combined population for 1870-90. I will assume that this proportion remained constant throughout the period, as there is no evidence to the contrary.

As can be determined from Table 18, in 1870, the Maricopa were 8.9% of the combined population; in 1882, 7.8%; in 1887, 6.9%; and in 1890, 6.6%. As mentioned above, in Table 18, all the combined figures but 1870 (and perhaps 1882) appear to exclude Maricopa, either because they were living off-reservation or classified as Pima. Therefore, I will assume that the Maricopa were about 9% of the combined Pima-Maricopa population (the 1870 proportion). The estimates of the combined population (Table 19) are thus obtained by dividing the estimates for the Pima by 0.91. As with the Pima figures, the results are rounded to the nearest twenty-five persons, and the growth rates are given only to the nearest tenth of a percent, so as not to give a spurious impression of accuracy.

During this period, several of the agents commented on whether they thought the Pima, Maricopa, or combined population was increasing or decreasing. In the light of the interpretation above, we can evaluate their hypotheses.

In 1870, Grossmann (1870:123) stated that the Pima population was stable, while the Maricopa were decreasing. Grossmann appears to be partly correct, in that both groups were decreasing at the time. In 1873, Ferris (1873: 180) felt that both the Pima and Maricopa were increasing. There is no support for this view, since 1872-73 was one of the poorest years of that decade (Stout 1873a:281). Even Ferris (1873:180) reported that the Gila River had been dry for three summers.

In 1882, Wheeler (1882:6) stated that both Pima and Maricopa were decreasing. Given the data, this seems unlikely, although if he was referring to the late 1870s, he was correct. Finally, in 1888, Johnson (1888:6) said both Pima and Maricopa were increasing in population, and there is no reason to dispute this.

Fertility

In that venereal diseases were reported to have increased among the Pima (but not the Maricopa) during this period, as well as because of poor maternal nutrition from food shortages among both the Pima and Maricopa, I assume that from 1869-80 Pima fertility was lower than during 1859-69, while Maricopa fertility remained relatively the same.

From 1880-89, with venereal diseases continuing, but less maternal malnutrition, I assume that fertility may have been slightly higher than during 1869-80.

The major data to test these statements come from the 1860 and 1890 Censuses. With no birth data available for the period, once again the child-woman ratio, with its imperfections, must be employed as a measure of fertility. In Table 20, the data fit the assumptions: the Pima child-woman ratio decreased considerably from 1860-90, while that of the Maricopa, allowing for the small size of the population, remained essentially the same. Unfortunately, what happened between 1860 and 1890 is unknown, and thus whether Pima fertility was lower in 1869-80 than 1880-89 is impossible to determine.

The Pima child-woman ratio would be lower in 1890 if enumeration of children 0-4 in 1890 were poorer than in 1860, or if enumeration of women 15-44 were poorer in 1860 than 1890. It does not seem likely that women 15-44 were more poorly enumerated than the rest of the population in 1860 (see Chapter Three). Children 0-4 appear to have been underenumerated in both censuses, probably more so in 1860, assuming that the census of 1890 was one of the most accurate to its date among the Pima and Maricopa. Moreover, it is unlikely that epidemics of childhood diseases caused greater deaths in the 0-4 age group in 1890 than in 1860, since the period 1885-90 was relatively free of epidemics. Thus the difference in child-woman ratios in the two censuses appears to be real.

Other data, although not as reliable, also tend to support my assumptions about fertility, or at least if contradictory, can be shown to be defective data. In Table 21, the adult to child ratio is shown for several censuses. I assume that a decline in fertility would be reflected by a higher ratio of adults to children.

The ratios of 1870, 1887, and 1890 are all higher than that of 1860, supporting my assumption. However, the data from 1870 and 1887 are both unsatisfactory for comparative purposes. In 1860 and 1890, I have divided the number of males above 18 plus the number of females above 14 by the remainder of the population, (and multiplied by 100 to obtain the ratio; for an explanation of why these ages were chosen, see Appendix C). In 1870, the ages of the "children" are unknown, as they are nowhere stated by the source (Andrews 1870a:166, 1870b:482). I have assumed that they are the same ages as for 1860 and 1890 only for purposes of comparison, but since the 1884 law requiring such an age tabulation had not been passed at this time (see Appendix C), there is no assurance that these are the ages of the children. Given the difference between this figure and those of 1860 and 1890, it is perhaps better to ignore the census of 1870 ratio.

The census of 1887 figure is from the summary by the agent, as I did not tabulate this census by single years of age. But as seen in Table 22, the agent (Howard 1887b) appears to destroy the credibility of his own summary.

We would expect that the number of males 18 or younger plus females 14 or younger would exceed the number of children 6-16 ("children of school age"). The latter group excludes those children of both sexes 0-5 as well as males 17 and 18, and includes only those females 15 and 16 not in the ages of "children." However, as seen in Table 22, for both the Pima and Maricopa at Lehi (i.e., T. 2 N., R. 5 E.) the number of school-age children in fact exceeds that of all children. For the enumerated Pima and Maricopa population of 1887 ("All areas;" this excludes Pima and Maricopa living off-reservation other than at Lehi), there is a difference of only 87 persons between the number of school-age children and all children. This is obviously impossible, and shows that the adult-child ratio for 1887 (Table 21) should be lower. Thus, we must reject the figures for males 18 or less plus females 14 or less ("children") reported by the agent in the summary of the census of 1887 (Table 21). This leaves the 1890 Census figure to compare to that of 1860, and as I assumed, the proportion of adults is greater in 1890, implying lower fertility than in 1860.

Thus, from 1869-90, it would appear that fertility declined among the Pima, while remaining low among the Maricopa. Besides the upsurge of venereal diseases among the Pima, presumably poor maternal nutrition, abortion, and possible infanticide (either direct or indirect) had an effect. Abortion and infanticide may have increased during a period of economic distress, when a family could not support as many children as previously.

Sex Ratio

As seen in Table 23, very few data are available by sex for this period; in fact, I found none for 1880-89. Further, the figures for 1874-77 must be rejected because they are estimates. The figures for 1872-73, including those for the Pima and Maricopa separately, are also suspect in that they are probably not new censuses, but rather updatings of the 1870 census based on births and deaths known to the agent, these figures being incomplete. The 1871 figure excludes off-reservation Pima (Blackwater). Nevertheless, because of the similarity of the sex ratios for 1870-73, let us assume that the Pima and Maricopa separate sex ratios for 1872 and 1873 are quite similar to those which would have been obtained for 1870 if they were available.

The 1870 and 1890 Pima-Maricopa (and probably Pima separately) sex ratios are both above 100, and well within probability by chance alone. The increase in the sex ratio from 1870 to 1890 (102.4 to 103.5) does not appear to be significant, given the different degrees of under-enumeration in the two censuses, but could have resulted in part from the end of hostilities with the Apache and Yavapai, in which I assume male mortality would have been greater. The value for 1870 for the Pima and Maricopa combined suggests that some underenumeration of males may have occurred in the census of 1868 (where the sex ratio was less than 100).

The Pima sex ratio, where shown, is slightly lower than the combined population, because the Maricopa sex ratio is higher. Although the Maricopa sex ratio seems quite high, the probability of occurrence by chance is above .05 because of the small size of the population. As discussed above, it is impossible to determine to what degree underenumeration has produced these figures, since in 1872 and 1873 some off-reservation Maricopa were not reported, and in 1890, some were classed with Pima. Nevertheless, the values do fit those of the Maricopa during preceding years (Table 14), when the sex ratio also expressed a considerable excess of males, except 1859 and 1868. The aberrant 1868 sex ratio may result from greater underenumeration of males than females in the census of 1868. However, in 1868, thirty-six Quechan and Mohave were reported among the Maricopa (Table 14) while in 1870 only five were found (Table 24). I have assumed that Quechan and Mohave resident among the Maricopa were predominantly female. If the decrease in their numbers from 1868-70 represents liberation of (mainly female) captives, the Maricopa sex ratio could have been below 100 in 1868 and above 100 in 1870 for this reason.

I assume that mortality from accidents would occur at a greater rate among males than females. Since the sex ratio appears to have increased (or at least stayed about the same) from 1868-90, it would appear that this cause of death was not affecting males disproportionately, or if it were, that there were sex-specific causes (such as maternal mortality) to keep female mortality at a level close to that of males.

Geographic Distribution

I assume that since young men without families appear to have been the first to go to farm the Salt River area for the Pima (but not the Maricopa), the Pima median age should have been lower at Salt River than Gila River, and that the sex ratio should have been higher. However, I found no data by reservation on either age or sex for this period, and evaluation of these hypotheses must await the next chapter, when the censuses of 1890 and 1895, as well as others, will be available.

I also assume that a higher rate of intermarriage between Pima and Maricopa occurred at Salt River than Gila River, since proportionally more of the Maricopa and fewer of the Pima were at Salt River. Similarly, I assume that Pima-Papago intermarriage occurred to a greater degree at Gila River than Salt River, because of the greater proximity of Gila River to the Papago.

While these hypotheses can not even be tested during the next period, much less this period, because of a lack of the necessary data, some assumptions about intermarriage in 1870, before migration to Salt River, can be made, based on the 1870 census (Table 24). While 9.4% of the Maricopa were living in predominantly Pima villages, 0.7% of the Pima were resident in predominantly Maricopa villages. Nevertheless, absolute numbers were more balanced: 36 Maricopa resided in predominantly Pima villages, while 27 Pima resided in predominantly Maricopa villages. Assuming virilocality, it would appear that Pima males married Maricopa females more often than the opposite tribe-sex combination. However, as determined in the preceding chapter, we can not necessarily assume virilocality, as some Pima males may have resided in Maricopa villages.

Papago were present only in predominantly Pima villages, while Mohave and Quechan ("Cocopa") were present only in predominantly Maricopa villages. This suggests a linguistic basis for ethnic intermarriage: the Pima and Papago speak a number of dialects of a single Uto-Aztecan language (Saxton and Saxton 1969:[vii]), while the Maricopa, Mohave, and Quechan speak dialects of one language or related Yuman languages (Spier 1933:ix). The "rule" was broken by the Pima and Maricopa, as they were adjacent to each other. "Apache" were present in both predominantly Pima and predominantly Maricopa villages, showing that these captives were probably married by both Pima and Maricopa. The "Apache" may well include some Yavapai, since the two groups were not always distinguished by white observers. About one-third of the "Apache" were residing with Maricopa, suggesting that Maricopa more often married captives than Pima (or perhaps sold Apache and Yavapai captives less often).

Finally, it is interesting to note two Pima-Apache in a predominantly Maricopa village, presumably offspring of the twenty-six Pima and six Apache there. Surely there were more persons of mixed ethnic ancestry (such as Pima-Papago and Pima-Maricopa), but only the two Pima-Apache were singled out, and presumably other Pima-Apache were not.

Notes to Chapter Four

1. The towns of Adamsville and Florence (Figure 2) were both founded in 1866 (Granger 1960:289, 294). By 1870, Adamsville had a population of 400 and Florence claimed 218 (U.S. Senate 1965:131-32). Ten years later, while Adamsville had disappeared, Florence had increased to 902 persons (USOC 1883:99). Whites in the Adamsville-Florence area constructed thirteen canals irrigating over 8,000 acres (3,200 ha) from 1868-75 (Farish 1918:50-53).

2. This situation was well-expressed at the time by Antonio Azul (in O. Howard 1872:167), recognized by whites and most Pima as spokesman regarding Pima interests:

> We always raised two crops a year, one of wheat and one of corn. Now since the Americans and Mexicans have moved on our land above us, and taken the water from our river (the Gila) to water their grain, we never raise but one crop, (wheat.) Some of us who live on the lower part of the land which you say is ours, (meaning their reservation,) do not get even enough to water our wheat, and much of it is even now lying down upon the ground dead. We cannot raise any beans, or pumpkins, or melons, or corn down there any more, because there is no water. [Punctuation is as in the source.]

3. The Pima were merely evening the score by harvesting for their own use the crops grown by the whites: the "stolen" food was grown with stolen water. Ironically, even by white law, the Pima and Maricopa had the right to first use of water for their needs when there was not enough water to meet the needs of all users of Gila River water. This is the legal principle

of prior appropriation (Hutchins 1971:14, 160) which in theory means that the first person to beneficially use the water will receive all of his accustomed amount during a year of scarcity. The second person to beneficially use the water will then receive all of his accustomed share, or the remainder available, if there is not enough for his entire share. The third person to beneficially use the water will receive none if the two users with prior rights have used up all the available water. The Pima and Maricopa were legally deprived of their prior right to Gila River water through the Gila River Decree of 1935 (U.S. District Court 1935).

    4. Much of the Blackwater area was eventually added to the Gila River Reservation by the Executive Order of 31 August 1876 (USDI 1912:24). In 1879, under the Executive Order of 14 June (USDI 1912:25-26), nearly all of what is now the Salt River Reservation was established, and the addition of Gila Crossing and the area northwest of it to the Gila River Reservation extended the boundaries of the latter to the Gila-Salt confluence.

    5. Those who produced more than they needed may still have sold some of their crop while others faced a food shortage. Wheeler's (1886:39) report of growing Pima involvement in the white economy as consumers is undoubtedly more candid than he intended: "Money received for crops is used in the purchase of clothing,

furniture, household utensils, and desirable personal property which before they had no use for."

6. The agent's report on the food situation for this year is poignant (Johnson 1889:120):

> In every house and "key" [the Pima word for their aboriginal dwelling] are found "varshroms" [i.e., storage baskets] full of wheat stored away for the winter, and Indian wagons have been busy since the beginning of harvest transporting their crops to market. General contentment prevails; in fact, when these Indians have enough to eat I truly believe that they are the happiest people on earth.

As we shall see in the next chapter, this was the end of an era for Pima agriculture: never again would they enjoy such a crop.

7. Agent Elmer A. Howard, of course, is not the O. O. Howard whom President Grant sent as special commissioner to the Apache of Arizona and New Mexico in 1872. E. Howard's (1887a:4) contradiction of previous reports is worth reporting in full:

> The reports that have gone forth from this agency for the several years past show that each succeeding year has been one of remarkable progress and advancement. As "distance lends enchantment to the view," and having embraced an opportunity to examine these reports prior to my arrival, I expected to find a settlement of Indians well advanced in civilization, with large and well-cultivated farms. I met with a disappointment, not bitter, yet not pleasant. While the annual reports have advanced apace the Indians, I should judge, for a considerable portion of that period have remained "in statu quo." Each year's report has shown an increased acreage of land cultivated. It is hard to reconcile this statement with the fact that the Pima Indians have always been a self-supporting people, and the amount of products raised by them now is barely sufficient for their maintenance. How they supported themselves before this increased acreage began I am unable to state. Intelligent men who have lived as neighbors

of these Indians for twenty years past inform me that their crop of wheat of to-day is no larger and the grade no better than twenty years ago.

Howard, however, is not an unbiased observer, as can be seen from his belief that among the Pima "The absence of any ambition or incentive to increase their holdings is remarkable. . ." (Howard 1887a:4). What this statement does show, other than Howard's acceptance of the lazy Indian stereotype, is that the water supply was so undependable that the Pima could no longer think of increasing their area of cultivation, much less farm what they still had.

8. The Southern Pacific Railroad, which ran off-reservation near the southern boundary of the Gila River Reservation, entered Arizona from the west in 1877 at Yuma. By 1879 the line had been built as far as Maricopa, just south of the Gila River Reservation, and by March 1880, Tucson was reached (Peck 1962:212). A connection to the east was made at Deming, New Mexico with the Atchison, Topeka and Santa Fe in 1881 (Bancroft 1888:604). This eliminated east-west stage traffic across the Gila River Reservation, but passengers bound for Phoenix got off at Maricopa and took a stage north, across the reservation to Phoenix. In 1887 a railroad line was built from Maricopa to Phoenix, also across the Gila River Reservation (Peck 1962:214), after which a stage station at Gila Crossing was removed (Russell 1908:60; calendar stick entry for 1887-88).

9. While Shaw (1974:128), a Pima, credits intoxication as a cause contributing to the deaths of persons falling off trains (as well as mentioning some relatives who were not intoxicated who rode the train to Tucson to visit her), Webb (1959:52) feels that the deaths were a result of train wrecks. At this time, trains were perhaps the only way Pima and Maricopa could travel long distances, as many must have been without horse and wagon.

10. The Pima obviously (and rightly) felt that since the murdered was a Pima, disposition of the murderer should rest with them and not the whites. The whites, of course, felt that they had jurisdiction over all crimes, regardless of whether they involved a case of a white against a white, a white against a non-white (such as a Pima), a non-white (such as a Pima) against a white, or a non-white against a non-white (such as a Pima against a Pima). Naturally, there are no reports from this period, or any other, of Pima supervising the trial of a crime committed by a white against another white.

11. Local whites, fearing that an attempt would be made to release the prisoners, clamored for the army to be stationed among the Maricopa near Phoenix. It was Pima, and not the Maricopa, who were involved in the incident, but this made little difference to the citizens of Phoenix (Bandelier 1970:122-23; <u>Daily Phoenix Herald</u>

4 June 1883:3, 5 June 1883:3).

    12. The most renowned Pima captive was taken in 1872, according to Shaw (1974:238). This was Dr. Carlos Montezuma, originally named Wassaja. He was sold by the Pima to an art gallery owner who happened to be in Florence at the time. The boy, an Apache or Yavapai (sources differ) of 5 years, spent much of his life in Chicago, New York, and at Indian Service installations as a doctor. Later in life, he returned to Arizona, by which time he had also become a spokesman for Indian rights. The fate of his two sisters, taken at the same time, was more typical of captives: becoming domestics, one wound up with a family in Mexico, the other in California. Shaw (1974:239) also states that captives were sold only when the captor could not provide the captive with enough to eat. While this may have been true of some cases during the 1870s, captives had been sold by the Pima to whites well before the Pima lost their Gila River water. Nevertheless, among the Pima, taking of captives does not seem to have reached the proportions practiced by the River Yumans against each other before 1860.

CHAPTER FIVE

FROM THE LOSS OF THE WHEAT CROP TO ALLOTMENT
(1890-1910)

Factors Affecting Pima and Maricopa Population
Food Situation

As during the preceding period, food shortages continued to affect the Pima and Maricopa. While the 1880s were a period of shaky maintenance of subsistence, the food situation worsened in 1889-90 (Crouse 1890a:4; Whited 1894:137) and continued to worsen for some time. Apparently the main constant factors were the operation of the Florence Canal, combined with continuing white settlement in the Safford Valley farther upstream on the Gila River.[1]

As during the 1870s, drought aggravated an already serious deficiency of water, for Castetter and Bell (1942: 15) report that a flood in 1891 ended a series of wet years --the years that saw the Pima and Maricopa raise enough wheat (along with gathering wild plants) for subsistence during the 1880s. Perhaps the final blow was more rapid runoff from erosion caused by overgrazing of cattle (C. Hayden 1965:59-81). This factor, unlike drought, was not to be reversed.

In 1890, only seepage water was available for irrigation on the Gila River Indian Reservation (Lee 1904: 9). Rations began to be issued at Gila River in 1892-93, but conditions were better at Salt River, where apparently there was enough for subsistence (Young 1894a:104). This state continued until 1896-97, when some improvement was noted at Gila River, with enough grown for subsistence (Young 1897:108). While adequate food was obtained again in 1897-98 (Taggart 1898:126), rations were issued in 1898-99 at Gila River (Hadley 1899:161). In the same year, Salt River still grew enough for subsistence in what Lippincott (1900:31) called the driest of the past 10 years. The Pima calendar sticks reported no crop at Blackwater, and Russell heard of five deaths from starvation during the year (Russell 1908:65).

Entering the twentieth century, starvation and deaths continued at Gila River (Fanning in Hadley 1900: 197; Russell 1908:65n). Now Salt River was having trouble raising enough food, and only the Indians at Lehi were still self-sufficient (Hadley 1900:196). By 1903, with the situation still critical at Gila River, rations were also issued at Salt River to the aged and blind (Wynkoop 1903: 134).

Conditions may have improved somewhat during 1903-5, although it is hard to understand why, and the reports by the agent (Alexander 1904:147, 1905:175) that there was no starvation perhaps do not reflect the situation.

Lee (1904:64), however, felt that at the time the Maricopa had enough to live on, and perhaps more, but considered the Pima in serious difficulty (Lee 1904:64-66).

Salt River experienced a bad year in 1905-6 when the Arizona Dam broke, and the water presumably washed out canals and was then unavailable at the right time (Alexander 1906:187). Nothing for that year was reported about Gila River. An increased crop was reported at Gila River for 1908-9, but it is not known if this was enough for subsistence needs (Valentine 1909:8). Thus it would appear that from 1889-1910 there generally was insufficient food for the Pima, and to a lesser extent, Maricopa populations. The situation for the Pima was apparently better at Salt River and Lehi until 1900, but then worsened. Government rations and a few good years eased the situation somewhat, but overall there was no assurance of sufficient food.

Some persons died from starvation, and while this in itself would affect population size, the more significant effect of food shortages would be to weaken the population so that diseases ordinarily not serious became so, and epidemics had a greater effect than if the people had enough to eat.

Epidemics

During this period there was an almost annual occurrence of epidemics. However, by now the Pima and Maricopa had been exposed to most common epidemic diseases for a considerable time, and the level of mortality was perhaps not much greater than among low income whites of that time. Nevertheless, the sheer number of epidemics must have had some effect on the population, especially infants and children. The following epidemics were reported by various sources:

1890-91. Measles and "la grippe" occurred at the school; two girls died (Dunagan in Crouse 1891:316).

1892-93. Chicken pox and whooping cough occurred throughout the reservation(s); measles occurred in two villages. Many persons were vaccinated for smallpox (Marden 1893:120).

1893-94. A general influenza epidemic occurred, but was mild; dysentery occurred in three villages east of Sacaton (Marden 1894:107). Cook (1894:107) reported malarial fevers at all times at Gila Crossing, an area of seepage of river underflow.

1895-96. Several cases of smallpox were reported, but no deaths (Young 1896a:114). Perhaps the smallpox vaccination program of 1892-93 was fairly successful, along with the immunity of those who already had smallpox. In the spring, there was a grippe or influenza epidemic (Wilson 1896:118).

1896-97. The calendar sticks reported a smallpox epidemic (Russell 1908:64) which turned out to be chicken pox (Crandall 1897:111). No cases occurred at the school.

There was also an influenza epidemic, followed by a few pneumonia cases (Crandall 1897:111).

1897-98. Whooping cough occurred in the fall and winter, with deaths of younger children, mainly from lung and bowel complications (Meriwether 1898:127).

1898-99. According to the calendar sticks, measles killed many children at the Phoenix Indian School and one child at Sacaton (Russell 1908:64). The agent (Hadley 1899:162) also reported the measles epidemic at Sacaton. Smallpox occurred in towns near the reservation, but no cases were reported on-reservation.

1899-1900. Measles occurred, with no deaths at the school (D. McArthur 1900:198). Two cases of typhoid fever were reported, both recovering (Fanning in Hadley 1900:197). Pneumonia occurred at the school, but of four cases there were no deaths (Hrdlička 1908:182).

1900-1. At the school, two deaths occurred from tuberculosis and two from enteric fever (typhoid) (Hrdlička 1908:182).

1901-2. There were two epidemics of influenza at the school with two deaths, as well as a fever epidemic with three deaths, and three deaths from tuberculosis (Hrdlička 1908:182).

1909-10. The Maricopa experienced measles, and whooping cough which often developed into bronchial pneumonia (Lumholz 1912:339).

One reason why more epidemics seem to have occurred during this period is probably better reporting. The report of the agency doctor appeared for the first time during the 1890s, and went into much more detail concerning illness than did the agent. The special investigations of Russell (1908) and Hrdlička (1908) also insured better reporting of diseases.

General Health

Reports go from unfavorable during the early part of the period to favorable with reservations, and back to unfavorable during the latter part of the period (Crouse 1890a:4; Hadley 1899:162; Lumholz 1912:339; D. McArthur 1900:198; Meriwether 1898:127; Young 1896a:114). This probably reflects the biases of the sources more than the health of the Pima and Maricopa.

Venereal Diseases

Evaluations of the effect of venereal diseases on the Pima and Maricopa vary, but all who discuss the two tribes separately felt that the Maricopa were more greatly affected than the Pima (Marden 1893:120; Russell 1908:268). Marden (1893:120) believed that venereal disease among the Maricopa was congenital, and led to high mortality for young children. He also estimated, apparently based on cases he saw as agency doctor, that 2% of the Pima had "syphilitic diseases" (Marden 1894:107). Russell (1908: 198) noted both congenital and acquired syphilis among the

Pima, but felt that it had not caused any population loss, and that overall, the Pima were fairly free from venereal disease. Meriwether (1898:127), another agency doctor, stated that while venereal disease was not rare, it did not seem to be increasing in occurrence.

Medical Services

During most of this period there appears to have been a doctor on the Gila River Reservation, but not at Salt River (Alexander 1903:132; Crouse 1890a:7, 1892:218; Fanning in Hadley 1900:197; Hadley 1899:161, 1902:159; Marden 1893:120-21, 1894:107; Meriwether 1898:127-28; Whited 1894:80; Young 1895a:123, 1896a:114). However, in 1909-10 Lumholz (1912:339) reported that treatment was being given by the agent at Gila River.

A hospital was built in 1891-92 (Crouse 1892:218), but by 1894-95 it was being used as the agency office (Young 1895a:123). In 1902-3 a small hospital was reported opened (Alexander 1903:132).

All reports were that the services of the doctor were well-used (Marden 1893:120-21; Meriwether 1898:127-28), but Fanning, a doctor at the agency, felt that the needs of the agency and school were enough to keep him busy and he could not devote time to other persons with health problems (Fanning in Hadley 1900:197).

Consequently, with a doctor generally in residence, perhaps a few less deaths occurred than would have without one, but medical services appear to have had a minimal effect on the population.

Hostile Encounters

Although violent acts occurred during this period between Pima-Maricopa and whites, there was no apparent group violence. Stealing of stock occurred in both directions (Crouse 1890a:7), with the Pima selling it for food. Nevertheless, in several reports, the agents mentioned peaceful relations between Pima-Maricopa and whites (Crouse 1891:213; Hadley 1902:159). A few reports of murders of Pima by whites appear in the Pima calendar sticks (Russell 1908:61-66), but these had no significant effect in causing Pima population decline.

Among the Pima, violence appears to increase for this period, as could be expected, given the lethal economic situation they faced. From 1889-97, eleven, and perhaps thirteen, murders were reported by the calendar sticks, plus one suicide (Russell 1908:61-64). Curiously, although the claendar sticks run to 1901-2, no murders were reported after 1897. While not a major cause of death, murder was a cause to be considered as fairly constant for the early part of this period, at the rate of about one per year.

Intermarriage

Russell (1908:186) and Hrdlička (1908:10) are the only sources from this period that mentioned intermarriage.

Both felt that most was between Pima and Papago, with some between Pima and Maricopa. The Pima were also mentioned by Russell as having married in small numbers Apache and Yaqui, and a "Hare-Eater" from Sonora.

It is impossible to determine whether intermarriage was greater in one direction than another and the effect it would have on population size and the sex ratio, especially for the Maricopa, where it could be significant.

Migration

Migration between the Gila River and Salt River Reservations and the off-reservation areas between them should have had some influence on Pima and Maricopa population figures. Persons living off-reservation were less likely to be counted. Part of the Maricopa moved during this period. Young (1894a:105) reported that in 1893-94, some Maricopa living off-reservation on the Salt River 3 miles (5 km) southwest of Phoenix moved to the Gila River Reservation, below the Pima at Gila Crossing (i.e., about as far downstream as possible on the reservation). This is a different group from those living at Lehi and received little attention from agents because of off-reservation residence.

Young (1895a:121) also reported some Papago living on the Gila River Reservation, while Alexander (1904:43) reported a Papago settlement near Sacaton. Whether these were Papago who had intermarried with Pima or a distinct group is not clear, nor is it clear how they were counted and classed by ethnic group. No Papago are reported as such in the population figures from this period, so presumably they were counted as Pima, if they were counted at all.

During the period, Pima (and perhaps some Maricopa) left the reservations temporarily for educational and economic activities. According to Spicer (1962:150), many older children went to boarding schools in order to relieve economic pressure on their families because conditions were so unfavorable on the reservation. During this period, at one time or another, Pima students were reported at Indian schools in Albuquerque and Tucson (Crouse 1890a:7); Genoa, Nebraska (Crouse 1892:216); Carlisle, Pennsylvania; Grand Junction, Colorado; Fort Lewis, Colorado; and Santa Fe (Young 1895a:123); and Chilocco, Oklahoma (Meskimmons 1902: 161). Again, according to Spicer (1962:150), some stayed off the reservation working where they could find employment. Thus, during this period, some on-reservation population may have been lost through migration to boarding schools and subsequent off-reservation residence outside the middle Gila and Salt River Valleys. Also keeping Pima school children off the reservation all year was the "outing system" practiced by Indian schools, including the Phoenix Indian School, in which during summer "vacation" female students were placed as maids in white homes throughout the territory, and males did farm labor, under the guise of education and employment (Young 1897: 108).

Non-students also engaged in various types of labor off-reservation. This included railroad work on the Southern Pacific (Young 1896a:114), constructing a railroad at the copper mine in Ray, Arizona (Hadley 1900:196), and working on a railroad in Nevada (Hadley 1902:159). Construction work on dams and other waterworks also employed some Pima and Maricopa off-reservation at this time, such as at Roosevelt Dam in Arizona (Brodie in Hayden 1965:90), the Laguna and Imperial Dams on the lower Colorado River (Alexander 1906:187; Leupp 1907:16)(in which it is reported that families migrated), and work on a levee along the Colorado River (Leupp 1908). Besides farm labor, such as fruit-picking, in the Salt River Valley (Crouse 1891: 213), Pima worked in the sugar beet fields at Rocky Ford, Colorado (Valentine 1909:5). Almost all of this off-reservation employment is reported for after 1900.

Thus it seems likely that some permanent (or semi-permanent) off-reservation residence occurred at this time, the Pima being faced with the impossibility of farming and the necessity of feeding themselves and their families. Even if the migration was seasonal, depending on when a census was taken, or whether the agent allowed for migration, the population figure for the Pima could be affected. Consequently migration becomes a factor of some importance in evaluating changes in population figures for the Pima (and perhaps Maricopa).

The rolls made by the agent were intended to be the de jure population, and persons moving off-reservation would not be removed unless the agent was notified of their death, nor would births be added unless reported to the agent. Thus while there should have been little effect on the rolls as a result of migration, since not all births and deaths of off-reservation residents were reported to the agent, and there was no good record of whether a person was residing off-reservation or not, the roll figure represents only very imperfectly the de jure Pima-Maricopa population at this time.

Consistency of Qualitative and Quantitative Data
Total Population

For both the Pima and Maricopa I would assume that population continually declined during 1890-1910. The overall rate of decline should have been about that of 1869-80, i.e., less than 1% annually. Although conditions during 1890-1910 sound worse than 1869-80, the rate of decline is assumed to be no greater because epidemics do not seem to have been as severe, the Pima and Maricopa by now probably had a greater immunity to certain diseases, and better reporting of diseases gave a false impression of more epidemics. Moreover, later in the period, some rations and off-reservation work should have prevented as large a loss as during 1869-80.

Nevertheless, food shortages and starvation were a reality the Pima and Maricopa had to contend with, as well as an absence of medical facilities and few medical services. Even though reduced in frequency, illnesses were at a level that would shock today's population.

Looking at the enumerated population figures for both the Pima-Maricopa combined and the Pima alone (Table 25), there is a decline from 1890-1910, but with considerable decline to 1895 (-0.9% annually for Pima-Maricopa and Pima alone), increase to 1900 (0.6% annually for Pima-Maricopa, 0.4% for Pima), followed by slight decline (0.2% annually for Pima-Maricopa, 0.3% for Pima).[2] Overall these figures support my hypothesis of decline, but not assumption of continual decline.

Although these figures are the most accurate or useful for the period, there are serious defects in them (see Appendix D for a fuller evaluation of these, and all other figures in Tables 26-28). I have attempted to reduce some of the error by presenting estimated figures in Table 25 (but have introduced other sources of error to the extent that my assumptions are incorrect).

Both the 1890 and 1895 enumerated population figures in Table 25 reflect serious age-specific and sex-specific underenumeration, as well as an unknown amount of overall underenumeration. As discussed in Appendix D, for the combined Pima-Maricopa population, the 1890 Census enumerated persons 40-79, and especially females, more poorly than did the 1895 roll. In both 1890 and 1895, children 0-4 were underenumerated, but to a greater degree in 1895. By making the adjustments described in Appendix D, I feel that I can eliminate the effects of age-specific and sex-specific underenumeration, and hence equalize the degree of overall residual underenumeration in the two censuses. As a result, it appears that in 1890 there should have been no less than 5242 Pima and Maricopa, and no less than 5074 in 1895. The annual growth rate for 1890-95 thus becomes -0.6%, compared to -0.9% before adjustment. The adjusted rate is closer to the value I postdicted, and is more consistent with rates during previous periods of decreasing population. The adjusted 1890 figure of 5242 is still less than the 5525 Pima and Maricopa I estimated for 1890 (Table 25), the basis of which was discussed in Chapter 4 and Appendix C. The adjusted 1890 census figure (5242) produces an estimate of underenumeration of 9.7%; my estimate (5525) from the previous chapter produces estimated underenumeration of 13.5% for the Pima and Maricopa combined (and 11% for the Pima alone; see Table 25). In that there must have been underenumeration in 1890 beyond what the adjusted figure corrected for, I will accept the estimate of 5525 Pima and Maricopa as fairly accurate, and for the Pima alone, will also continue to use the estimate of 5025. The difference between the two estimates (500) is assumed to be Maricopa, but this estimate is not to be taken too seriously, as it is small and subject to extreme error. The estimated underenumeration of Maricopa in 1890 is thus (315 ÷ 500)-1, or 37%. As discussed below and in Appendix D, such a high figure for the Maricopa is valid, since it appears that some Maricopa were erroreously enumerated as Pima in 1890 and 1895.

Assuming the 1890 rates of underenumeration for the 1895 data (Pima-Maricopa, 13.5%; Pima, 11%), the Pima and Maricopa estimate is about 5275, and the Pima alone 4800. The annual growth rate from 1890-95 in this case is about -0.9% to -1.0%, as would be expected, since the enumerated figures (Table 25) have been inflated to the same degree. As stated above, this rate seems a bit high for the time. If underenumeration were greater in 1895 than 1890, the 1895 population estimate would be increased. Assuming that persons were leaving the reservation from 1890-95 to seek work off-reservation (and to look for wild plant foods), the 1895 enumeration would have been poorer since more Pima or Maricopa would have been missed than in 1890. Thus, for the Pima and Maricopa combined, I will assume that underenumeration was 15% in 1895, giving a revised estimate of 5375, and a -0.5% annual growth rate from 1890-95. It is important to remember that in this case I estimate the *de jure* Pima and Maricopa population, and not just those residing on-reservation; thus, it does not matter where a Pima or Maricopa may have been living at the time of the enumeration, since all Pima and Maricopa should be on the roll.

For the Pima, I will assume that the Pima proportion of the combined population was the same in 1890 and 1895, producing an estimate of about 4900. As before, the residuum (475) is the estimate for the Maricopa, and should not be taken very seriously. These figures give estimates of about 13% underenumeration for the Pima, and 38% for the Maricopa.

The figures for 1900 are much less useful than those from 1890 and 1895. As discussed more fully in Appendix D, the 1900 figures are not from a census or roll, but rather an estimate of a census. Thus I am hesitant to produce any estimates, as I have no idea of the degree of underenumeration for partly estimated figures.

The 1910 estimate for the Pima and Maricopa (Table 25) was obtained by retrojection from 1920, based on an assumed annual growth rate, the basis of which is discussed in the next chapter. The estimate (5890) assumes that underenumeration was considerable in 1910, being about 21.5%. In that later censuses produce even higher estimates of underenumeration, this is not impossible. Moreover, the Pima-Maricopa combined sex ratio for this census (107.4) seems too high in relation to 1890 (103.5), 1895 (105.8), and 1900 (103.2). This most likely indicates proportionally greater underenumeration of females in 1910, as compared with 1890, 1895, and 1900, which I assume contributed to the high degree of underenumeration estimated for the

1910 Census.

For the estimated figures, the Pima-Maricopa annual growth rate from 1895-1910 is 0.6%. The estimate for 1900 is obtained by projection from 5375 in 1895 at 0.6% yearly, and of course assumes that growth was constant from 1895-1910.

For the 1910 Pima estimate, I have multiplied the proportion Pima in the 1910 Census Bureau figures (91.6%) by the combined estimated population. The annual growth rate (1895-1910) is 0.7%.

Although I originally felt that population would be declining throughout from 1890-1910, these estimates make it appear that decline took place at least through 1895, but some time after that, probably no later than 1900, population began to increase. I feel the estimates present a more realistic situation than the fluctuations of the enumerated figures, as I can think of no reason (in terms of the factors discussed above) that the de jure population would increase from 1895-1900, but decrease from 1900-1910. The turn of the century thus appears to have been a turning point for Pima-Maricopa population, as I have found no evidence of population decline in the twentieth century. A combination of factors presumably acted to permit a small increase in Pima-Maricopa poulation sometime after 1895. Rations certainly must have helped some persons, while off-reservation employment was obtained by others. The drilling of wells on the eastern part of the reservation from 1903-10 (Spicer 1962:150) may also have permitted yet others to grow some food. Finally, there were no devastating epidemics from 1900-10, although infant and child mortality continued at a high level. Thus, while conditions could not be described as good, they were relatively better than 1890-95, and with an assumed high birth rate, could well have produced population increase.

Assumptions regarding Pima population dynamics by some sources from this period support my conclusions, while others do not. For 1893, three sources promoted three different views. According to the agent (Crouse 1893: 114), population was slowly declining, which appears to have been true at the time. The agency physician (Marden 1893:120) estimated a slight increase, apparently based on the number of births and deaths he was aware of, which no doubt was woefully incomplete. Whittemore (1893:80) felt that Pima population was stable, based on his estimates for 1873 and 1893. He is in error, as his figure (4000) is too low for 1873 or 1893, and he ignores what occurred between 1873 and 1893, which was anything but stability.

Taggart (1898:126) also considered Pima population to be stable, while Alexander (1903:132) and Lumholz (1912: 339) (the latter in 1909-10) felt that the Pima were increasing in numbers, which appears to be true.

Up to this point, I have mentioned the Maricopa alone only briefly. There are no estimates of Maricopa population in Table 25 (although a figure can be obtained for any of the years shown by subtracting the Pima estimate from that of the Pima-Maricopa). As the Maricopa population is very small, a difference of only ten persons can cause a 0.2% difference in the annual growth rate over 10 years. Besides this objection, as in preceding periods, the figures for the Maricopa make little sense, showing great fluctuations that could not be a result of natural causes (Table 27). Only three figures, those of 1890, 1896, and 1910 (column 2), are useful in analyzing Maricopa population dynamics for this period, and the situation still remains confusing.

In Table 27, all figures of 325 or less may be considered greatly in error because they appear to leave out some off-reservation Maricopa, or reflect Maricopa enumeration as Pima (or both). This includes the 1890 Census (which is also the roll) figure.

As discussed in Appendix D, the 1895-96 Maricopa population increase represents reclassification of Pima as Maricopa. The 1910 figure in Table 27, column 2 also appears to represent a more complete Maricopa enumeration. Assuming these figures represent equal rates of both ethnic classification and underenumeration, population increased 0.7% annually from 1896-1910. During the same period, the enumerated Pima population figures showed an annual decline of less than 0.1%. However, while in 1896, Maricopa were 7.4% of the combined population, in 1910 they were 8.4%. While this probably represents better ethnic classification in the 1910 Census, the figures support the assertion than the Maricopa were living under relatively better conditions than the Pima (Lee 1904:64).

Assuming that in 1890 the Maricopa should have been 7.4%-8.4% of the enumerated census population (4779), about 350-400 Maricopa should have been reported. (The true figure[3] should be larger, because of remaining under-enumeration.) These figures imply a small to considerable decrease from 1890-96.

It thus appears that until the Maricopa living south of Phoenix (not to be confused with those at Lehi) moved to the Gila River Reservation below Gila Crossing in 1893-94, they were suffering population loss just as were the Pima. They presumably moved back to Gila River because of white encroachment and expansion. The area they moved to was an underground water seepage area of the western part of the reservation.

All sources which commented on Maricopa population dynamics for this period assumed that the Maricopa were declining in numbers (Crouse 1893:114; Hrdlička 1908:43; Whittemore 1893:80). Crouse and Whittemore are probably correct, but Hrdlička probably is not. His reason for assuming a declining population is obscure. For both the Pima and Maricopa, Hrdlička reported the RCIA and RITINT figures (reproduced here for the Maricopa in Table 27) for 1890, 1900, and 1903-6. Although he commented on the credibility of the Pima figures, for the Maricopa he stated only that "Of late the Maricopa are decreasing in number, though the reason is not clear. The people are strong physically and in no way degraded" (Hrdlička 1908: 43).

If one thing is clear by now concerning Maricopa population, it is that no one except perhaps the Maricopa knew what was going on. The Maricopa, because of their small numbers, have always been neglected in favor of the Pima, not just in information on population, but in all studies, as a count of entries in Murdock (1960) shows.

Geographic Distribution

From 1895-1900, there may have been net migration to Salt River from Gila River, although the evidence is not overwhelming. As seen in Table 29, the proportion of the combined population increased at Salt River from 1899-1900. Unfortunately, the 1900 population figures include non-Indians resident on both reservations, and these numbers were not reported. But I assume that a greater proportion of non-Indians would be found in the Gila River population, as Sacaton was the administrative center for the two reservations, with the agency office. Moreover, the Salt River figure for 1900 does not include persons living off-reservation in the Lehi area. Thus, if the 1900 figures are biased because of inclusion of non-Indians, the proportion at Salt River should be increased rather than reduced. This argues for migration to Salt River.

It also appears that this migration did not occur only from 1899-1900, but from about 1895-1900. The 1899 figures appear to be rounded versions of the 1896 figures. These figures, in turn, are largely based on the 1895 roll, which was originally taken in 1894 (see Appendix D). Thus, the migration does not seem so sudden since it occurred over 5 years. Migration to Salt River was presumably in response to the relatively better farming situation there. From 1900-10, however, migration seems to have been from Salt River to Gila River, presumably in response to the opening of new wells on the eastern part of the Gila River Reservation (Spicer 1962:150). In this regard, it is also significant that population within the Gila River Reservation increased in the Pinal County part and decreased in the Maricopa County part. Thus, persons in the western part of the reservation, much of which lies in Maricopa County, shifted residence eastward also (see Figure 2).

Together, Salt River and the Maricopa County portion of the Gila River Reservation lost 415 persons (Table 29). The Pinal County portion of the Gila River Reservation gained 575. This allows for some additional persons returning to the Gila River Reservation from off-reservation, as well as an increase in white residents in the agency at Sacaton, which is in Pinal County.

Geographic Variation in Sex Ratio and Median Age

In the previous chapter, I postdicted that the sex ratio at Salt River should be higher than at Gila River for the Pima, and the median age lower, assuming that young, unmarried males first settled the new area. By 1890 and 1895, the only years for which data are available to test this assertion, the sex ratios are contradictory. The 1890 figures, 103.2 at Gila River and 101.6 at Salt River (RCIA 1890:545), do not provide support, but in 1895 the situation was reversed, with the higher sex ratio (109.7) reported at Salt River, and 104.8 at Gila River (Young 1895a:121). Since the 1890 Census underenumerated women to a greater degree than 1895, and erroneously included some Maricopa as Pima, the 1890 data are defective and can not be used to deny the hypothesis.

The median age data from 1890 and 1895, however, show that in both cases, median age was higher at Salt River, the opposite of what I expected (Table 30). By this time, factors other than the sex of the original settlers at Salt River were affecting the sex ratio, since 20 years had elapsed from first settlement to the 1890 and 1895 censuses.

Fertility

While economic conditions were serious from 1890-95, it does not appear that fertility declined. However, because of the inaccuracies in the 1890 and 1895 censuses, the child-woman ratio, even when adjusted for underenumeration, cannot be considered very accurate. For the Pima-Maricopa combined, the reported data (from Crouse 1890b and Young 1895b) produce a child-woman ratio of 618.9 for 1890 and 538.9 for 1895. This appears to indicate that either fertility declined or infant mortality increased (or both) from 1885-95. However, while infant mortality from 1890-95 may have been higher than 1885-90, a large part of the deficit of children 0-4 reported in 1895 (Table 31) is the result of extreme underenumeration of children 0-4 (see Appendix D). Moreover, if infant mortality was high as a result of lack of food and decreased resistance to disease, a higher proportion of women 15-44 would also have died from 1890-95 compared to 1885-90. Thus I doubt that the decrease in the child-woman ratio from 1890-95 is real. In fact, correcting the figures for underenumeration reverses the situation. Although women 40-44 were propotionally more poorly enumerated in 1890 than 1895, I will not adjust this number, as the increase should be less than 3%. However, in 1890, children 0-4 should be increased from 799 to 850; for 1895 from 561 to 1312. With these adjusted figures, the adjusted child-woman ratios become 658.4 for 1890 and 988.0 for 1895. These figures imply a considerable increase in fertility or decline in infant moratlity over 10 years. I feel that infant mortality probably did not decrease at this time because of the very unfavorable economic situation. It remains to be determined whether fertility increased or stayed relatively the same.

Probably differential underenumeration of women 15-44 in the 1890 and 1895 censuses had a considerable influence on the widely different child-woman ratios of 1890 and 1895, or I may have estimated too many children 0-4 for 1895. There are considerably fewer women reported from 15-44 in 1895 (1041) than 1890 (1291). In either case, the child-woman ratio would be reduced, but probably not below that of 1890.

It is also possible that the remaining fewer women were having more children, but overall I feel it safest to merely state that there most likely was no decline in the child-woman ratio from 1890-95.

Once again during this period, venereal diseases were reported to be more common among the Maricopa than the Pima. The child-woman ratios of the 1890 and 1895 data provide no support for this assertion. In 1890, the Pima child-woman ratio was 620.8; the Maricopa, 593.0. But in 1895 the Pima was 536.4; the Maricopa, 575.8. I do not feel it would be valid to adjust the Maricopa figures, as in such a small population a few persons more or less could affect the child-woman ratio considerably.

Thus, overall, I feel that the fertility of both Maricopa and Pima was fairly high at this time, as represented by a child-woman ratio of at least 650.

Median Age

The differences between the 1890 and 1895 data in Table 30 most likely reflect differences in age-specific and sex-specific enumeration rather than real change. In 1890, for the Pima and Maricopa combined, there is a larger difference between male and female median age than for 1895. This reflects greater underenumeration of females aged 40-79 in relation to males of the same ages in 1890. However, the 1890 female median age is higher than that for males, which is the opposite of what would be expected if females were underenumerated to a greater degree than males at older ages. Apparently overstatement of female ages and understatement of male ages (see Appendix D) more than offset the effect of sex-specific underenumeration at older ages. The similar median ages by sex for 1895 argue that coverage by sex was about equal in 1895.

For all groups, the median age is lower in 1890 than 1895. This reflects proportionally greater underenumeration of children 0-4 in 1895, which would act to raise the median age.

Notes to Chapter Five

1. 1886 marked the beginning of construction of the Florence Canal. When completed in 1888, it left the Gila River 12 miles (19 km) above the town of Florence and ran for 50 miles (80 km) with an average width of 20 feet (6 m) (USOC 1894b:31). By 1890, lands served by it would have been in cultivation. From 1889-99, area irrigated in Pinal County increased from 6,919 acres to 11,297 acres (2,802 ha to 4,575 ha) (USOC 1902:825).

The Safford Valley lies a straight line distance of about 135 miles (220 km) upstream from Sacaton. Bancroft (1888:627) says that in 1887, the area was still sparsely settled, although most of the towns had been founded by then (Granger 1960:124-26, 130-31). Much expansion took place during the 1890s: Solomonsville, one of the earliest settlements, grew from 175 persons in 1880 to 287 in 1890 and 629 in 1900 (USOC 1883; USBC 1913:Table 1). While the population of Arizona increased 39.3% from 1890-1900, that of Graham County increased 149.8% (USBC 1913:Table 1, 1971a:Table 1). From 1889 to 1899, area irrigated in Graham County increased from 7,556 acres to 18,297 acres (3,060 ha to 7,409 ha) (USOC 1902:825). Besides the Safford Valley, the other major area of white settlement in Graham County was Clifton-Morenci, which relied economically on copper mining and smelting, also heavy uses of water. Mining activity increased from 1890-1900 (Dunning 1959:138, 140).

Ironically, the whites farming in the Florence area who deprived the Pima and Maricopa of the Gila River Reservation of water in the 1870s were in turn deprived of the water during the 1890s by their fellow whites in the Safford Valley. By 1897, whites were beginning to abandon farms near Florence because of a lack of irrigation water (Davis 1897:44).

2. The 1890 population is a Census Office figure for the de jure Pima-Maricopa population; i.e., all persons identifying themselves as Pima or Maricopa, regardless of place of residence, are included. The 1895 figure, from the Office of Indian Affairs, is from the roll, which also was supposed to enumerate the de jure Pima-Maricopa population, not just those living on-reservation. The 1910 figure is from the Census Bureau and again is intended to represent the de jure Pima-Maricopa population. See Appendix D for further information.

3. My estimate of the entire Maricopa population in this year is about 500, the difference between the two population groups in Table 25.

CHAPTER SIX

FROM ALLOTMENT THROUGH THE DEPRESSION

(1910-40)

Availability of Data

Very little historical information on the Pima and Maricopa has been published for this period. The annual report of the local Indian agent (or agency superintendent, as he had by now come to be called) to the Commissioner of Indian Affairs was no longer published after 1906, and the Pima calendar sticks ended before 1910. This eliminates the two major sources of Pima-Maricopa history, on which heavy reliance was placed in earlier chapters. Consequently, what history can be learned must be gathered piecemeal from a variety of sources, notably Kneale (1950), Shaw (1974), Spicer (1962), U.S. Senate (1931) and Webb (1959). None of these sources go into much detail other than over very short periods. As during the previous period, much less is reported of events at Salt River than at Gila River, because the two reservations were administered from Sacaton, on the Gila River Reservation (or in the case of Salt River, for a short time from Phoenix).

Population figures for this period represent three different populations, and differ in the geographic area covered so as to conform to the target population of the agency making the estimate. Johnston (1966:9-18) recognized this problem in his pioneering study of Navajo population.

Using Johnston's terms for these three populations, the largest group is the "de jure" population. All persons with sufficient Pima or Maricopa ancestry to be enrolled on the tribal roll comprise this population. In general, it may be said that a person must be at least one-fourth Pima or Maricopa to be enrolled (Kelly 1953:61, 67). This population thus includes (ideally) all Pima or Maricopa, regardless of where they live. The roll is the source of this figure.

The Bureau of the Census has attempted to enumerate the entire Indian population of the United States by tribe in 1910, 1930, and 1970, but on a different basis from the BIA. The initial Census Bureau basis for classification by tribe is the tribal affiliation stated by the person being enumerated; these categories are then often classified into larger groups, generally based on linguistic similarity (USBC 1915:71-78, 1937:33, 1973:XI-XVI). If the Bureau of the Census figures were a complete enumeration, an estimate could be made of how deficient the tribal roll is, but unfortunately, the Bureau of the Census figures by tribe are also inaccurate to a great degree because of underenumeration.

The second population for which figures appear is persons on-reservation, referred to by Johnston as the "cultural" population.[1] Strange as it seems, it is not always as easy to obtain this figure as the tribal enrolment figure (or the figure for the reservation and adjacent area population, discussed below). The Bureau of the Census generally provides this figure, one way or another, but only every 10 years. However, the figure sometimes includes persons of all races or ethnic groups living on-reservation, not just Indians, and thus does not report Indians separately. Nor does the Bureau of Indian Affairs always provide this figure. They are mainly concerned with the preceding population, all those enrolled, as potential users of BIA services, and the following population, reservation and adjacent areas, as actual users of their services. Thus, for this period, the BIA provides figures for persons on-reservation only for 1930-37; for 1910-29 the roll (i.e., <u>de jure</u>) population is reported ("Table" in RCIA 1910-37).

Until this period, the roll and on-reservation population generally were fairly close, since most off-reservation migration was within the Salt and middle Gila River Valleys, and usually was not permanent. Thus the BIA (and I) did not distinguish the two populations in previous periods. With the end of the wheat crop, and thus farming as the main economic pursuit for the Pima and Maricopa, permanent, or at least seasonal, off-reservation residence became a necessity: the jobs available were not in the vicinity of the reservation, but rather in farms around the southern part of Arizona, in Phoenix, or even farther away. Because of the distance from the reservations to work, many persons could not have lived permanently on-reservation. This is the situation in which Anna Moore Shaw and her husband found themselves during this period (Shaw 1974:148, 150). The increasing semi-permanent out-migration from 1890-1910 caused some difficulties in interpreting those data; for this period the BIA at least produced a few estimates of population on-reservation.

The third type of population figure covers the reservation and adjacent areas. Johnston terms this the "administrative" population because this group regularly uses services provided by the BIA. Sometimes BIA figures are given for both reservation and reservation and adjacent population; at other times, only one of the figures is given, generally the latter, as will be seen for the next period (1940-72).

It is not possible to compare Bureau of the Census figures from reservations and adjacent areas with such BIA figures because Indians are not reported by tribe in the Census for such small geographic areas; in fact, sometimes it is extremely difficult to find the number of Indians regardless of tribe in geographic areas smaller than counties. Furthermore, tribe is not reported in every Census, only those of 1910, 1930, and 1970.

During this period, even the BIA frequently did not produce population figures by tribe. After 1924, the

BIA no longer did so for Salt River, and from 1910-40, the population at Gila River was not reported by tribe for 1925-29 and 1938-40. Since both Pima and Maricopa lived on the Gila and Salt River Reservations, and were equally entitled to services, the tribal identity of an enrolled Indian at Gila River and Salt River was irrelevant to the BIA (just as the tribal identity of the "Maricopa" was to whites during the mid-nineteenth century).[2] Yet even today the Maricopa tend to reside in certain areas of the Gila River and Salt River Reservations.

Even for the existing figures by tribe, there is continued fluctuation in Maricopa numbers, reflecting more an uncertainty of how to classify Indians living at Gila and Salt River than any possible natural (or unnatural) change in Maricopa population independent of classification.

As seen in Table 32, the Gila River Maricopa (as well as Pima) population is reported to increase rapidly from 1911-13 at the unlikely annual rate of 13.9% (compared to a still unbelievable 4.4% for the Pima). The Maricopa population fluctuates between 267 and 300 from 1913-25 (with the Pima population reported as increasing considerably during this time). After the hiatus from lack of data, the Maricopa population is reported as almost doubling to 505 in 1930, clearly impossible. The Pima population was reported to decline at the same time, so the larger number of Maricopa reflects reclassification of Pima as Maricopa in 1930: the Pima population lost 237 persons from 1925-30,

and the Maricopa gained the same number. By 1932 there are
even more Maricopa and fewer Pima, again very likely
reflecting reclassification of some Pima in 1930 as Maricopa
in 1932. A rapid decline in Maricopa numbers is shown for
1936-37 (-1.54%), but there is not a large enough increase
among the Pima to account for this through reclassification.
By 1950 (more properly covered in the next chapter), the
Maricopa population was reported to have shrunk into acute
insignificance in relation to the Pima.

At Salt River, the reported situation is somewhat
different, and fewer data are available. After an overall
decline from 1911-17 (especially heavy 1913-14), the
Maricopa population was reported to increase considerably
from 1917-18 (the year of the worldwide influenza epidemic),
and remain relatively stable until 1923 when a cataclysmic
increase took place. Only two figures were reported after
this year, showing great decline: 1937, and the miniscule
figure for 1950. Here again, perhaps more strongly than
for Gila River, it would appear the Maricopa population
size is inversely related to Pima population size, implying
classification of the same persons in different ethnic
groups at different censuses.

To further complicate matters, from 1930-37, the
"Table" in the RCIA presented an extremely detailed ethnic
classification of part-Pima and part-Maricopa. 1933 and
1934 saw the greatest detail, with eighteen categories of
offspring of Pima-other Indian intermarriage, and seven for

the Maricopa. These included Pima-Navajo, Pima-Hopi, Pima-Oneida, Pima-Pueblo-Seneca, and sixteen persons reported as Maricopa-Klamath-Pima, Maricopa presumably predominating. Significantly, up to twelve Pima-Maricopa (in 1932) and eight Maricopa-Pima (in 1933 and 1934) were reported. The criteria for distinguishing Pima-Maricopa from Maricopa-Pima were not stated; presumably the ethnic group of the father came first. Considering the number of offspring at Gila River of mixed Indian ancestry (144 in 1933 and 1934), the reported number of Pima-Maricopa and Maricopa-Pima would appear to be too small. At Salt River the number of children resulting from intertribal marriages was considerably smaller, both absolutely and relatively.

For the above reasons, it is impossible to carry out an analysis of data by tribe for this period, and comparisons will be made between the combined Pima-Maricopa populations at the Gila River and Salt River Reservations, rather than between the Pima and Maricopa. Fortunately, data by reservation are more abundant than in the past, when information about Salt River was much less abundant than for Gila River.

Factors Affecting Pima and Maricopa Population

As during the previous period, relatively more has been published on the history of the Gila River Indian Reservation than the Salt River Indian Reservation. Absolutely, however, this means that very little has been published on Gila River for this period, and almost nothing for Salt River.

At Gila River, land allotment was carried out from 1914-20 (Spicer 1962:150), and persons living off-reservation reportedly returned to Gila River to attempt to take up farming on their allotment, in the expectation that irrigation water would be coming. Each person, regardless of age or sex, received 10 acres (4 ha) of farm land and 10 acres (4 ha) of desert land. No one received any more water than there had been before allotment, since depletion of river water occurred through continued farming above the reservation by non-Indians. Allotment also dispersed the population across certain areas of the reservation, in contrast to much denser settlement in villages before allotment. Consequently, population was no longer reported by village.

With no water forthcoming, presumably persons once again left the reservation to find work, for in 1924, when Congress approved the construction of a dam and reservoir at San Carlos on the Gila River and the San Carlos Irrigation Project (which included the Gila River Indian Reservation as well as certain non-Indian lands upstream), Pima working off-reservation were once again reported as returning to the Gila River Reservation (Spicer 1962:151). The dam was not completed until 1930, and until then the Pima reportedly attempted to make a living from wage labor and collecting wild foods (Kneale 1950:395, 405). During the early 1930s, some Pima, perhaps 400-500 (Kneale 1950: 412), found work clearing and otherwise preparing allotments for irrigation, as well as constructing irrigation canals and ditches (Kneale 1950:407; U.S. Senate 1931:8234).

The irrigation project did not bring the highly touted prosperity to the Pima that proponents had forecast, since there was never enough water for all allotments. Although the Pima were adjudged to have immemorial water rights to 35,000 acres (14,000 ha), this right was not fulfilled before non-Indian lands of later priority were irrigated, under the provisions of the Gila River Decree (U.S. District Court 1935). Lured to the reservation with the promise of water when none was to come, a number of Pima had to seek work elsewhere after construction activities for the San Carlos Project ceased, in the midst of a national economic depression.

At Salt River, allotments were also made, from 1912-14 (Munsell 1967:111; RCIA 1916:98). There is no information whether Pima returned to the Salt River Reservation from off-reservation residence at this time.

Besides the reports concerning migration resulting from allotment and construction of irrigation projects, government publications provide some information on the health status of the Pima and Maricopa.

Up to three doctors were present at one time at Gila River in 1930 or 1931 (U.S. Senate 1931:8239), but there were no public health nurses. All school children, and some pre-school children, were reportedly vaccinated against smallpox. All school children were reportedly immunized against diphtheria, and some against whooping cough and typhoid fever. Nevertheless, diphtheria and whooping cough, as well as measles, for which there was no vaccine at that time, were reported to be problems. Leading the most prevalent diseases at Gila River was pulmonary tuberculosis (U.S. Senate 1931:8240). Skin diseases and dysentery and allied gastroenteric diseases were also of frequent occurrence. Syphilis was considered uncommon, but gonorrhea was reported as widespread. The level of infant mortality was felt to be about like that of urban slums of the period (U.S. Senate 1931:8341). Somewhat contradictorily, the agency doctor felt that health among the Pima and Maricopa at Gila River was as good as that of whites in surrounding communities, except for a higher incidence of tuberculosis, with up to 62% of the population showing a positive skin test (U.S. Senate 1931:8261).

At Salt River, a doctor was apparently resident in 1930 or 1931 (U.S. Senate 1931:8139). He reported that all school children were vaccinated against smallpox. TB was also a considerable health problem at Salt River, and was reported as more common than among whites (U.S. Senate 1931:8159).

At both Gila River and Salt River, reporting of births was considered quite low, with most births outside the hospital (U.S. Senate 1931:8241, 8262-63). At Gila River, death reporting was considered better than birth reporting, because the person reporting the death at the agency office could obtain a coffin (U.S. Senate 1931: 8241).

Population Dynamics

De Jure Population

In this section, I attempt to determine the size and factors affecting the size of the entire Pima-Maricopa population, regardless of residence.

Gila River Indian Reservation roll

For reasons presented in Appendix E, the roll population figure is more accurate for some years than others. I consider the most accurate figure for this period to be the final allotment roll, since all persons, regardless of residence, had a considerable incentive to be included. Minor children were allotted, so the roll should be as accurate a count of the entire Pima-Maricopa population of Gila River as was possible.

From 1914-20, 4894 or 4898 allotments were made at Gila River (U.S. Senate 1931:8245; Van Cleve Associates 1972:30). Nevertheless, some persons were certainly missed, and children who were born shortly after allotment were not allotted. Consequently, I estimate a good round 5000 Pima and Maricopa should have been on the allotment roll in 1920. Other roll figures are much less reliable than this, since they relied on reporting of births and deaths after an initial enumeration. It is not clear when such a count was made, if at all, other than for the allotment roll. As a result, I will project and retroject the Pima-Maricopa de jure population for Gila River from the above assumed number for 1920, assuming certain annual growth rates in accordance with medical and economic factors acting during this period.

Salt River Indian Reservation roll

Here again, the most accurate figure should be based on the allotment roll. From 1912-14, 804 allotments were made at Salt River (RCIA 1916:98). But 950-75 persons were on the roll from 1912-14 (Table 33). Apparently the allotment excluded the Lehi area, since the 1911 roll reported 241 persons at Lehi (Coe 1911). I estimate about 1170 Pima and Maricopa should have been on the Salt River roll in 1915, and will project and retroject the roll population from this figure at assumed annual growth rates. Appendix E gives more details on how this estimate was made.

1920-30

Let us first consider the probable change in population from 1920-30 because birth and death data are available for 1 April 1928 to 31 March 1931. The mean number of births and deaths for the 3 years is used so as to smooth abnormal fluctuations that may occur in a single year. The mean number of births and deaths, mean number of infant deaths, birth rate and death rate calculated on the reported 1930 roll population, natural increase, infant death rate, and infant deaths as proportion of all deaths, are shown in Table 34. The rates were calculated with unadjusted numbers of events and population.

Both the birth and death rates are higher at Salt River than Gila River, but the natural increase is near stability, with 0.29% at Gila River and -0.23% at Salt River. The lower rates at Gila River probably reflect poorer reporting of vital events in a larger, more dispersed population. However, as mentioned before, BIA personnel felt that deaths were better reported than births; thus, the birth rate should be higher at both Gila River and Salt River. The excess of deaths over births at Salt River should then not be taken seriously, since deaths were apparently more completely reported than births.

I feel that a moderate increase is thus likely for both the Gila River and Salt River roll populations. With a continuing high death rate from infectious diseases, the rate should be less than 1% annually, and I estimate it as 0.5%.

Supporting this assertion, it is seen in Table 34 that infant deaths were 15.8% of all deaths at Gila River, and 28.1% at Salt River for the respective enrolled populations. The lower rate at Gila River again probably reflects greater underreporting. The infant death rate (Table 34) is also quite high. Adjusted values for infant deaths as proportion of all deaths would probably be about 20%-25%, and the infant death rate about 200.

For deaths at all ages for Gila River and Salt River combined, tuberculosis, pneumonia, and influenza accounted for 46% of all reported deaths, while unknown causes were responsible for 18.6%. The leading causes of infant deaths were unknown, but diarrhea, influenza, pneumonia, and congenital anomalies were among the more frequently specified causes. (These figures have been calculated from data in USOIA 1924a-32a, 1924b-32b.)

The child-woman ratio for the roll population of Gila River and Salt River combined was 518.9; when adjusted for age-specific and sex-specific underenumeration, it would probably be about 650. This also suggests a low rate of increase and high infant mortality, with an apparent high birth rate. (Data are found in Brown 1930 and Kneale 1930).

Assuming a 0.5% annual growth rate from 1920-30, Table 35 shows the estimated *de jure* Pima-Maricopa population by reservation of enrollment for 1930.

1910-20

With a high crude and infant death rate, and severe economic distress during this period, there is no reason to assume a growth rate greater than that of 1920-30, and thus I assume 0.5% as a credible growth rate for this period. In fact, it may have been lower, as a result of the influenza pandemic of 1918, which Spier (1933:142) reports was remembered among the Maricopa as causing many deaths. The rate for 1890-1910 was a bit over 0.6% annually. As during that period, I assume a number of persons supported themselves by working on and off the reservation in such assorted low-paying occupations as farm and nonfarm laborer, maid, firewood seller and gatherer, arts and crafts, and for some near wells, farming. The retrojected figures for 1910, by reservation of enrollment, are shown in Table 35.

1930-40

During this period it must be assumed that the population grew by a lower rate than during 1920-30. This is supported by a small 1935-45 birth cohort in the Gila River and Salt River populations in the 1970 Census (Table 36, ages 25-34). Consequently, I assume that the growth rate during this period was only 0.25% annually. This produces the estimates shown in Table 35 for 1940. Unfortunately, I could find no roll figures for 1940, and thus it is impossible to compare the estimate with the official BIA enrollment figure.

On-reservation Population

Although both the Bureau of the Census and BIA have published on-reservation population figures for the Gila River and Salt River Reservations for this period, in no one year do both agencies provide a figure. In the discussion below, the 1910 and 1920 reported figures (Table 37) are from the Bureau of the Census, and include all races or ethnic groups resident at Gila River or Salt River at the time of enumeration. There is no such BIA figure for the on-reservation population, only the roll population.

In 1930, only the BIA figure is available for on-reservation population, since the Census Bureau no longer used Indian reservations as minor civil divisions (the next smaller level than the county for presentation of data).[3]

The last year that the BIA published the "Table" as a part of the RCIA or RSI was 1937; I could find no figures for either roll or on-reservation population for 1940. The Bureau of the Census figures were also not published in an official report, but appeared in a local newspaper (Arizona Republic, 28 May 1940). The minor civil divisions for 1940 were very large, being the supervisorial districts of each county, of which there were three, regardless of county area or population (USBC 1942:88, 91).

All these figures, as well as the Bureau of the Census Indian population for Maricopa and Pinal Counties in 1910-40, are shown in Table 37.

Gila River Indian Reservation

1910-20. I postdict that the Gila River population from 1910-20 should be essentially stable. Natural increase, as shown in the preceding section, was low from "normal" mortality, as well as the influenza epidemic of 1918. Although an unstated number of persons took up reservation residence during the allotment period, many had probably already left by the completion of allotment in 1920, when they saw that no water was likely to arrive for farming.

The 1910 and 1920 Census figures support this assertion (Table 37, "Reported Population"). The annual rate of population growth was -0.3% for the 10 year period. Because of inaccuracies in the data, I feel this rate implies stability rather than a decline, which was small. There could also have been a slight increase, for that matter; the important point is that the population appears to be pretty much the same size in 1910 and 1920.

My assumption that net out-migration occurred at this time is supported not only by the lower figure in 1920 for the Gila River population, but also by its distribution (Table 38). While the number of persons in the Pinal County part of the reservation, where the allotments were made, was greater in 1910 than 1920, the number of persons in the Maricopa County part of the reservation was greater in 1920 than 1910. Moreover, as will be seen below, the rate of increase at Salt River from 1910-20 implies net in-migration, presumably at least in part from Gila River. The people migrating from the Pinal County part of Gila River to its Maricopa County part and Salt River were perhaps largely those who went the other direction from 1900-10, mentioned in the preceding chapter.

Although I am reluctant to estimate the true size of the Gila River Reservation population at this time, based on fuller information from later censuses, it would be fair to assume about 10% underenumeration in the reported population. It was probably higher but this simultaneously corrects for an assumed 5% non-Indians in the reported population figure. Although the amount of underenumeration probably differed in 1910 and 1920, it is not possible to correct for this. The population estimates appear in Table 37 and are highly speculative.

<u>1920-30</u>. By 1930, I feel that the rate of annual growth should exceed natural increase to a considerable degree because persons residing off-reservation were returning to take up reservation residence in preparation for farming. I feel that the rate of growth was higher than for 1910-20 because during 1920-30 some employment was available on-reservation, and with the construction of Coolidge Dam, there was more reason to expect the imminent arrival of irrigation water. People thus had more incentive for remaining on-reservation.

The reported population figures in Table 37 support this assertion, but caution is necessary in interpretation to an even greater degree than for the 1910 and 1920 figures. The 1920 figure is from the Census Bureau and includes all races resident at Gila River; the 1930 figure is the

BIA on-reservation population figure. Thus the rate of growth in the reported figures should be higher, because the 1920 population should be reduced by perhaps 5% to allow for non-Indians included in it.

The reported figures produce an annual rate of population growth of 1.2%. From the birth and death data in Table 34 for 1928-31, we see that the estimated crude birth and death rates are about equal for the reservation population, compared to a small increase for the roll population. If the incentive to report deaths to a greater degree than births was cost-free acquisition of a coffin, there would be less reason for off-reservation residents to report deaths, since they would have to travel a considerable distance to the agency to report the death, and have to possess or obtain some means of transporting the coffin. Thus the number of deaths not reported among off-reservation residents may well have been greater than deaths not reported among reservation residents, making the difference in rates between on and off-reservation residents spurious. Consequently, I feel it is safe to assume that natural increase on-reservation (where the majority of Pima and Maricopa lived) was about 0.5% annually in 1930.

Indirect support for assuming a slightly decreasing or stable Gila River Reservation population from 1910-20 and increasing population to a considerable degree by migration in 1920-30 is provided by the Bureau of the Census figures for Indians in Pinal County (Table 37). However, these figures exclude Gila River Reservation residents in Maricopa County, and include reservation residents of the Ak Chin and part of the Papago Reservation (1920 and after) (see Figure 1), as well as all off-reservation Indians in Pinal County.

The figures for 1910 and 1920 are almost the same, supporting the assumption of stability or slight decrease. From 1920 to 1930 the population was reported to increase by about 1.0% annually, close to the 1.2% for the Gila River population data. This should not be surprising, since well over half the Indians in Pinal County were living on the Gila River Reservation.

I am again reluctant to estimate the true size of the Gila River Reservation population in 1930, but feel that since a greater proportion of all Pima and Maricopa were living on-reservation in 1930 than 1920, and they were more likely to be enumerated, perhaps underenumeration was about 12.5%. (As no non-Indians are included in the reported figure for 1930, and I assumed about 5% non-Indians in the reported figures for 1910 and 1920, the degree of underenumeration I assume for 1930 actually is greater than 1910 or 1920, even though the enumeration of Indians may have been more accurate.) While there is no reason to assume that BIA reservation population figures are always more accurate than those of the Census Bureau, at this time the BIA was interested in ascertaining the number and identity of allottees and heirs of allottees. According to the provisions of the law authorizing the San Carlos Project, the cost of construction of the project and preparation of the land for farming was reimbursable to the United States Government, but was deferred until or unless the land passed out of Indian ownership. Nevertheless, since this apparently was anticipated, a record was kept of who had their land cleared, and at first, the actual cost of clearing each allotment (U.S. Senate 1931: 8284-86). Later, it was decided to prorate the total cost of clearing the land for all allotments, so as not to charge some a very high amount for land clearing, and others very little. The BIA should thus have had a good idea of the number of allottees and descendants of allottees living on-reservation, but not necessarily of their descendants. The lower BIA figure (roll, not on-reservation) for 1930 as compared with 1923 (Table 33; the 1923 figure appears to be the final allotment roll; see Appendix E) shows that considerable underenumeration still occurred. The annual rate of population growth for 1920-30 for the estimated figures in Table 37 comes out to 1.4% annually.

For 1940, no population figure was available by reservation; the estimates I have made by reservation are discussed below, after the following section on Salt River from 1910-30.

Salt River Indian Reservation

1910-20. For this period, the Census Bureau reported figures show an annual rate of growth of 2.7%, compared to stability or slight decline at Gila River. The rate itself is too high to have occurred by natural increase alone (at this time), and thus implies (among other less likely possibilities) that either underenumeration at Salt River was greater in 1910 than 1920, or considerable in-migration took place from 1910 to 1920.

Supporting assumption of greater underenumeration in 1910, for that year 85% of the Census Bureau population was reported at Gila River and 15% at Salt River. For 1911-20, BIA figures (although of the roll, not reservation population) reported 18%-21% at Salt River and 79%-82% at Gila River.

But since the 1910 Census figure includes non-Indian residents on the reservation and the BIA figures do not, it seems likely that proportionally fewer persons were reported by the Census at Salt River because proportionally more non-Indians were very likely living at Gila River than Salt River. Gila River was the agency headquarters, and a greater number of government officials and employees, including school teachers, would be there.

In 1920, the Census Bureau and BIA essentially agree on the proportion of persons at the two reservations: 19.3% at Salt River according to the Census Bureau (Table 37), and 19.0% according to the BIA (roll, not reservation population, Table 33). The high rate of increase from 1910-20 at Salt River, along with this change in proportions from 1910, is consistent with the assumption of considerable in-migration at Salt River, especially from Gila River. Since allotments were made at Salt River in 1912-14, a number of persons, including some living off-reservation, would have returned to the reservation.

Providing further support, while the population at Salt River (and the Maricopa County part of Gila River) increased from 1910-20, the Indian population of Maricopa County was reported to have decreased (by 1.6% annually) (Tables 37 and 38). If we look at the population for Gila River and Salt River combined in 1910 (Table 37), it was 4779; in 1920 it was 4898, or an annual rate of growth of about 0.2%. This is consistent with assuming a natural increase of less than 1% for this period, as was done for the roll population.

It would thus appear that the higher rate of growth at Salt River is real (although not necessarily the value shown here); the increase at Salt River is in part proportionally greater than the decrease reported at Gila River because the population base is smaller. Because of the smaller Salt River population, making an estimate of true population on-reservation is even more hazardous than for Gila River, but I assume about 15% underenumeration for both 1910 and 1920, as shown in Table 37 ("estimated population").

1920-30. The annual rate of growth for this period is reported as 0.3%, less than the 1.2% at Gila River. However, the 1930 figure is Indian only, while that of 1920 is all Salt River residents (Table 37). Thus the growth rate should be higher, but not by much (probably less than 1%, assuming between 5% and 10% of the 1920 Salt River population was non-Indian).

There is no good evidence to support a higher rate of growth at Salt River at this time, other than a larger increase (and hence high growth rate) for the Indian population of Maricopa County from 1920-30 (Table 37). However, since most off-reservation Salt River Pima and Maricopa would presumably be in Maricopa County, other groups of Indians must have contributed to this high rate of growth (3.8% annually). Part of the answer is that 1930 was one of the years when identification by tribe was sought from Indians by Census enumerators. Consequently, persons who previously may have been classified as non-Indian were more likely to be counted as Indian in 1930. This is perhaps especially true of the Yaqui, about 500 of whom lived in the village of Guadalupe, south of Tempe, and at other places in Maricopa County at this time (Spicer 1940:5). Many Yaqui must have been reported as white in 1920, as many spoke Spanish better than English as a second language, being recently arrived from Mexico at the time.[4] Reclassification of "Mexicans" as Yaqui, as well as continued Yaqui migration to Arizona thus should have accounted for a considerable portion of the Maricopa County Indian population increase from 1920-30.

With considerable migration to Salt River taking place from 1910-20, but no reason for much to occur from 1920-30, it is entirely credible that the 1920-30 growth rate at Salt River was less than at Gila River, where persons were returning in expectation of farming. The construction of Coolidge Dam and San Carlos Reservoir had no effect on the Salt River, as it enters the Gila River below the Salt River Indian Reservation.

1930-40

For 1940, only a Census Bureau figure is available, and it is for the combined populations of the Gila River, Salt River, Ak Chin, and Fort McDowell Indian Reservations. I will thus estimate the Census Bureau population at Gila River and Salt River, based on the BIA proportions by reservation as reported in 1937, the nearest date for which such data are available. From the "Table" (RCIA 1937:252), 76.8% of the population residing at jursidiction of enrollment (i.e., on-reservation) for the four reservations was at Gila River, and 17.3% at Salt River. The proportions of the 6087 Indians reported for all four reservations were used to make the estimates in Table 37 for the reported population.

Given these estimates, the 1930-40 growth rate at Gila River is 0.50% annually, and at Salt River, 0.76%,

both quite moderate. In the preceding section on the
de jure population, I estimated the natural increase for
this period to be 0.25%. It thus appears that net in-
migration was occurring at this time, contributing to the
growth rate at both reservations. This assumption is
supported by the Census Bureau figures for Indian population
in Maricopa and Pinal Counties in 1930 and 1940 (Table 37).
The Indian population of Pinal County, which resided mainly
on reservations, reportedly increased 1.9% annually. That
of Maricopa County, where many more persons resided off-
reservation in Phoenix, decreased 1.5% annually. Part of
the decrease in Maricopa County could be enumeration of
Yaqui as white in a Census which did not seek tribal
identity of Indians, and in which racial classification
was made on sight by the enumerator, not supplied by the
respondent. But the increase in Pinal County, in a year
when Indians were not sought out by the Census, argues for
net in-migration at Gila River, at least.

However, for Gila River, part of the increase
could have been continued relocation on-reservation in
the expectation of being able to farm. At the same time,
the national economic depression also left a number of
persons with no choice, as Indians, in whatever job, would
have been among the first to be laid off. As shown in
the next chapter, I believe that enumeration was somewhat
better at this time, with only 10% of the population missed
at Gila River but still 15% at Salt River; the estimates

in Table 37 reflect these rates.

Proportion of Population On-Reservation

With estimates of both the de jure Pima-Maricopa population by reservation (Table 35) and the on-reservation population (Table 37) at 10 year intervals from 1910-40, the estimated proportion of persons on-reservation may be calculated (Table 39). These figures support the assumptions above concerning migration.

In 1910, the on-reservation proportion of the de jure population of Salt River is less than Gila River, although not necessarily to the extent in the estimated figures. This is presumably a result of prior migration to the eastern part of the Gila River Reservation where wells had been drilled. By 1920, the Gila River figure is lower, reflecting the departure of persons who had been expecting to receive water for their allotments, as well as persons returning to Salt River to be allotted. Thus, the on-reservation proportion of the enrolled population at Salt River increases.

In 1930, the proportion on-reservation at Gila River is greater than in 1920 because of return to the reservation in expectation of water from the San Carlos Project, as well as some local employment. At Salt River, the proportion is about the same. By 1940, the proportion at Gila River is about the same, while that at Salt River has increased, reflecting a high rate of on-reservation residence at both reservations during the Depression, when there must have been little work off-reservation.

Sex Ratio

For reasons discussed in Appendix E, the 1923 figure for Gila River (Table 33) appears to be the allotment roll, and is thus assumed to present the most accurate sex ratio, 104.0 (Table 40). This is well within probability by chance alone, and is consistent with past sex ratios which also showed an excess of males.

During the 1930s, comparing the roll sex ratio to the on-reservation ("at jurisdiction") sex ratio (Table 41), it appears that at Gila River females were more likely than males to live off-reservation, because the on-reservation sex ratio is higher for all but 1936-37. This is also true of Salt River for much of the 1930s. This assumption is also supported by the Bureau of the Census figures for the Indian population of Maricopa and Pinal Counties and Phoenix (Table 42). Phoenix, in which all Indians would be migrants or descendants of migrants, has a very low sex ratio (whose probability in 1930 is between .01 and .05 even for such a small population). The sex ratio of Indians in Maricopa County, where more Indians were living off-reservation than in Pinal County, is lower than that of Pinal County for both 1930 and 1940. If more women were living off-reservation than men, women would more likely be missed by enumerators, and this could explain in part the improbable sex ratios for Pinal County in 1930 and 1940 and Maricopa County in 1930. A greater number of women living off-reservation would also make the Pinal County sex ratio higher than the Maricopa County sex ratio, since much migration would be to Phoenix, in Maricopa County.

For Salt River, the sex ratio is usually higher than Gila River (Table 40 and 41), especially from 1911-28. Chance is probably the best way to account for this. I consider the 1914 Salt River figure of 109.4 the most accurate of all those presented (Table 40), but the lower figures for the 1930s (Table 41) may not be greatly in error. In 1929 some minor allottees were transferred from the Salt River roll to the Gila River roll; with the small number of persons at Salt River, a greater number of males being transferred would lower the sex ratio. The sex ratio at Gila River is also generally higher during the 1930s.

In that the population figures for this period are extremely inaccurate and the sex ratios show correspondingly wide variation, even from one year to the next, I do not feel able at this time to draw any further conclusions. However, the 1915 sex ratio for Salt River (Table 40) is obviously an error, and should be the reciprocal of its value as a proportion (.936), viz., 1.068, or a sex ratio of 106.8.

Age Distribution

The BIA and Census Bureau age distributions for the de jure Pima-Maricopa combined population are shown together in Table 43. For reasons why more age distributions were not available or presented in this work, see Appendix E.

Both distributions show the usual underenumeration in the 0-4 age interval, principally at ages 0 and 1. For the BIA roll ("enrolled population"), there should probably be at least 150, and perhaps as high as 250 additional males and at least 100, and perhaps as high as 150 more females in the 0-4 age interval, reflecting greater underenumeration of males, and loss of up to 40% of persons during their first 5 years of life. There also appears to be greater underenumeration of females than males aged 5-9 in the Census age distribution, as well as to a lesser degree in the BIA roll distribution.

The deficit in the 10-14 age interval seems to be real, however, since this age group is the 1915-20 birth cohort, and presumably suffered heavy mortality as infants and young children during the influenza epidemic of 1918.

All other things equal, the Census age distribution appears to be more accurate in a relative sense, while the BIA roll appears to be more accurate in an absolute sense. The age groups in the Census age distribution always show a decline in number after 10-14, while there is some fluctuation in the BIA roll figures, reflecting age heaping at ages ending in 5. The age-specific sex ratios in the Census distribution are less divergent than those of the roll. However, overall, the Census population is only 83.9% of the roll population.

In both distributions, females appear to have been more greatly underenumerated than males at ages 30 and above. The roll produces a sex ratio of 121.8 for these ages, while the Census produces a similar 121.5. There should probably be at least an additional 100 females on the roll at these ages, reducing the sex ratio to 110.8.

Correcting the roll for underenumeration by sex and age, the new total is 5940-6090, with 3039-3139 males and 2901-51 females, and a sex ratio of 104.8-106.4. This does not correct for general underenumeration, however. The estimated 1930 de jure population (Table 35) is 6510, still leaving a deficit of 6.5%-8.8%.

The median age of the population is 24 in both distributions, but should probably be around 23 because of proportionally greater underenumeration at ages 0-9. More detailed information is presented in Appendix E on median age (and the child-woman ratio) by reservation and tribe, but there are no great divergences from the above figure except to express differing underenumeration by tribe or reservation.

Notes to Chapter Six

1. The choice of this term is unfortunate, as it implies that when Indians of a particular ethnic group live on-reservation they are more Indian or "tribal" than when off-reservation. While it is true that more of the indigenous cultural practices will be found on-reservation, the stereotypes implicit in this term make me feel that it should be replaced by a substitute, such as "reservation." The basis for this population is geographic, not cultural.

2. Combining politically and culturally distinct groups into an administrative unit is not unique to the Pima and Maricopa, of course, and similar situations have occurred in all parts of the United States, usually formalized by the creation of a political entity under the Indian Reorganization Act titled by a geographic or political, rather than cultural name: e.g., Fort Belknap Community in Montana; Three Affiliated Tribes in North Dakota.

3. The 1930 minor civil divisions for Arizona were election precincts, which included both on-reservation and off-reservation areas (USBC 1931:93-97).

4. All Yaqui originally lived along the lower Yaqui River in Sonora, Mexico. They began settling in the United States in small numbers as early as 1880, with family groups taking up residence after 1900. Although fairly mobile from 1900-10, traveling as far as

New Mexico, California, and Oregon, the demand for farm labor in the Tucson, Phoenix, and Yuma areas in Arizona led to the major settlements in the Tucson (Pascua and Barrio Libre) and the Phoenix areas (Guadalupe, with another group of perhaps 400 in 1937 near Scottsdale) (Spicer 1940:4-5, 20-21).

The Yaqui originally fled to the United States because their resistance to Mexican attempts to gain control of their lands and integrate them into Mexican society was met with military action. Prisoners were shipped to plantations in Yucatán in Mexico. As late as 1926-27 the Yaqui and Mexican Government were engaged in warfare, and Yaqui were fleeing to the United States during this period (Spicer 1962:83).

As an aside, the curious nature of political repression may be seen in contrasting the Yaqui and Kickapoo: the Yaqui fled persecution in Mexico by entering the United States, while the Kickapoo fled persecution in the United States by fleeing to Mexico.

CHAPTER SEVEN

FROM THE SECOND WORLD WAR TO THE PRESENT

(1940-74)

Population Dynamics

De Jure Population

For this period, I found statements of the enrolled population for only 1950 and 1969. Because the rolls were so obviously deficient, it was not possible to estimate the de jure Pima-Maricopa population for this period. For further information on the roll figures, see Appendix F. The 1970 Census figures by tribe (USBC 1973) are also useless for this study, for the Pima were included with the Papago in all tabulations.

Reservation Population and Reservation and Adjacent Areas Population

1940-52

From 1940-46, for both Gila River and Salt River, I expect a very low annual rate of growth occurred, probably negative, resulting from a presumed low birth rate and considerable off-reservation migration and subsequent residence. The low birth rate is assumed to be a result of severe economic conditions in the early years (1940-42), while later on a result of the absence of many males in the armed forces. More than at any other period, Pima and Maricopa were perhaps successful to a greater degree in finding off-reservation employment, because of the labor shortage during World War II. Ethnic minorities and women were hired at this time for jobs they ordinarily would have been denied.

The figures in Table 44 show my estimates, derived from BIA and Census Bureau figures, of the population by reservation for 1940 and 1952. The original data, shown in Tables 45 and 46, and the bases for my estimates in Table 44 are evaluated and discussed in Appendix F. These figures, as well as other data below, support the situation I have sketched.

Age distribution in the 1970 Census. Table 36 shows that in the 25-34 age interval (approximate 1935-45 birth cohort), there were fewer persons than expected assuming a constant decline in numbers by age group. At Salt River, there is actually a gap. At Gila River the number seems rather low, being nearly as small as the next age group. It seems likely that this pattern is a result of a low birth rate from 1935-45 rather than an age-specific pattern of mortality. Table 47 shows the number of deaths by reservation for 1969-71 for ages 15-44 (grouped data). Although the number of deaths from 25-34 is greater than those from 15-24 for Gila River, this is not the case at Salt River. Moreover, the number of deaths from 35-44 is greater than those 25-34 at both reservations. Thus, while we would expect a decline in numbers from 15-24 to 25-34, we would expect at least as great a decline from 25-34 to 35-44, unless either the death rate for persons 25-34 had increased or the death rate for persons 15-24 had declined in the last 10 years. The greater number (at Salt River) or similar number (at Gila River) of persons 35-44 compared to those 25-34 leads to the conclusion that the small number of persons 25-34 is the result of a low birth rate during 1935-45. Migration of persons 25-34 to a greater degree than those 15-24 or 35-44 also seems unlikely, as all three age groups should be affected by migration.

Population figures. From Table 44, I estimate that for the combined Gila River-Salt River population, fewer persons were living on-reservation in 1952 than 1940 in spite of an assumed small population increase of the de jure population (not estimated). This decrease is a result of the figures for Gila River, while for Salt River a small increase is shown.

Nevertheless, by 1952 I would have expected that a high post-war birth rate and return migration to the reservations would have increased the on-reservation population. The 1970 age distribution in Table 36 shows a considerably greater number of persons in the 1945-55 birth cohort (15-24 age interval) as compared to those 25-34, and it appears this difference is a result of differential fertility. However, women coming into childbearing age (15) from 1945-55 were born 1930-40. This is a small birth cohort, especially 1935-40, and thus the increase through births is probably not as great as would be expected.

It appears that considerable off-reservation migration took place during World War II, and that a large number of persons did not return to the reservations afterward, leading to a net loss of population from at least 1940-46, which an increased postwar higher birth rate could not compensate for even by 1952 at Gila River. For Salt River, it is unclear whether there was less migration during the Second World War, a higher birth rate, a lower death rate, or some combination of these factors.

Although the Gila River and Salt River populations look relatively stable from 1940-52, there was most likely considerable fluctuation, with a low point reached about 1944-45, and high points at 1940, when a large number of persons had returned from off-reservation residence, and 1952, after the post-Second World War birth rate increase.

1952-60

During this period, I expect a considerable increase in population occurred from a continued high or increasing birth rate and a decreasing death rate (especially infant), as medical services were assumed from the BIA and expanded by the Public Health Service. The effect of migration on the reservation population is hard to postdict, but perhaps there was a net gain, or at least fewer leaving the reservation because of the economic recessions of the 1950s.

The assumption of a high rate of population growth on-reservation is supported by the population data. Table 44 shows that the combined reservations population grew an estimated 2.2% annually for the period. The estimated rate of growth at Gila River was 2.1% while that at Salt River was slightly higher, 2.4%. However, because all these figures are estimates and hence subject to considerable error, it is difficult to say whether the difference in growth rates between the two reservations is significant. Besides the population estimates, other data also support the assumption of a high rate of growth at this time.

Birth data. Unfortunately, the number of births by reservation is not available for this period. However, the number of Indian births by county is. For Maricopa County, the figures are of little use in attempting to infer the number of births at Salt River, because most of the Indian population is not at Salt River. The Fort McDowell (Yavapai and Apache) and Gila Bend (Papago) Reservations are entirely located in the county, and parts of the Gila River and Papago Reservations are also in Maricopa County. A considerable number of Indians live off-reservation in Phoenix and surrounding cities, as well as the Yaqui at Guadalupe. The figures for Pinal County are more useful. Besides the majority of the Gila River Reservation, the Ak Chin (Papago) Reservation and part of the Papago Reservation are located in the county. Indians live off-reservation in Coolidge, Casa Grande, Florence, Maricopa, and Stanfield (USBC 1971b:Tables 27,31, 33), but the majority of the county Indian population resides on the Gila River Reservation. Consequently, the birth figures for Pinal County may be assumed to roughly represent the trend at Gila River.

As seen in Figure 7, the number of Indian resident births in Pinal County increased steadily from 184 in 1952 to 245 in 1957, then fluctuated from 230-43 to 1960. By itself, an increasing number of births does not imply an increased birth rate. If a large number of women were attaining child-bearing age during the period, the General Fertility Rate (see Appendix A) could remain the same as before, yet more children would be born. But the women entering childbearing from 1952-60 were those born 1937-45, which is a small birth cohort. Under these conditions, the number of births would be expected to decrease assuming constant fertility. That the number of births increased supports the assumption that a good part of the population increase at this time can be ascribed to an increasing birth rate.

The mean number of births per year from 1950-54 in Pinal County was 178.6; from 1955-59, 228.6. This is a 4.94% increase, which is larger than the population of childbearing women could have been increasing at this time.

Moreover, the 1955-65 birth cohort (ages 5-14) in the 1970 Census age distribution (Table 36) seems to me considerably larger in relation to the number of persons 15-24, especially at Gila River, than would be expected from the small number of deaths recorded for the 5-14 age interval at both reservations for 1969-71 (4 of 230, or 1.7%). Migration off-reservation of persons 15-24 may have reduced somewhat the true size of the 15-24 year old population in 1970. Nevertheless, older persons (25-44) migrating off-reservation would take children (aged 5-14) with them, decreasing the size of that age group. Since the birth rate may decrease somewhat from 1960-64, or at least remain the same (given the number of births shown in Figure 7 and an increasing population), not all of the greater number in the 1955-65 birth cohort in 1970 as compared to the 1945-55 cohort should result from births in 1960-64.

Somewhat less trustworthy data on the child-woman ratio also suggest an increasing birth rate from 1950-60, as well as a possible reduction in infant mortality. The Pima Indian Agency Area population for 1950 (see Appendix F for definition) showed a child-woman ratio of 708.1, while the ratio for the Indian population of Pinal and Cochise Counties in 1960 was 986.0. The main deficiencies in this comparison are that two different populations are compared, and both sets of data are based on samples of populations of around 5000, which is quite small, and entails large sampling error when divided into age groups (Appendix F).

Finally, the unadjusted birth rates for Indians in Pinal County in 1950 and 1960 can be compared. That of 1950 was 34.9; that of 1960, 39.9 (or 44.0 if the mean births for 1959-61 are used). There is probably relatively greater underenumeration of the Indian population of Pinal County than underreporting of births, so the birth rate may be too high.

An unknown factor concerning the number of births is to what degree reporting of births improved from 1952-60. Nevertheless, I feel that taken together, the above data support the assumption that an increased birth rate from 1952-60 as compared with 1940-52 was largely responsible for the higher rate of population growth in 1952-60.

Death data. Some of the population growth could also be a result of a decrease in the crude death rate, and perhaps especially the infant death rate, in 1952-60 as compared with 1940-52. I would not expect this factor to have as much influence as the increased birth rate, however.

Deaths by cause are available for the combined reservation populations of Arizona counties for 1959-61 (as well as other years following). Although this prevents comparing Gila River and Salt River, the inclusion of the other reservations in Maricopa and Pinal Counties does not seriously distort the data. In 1969-71, deaths on reservations in Maricopa County other than Gila River or

Salt River were 5 of 95, or 5.3%. For Pinal County in the same years, deaths on reservations other than Gila River were 9 of 149, or 6.0% (unpublished data from Arizona State Department of Health, Division of Records and Statistics).

Unfortunately, no death data are readily available, even by county, for any years preceding 1959 until we arrive back at the 1928-31 data for Gila River and Salt River presented in the preceding chapter.[1] Incompleteness of these data prohibit comparing death rates. As a result, the leading causes of death in the two periods will be compared, along with some data on infant deaths.

The data presented below support the assumption that mortality decreased from 1930 to 1960; this does not necessarily imply that the decrease was smooth. I would imagine that the main improvement came in the post-Second World War period, especially after the Public Health Service assumed administration of health services to Indians in 1954. In 1950, then, health conditions were probably not as bad as 1930, but not as good (in relative terms) as 1960. This should be kept in mind in attempting to determine to what extent a reduction in the death rate could have contributed to greater population growth in 1952-60 as compared with 1940-52.

Because of the inaccuracies of the birth and population data, I do not feel justified in calculating infant death rates for comparative purposes for 1928-31 and 1959-61. The latter requires an estimate of the

on-reservation populations of Maricopa and Pinal Counties
which I am not prepared to provide at this time. As a
result, I will compare infant mortality through expressing
infant deaths as a proportion of deaths at all ages. In
1928-31, infant deaths were 19.6% of all deaths for the
combined data from Gila River and Salt River. As mentioned
in Chapter Six, this should probably be at least 20% to 25%
to allow for underreporting at Gila River. This
figure for the on-reservation Indian population of Maricopa
and Pinal Counties in 1959-61 was 15.0%. There appears
to have been some, but not overwhelming improvement in
reducing infant mortality from 1930 to 1960. The proportion
for Gila River alone in 1928-31 was 15.8%; for Salt River
28.1%. Although not strictly comparable, the proportion
in 1959-61 for Indians on-reservation in Pinal County was
12.1%, and for Maricopa County, 20.0%. Thus, Maricopa
County, which contains Salt River (as well as part of
Gila River), had a higher proportion of all deaths to
infants, while Pinal County was lower. It appears likely
that the higher proportion at Salt River in 1928-31 was
still present in 1959-61, but I am at a loss to explain why,
other than differential rates of death registration,
presumably less complete reporting at Gila River, where the
agency and hospital are farther away for some persons.

    The problem of calculating crude death rates is
similar to that for infant death rates, and thus this has
not been done. The smaller absolute number of deaths

and larger population in 1959-61 compared to 1928-31 produces a lower mortality rate in 1959-61. Moreover, the 1959-61 data include persons residing on all reservations in Pinal and Maricopa Counties, not just those at Gila River or Salt River, as do the 1928-31 data (Table 48). In Table 48 are shown the seven leading major classes of death for the combined Gila River-Salt River data of 1928-31 and the combined on-reservation Indian resident population of Maricopa and Pinal Counties in 1959-61. The seven leading classes for 1928-31 represent 88.1% of all deaths, while those for 1959-61 represent 84.6%.

The leading class of deaths in 1928-31 was infective and parasitic diseases, mainly tuberculosis (ICD 010-019, seventy-two deaths), and intestinal diseases (ICD 000-009, twenty-four deaths). By 1959-61, this class was considerably less important, representing only 8.6% of all deaths, including only one death from tuberculosis. However, intestinal diseases still caused thirteen deaths, or 68.4% of those in the class.

The second most frequent class of deaths in 1928-31 was symptoms and ill-defined conditions, with 18.6% of all deaths. This class was third most common in 1959-61, with 10.9% of all deaths. This high frequency must reflect a high degree of non-hospital deaths, where the cause of death was vaguely reported by a relative of the deceased, without examination for cause of death by medical authority. It indicates either insufficient or underutilized medical services. This class includes senility when given as a cause of death.

The third most frequent class of deaths in 1928-31 was respiratory diseases, with 15.8% of all deaths. These were almost entirely pneumonia (71.4% of all deaths in the class) and influenza (26.5% of all deaths in the class). By 1959-61, this class had dropped to sixth place, with 7.3% of all deaths. Nevertheless, pneumonia represented twelve, or 75% of the deaths in the class, but influenza was responsible for only one death (6.25%) in the class.

The fourth most common class of deaths in 1928-31 was digestive diseases, with 5.8% of all deaths. The first three classes caused so many deaths that this class was considerably less significant. "Stomach trouble" (which may be cholelithiasis) and peritonitis (presumably from ruptured appendices) represented ten, or 55.6% of the deaths in this class. In 1959-61, this class of deaths ranked lower, but actually represented a greater proportion of all deaths than in 1928-31, 6.4%. In this case, cirrhosis of the liver (six deaths) and diseases of the pancreas (three deaths) were responsible for 64.3% of the deaths in the class. In 1928-31, only one death from cirrhosis of the liver was reported, but it is difficult to determine whether the increased number in 1959-61 is significant, given the large number of deaths from unknown causes for both periods.

The fifth largest class of deaths in 1928-31 was

genito-urinary diseases, with 5.1% of all deaths. These deaths were mostly from nephritis (fourteen; 87.5%). This class was not among the leading seven classes of death in 1959-61, but nephritis and kidney infections caused all seven deaths in the class.

The sixth most frequent class of deaths for 1928-31 was accidents, poisonings, and violence, with 4.5% of all deaths. This seems quite low, especially as these causes of death would be better known and reported than some others. Motor vehicle deaths caused two of the deaths in the class, or 14.3%. The other causes were diffuse, mainly one death per cause, except for fire and burns, which accounted for three deaths, or 21.4%. By 1959-61, deaths from this class had become the leading cause. Most of these (twenty-seven, or 51.9%) were motor vehicle deaths. As before, other causes were diffuse, but accidental drownings accounted for six deaths (11.5%) and fire and burns led to three deaths (5.8%). It would appear that few persons had cars in 1928-31, but by 1959-61, enough persons had acquired them in sufficient numbers to make motor vehicle deaths among the most significant causes of death.

The seventh most common class of deaths for 1928-31 was nervous and sensory diseases, with a very small 2.9% of all deaths. Six of these deaths (66.7%) were meningitis. In 1959-61, this class did not appear among the most frequent classes, but still represented 2.3% of all deaths, with two deaths (40%) from meningitis.

Two of the seven leading classes in 1959-61 were not represented among the leading classes of 1928-31. These are circulatory diseases, the second most frequent class in 1959-61, with 17.3% of all deaths, and neoplasms, the fourth most common cause, with 10.5% of all deaths. These two causes are significant because they are typical of populations with low death rates and a relatively long life expectancy, as, for example, the United States population of 1970 as a whole.

The significant changes in classes of death from 1928-31 to 1959-61 appear to be:

1. The elimination of tuberculosis as a significant cause of death, but probably not as a disease. A means of treatment had been developed.

2. The rise of motor vehicle deaths as a major cause, the result of greater ownership of automobiles.

3. The appearance of heart diseases and cancer as major causes of death, probably as a result of fewer deaths from infective diseases and better diagnosis.

4. A general reduction in the most frequent causes of death; i.e., causes were becoming more diffuse, as represented by a more even distribution among the seven leading classes of death, and the seven leading classes of death representing a smaller proportion of all deaths.

5. Elimination of influenza as a significant cause of death.

6. Reduction, but not elimination, of the frequency

of diarrheal diseases as a cause of death.

<u>Difference in growth rate by reservation</u>. The difference in growth rates between Gila River and Salt River is 0.3%. I feel that to a large degree this is a spurious difference because of the inaccuracy of the population estimates. In fact, the closeness of the two rates should rather support the assumption that the growth rate at Gila River and Salt River was quite similar, unlike during 1960-74.

However, if there was in fact a true difference, several factors provide support. If natural increase were greater at Salt River than Gila River, as it was during the next period, the difference in growth rates could have resulted largely from a higher birth rate at Salt River, which is the case in the next period. However, presence of this factor in the next period does not necessarily mean that it occurred in this period, and the data are not available to test the assertion.

On the other hand, the rate of natural increase could have been the same (or higher) at Salt River as compared with Gila River, but the rate of migration to Salt River could have been higher than at Gila River. This position is supported by migration data from the 1960 Census. However, the comparison is indirect in two ways: the Gila River data include only the reservation segment in Maricopa County, and the Salt River data include the Fort McDowell Reservation and some adjacent off-reservation

areas (but with few Indians). Moreover, the data include
a few blacks (but not whites) residing in both areas.
These data, in Table 49, show that a greater proportion
of 1960 "Salt River" residents moved from 1955 to 1960
(33.8%) than persons who moved during the same period
living at "Gila River" in 1960 (20.8%). However, since
15.1% of those living at "Salt River" in 1960 moved from
1955 to 1960 but did not report their previous residence,
many could have merely moved from one house to another
on-reservation. Those who lived outside Maricopa County
("outside this SMSA") in 1955 (and hence not at "Salt
River") but at "Salt River" in 1960 were 7.3% of all 1960
"Salt River" residents, while of all persons living at
"Gila River" in 1960 only 1.0% were living outside Maricopa
County in 1955. But 16.3% of all persons at Gila River
in 1960 were living in another part of Maricopa County in
1955, (either on or off a reservation), while only 7.3% of
those living at Salt River in 1960 were. As a result, it
seems much safer to assume that the difference between
growth rates at Gila River and Salt River, if there be one,
is a result of differential fertility, and to some degree
mortality, as well as possibly a different age structure.

Summary. Birth or death data from 1928-31 and
1950-61, as well as population estimates, support the
assumption that the growth rate at Gila River and Salt
River was over 2% from 1952-60, mainly because of high
fertility and to a lesser degree, lower mortality than

during 1940-52. Migration off-reservation (and back) was not as significant as during 1940-52. The difference in estimated annual growth rates for 1952-60 between Gila River (2.1%) and Salt River (2.4%) may result from different age structures or vital rates.

1960-72

Population estimates. Some rather curious trends appear at this time as a result of the population estimates for 1960, 1970, and 1972 in Table 44. The combined populations show an annual growth rate of 1.6% from 1960-70. This is somewhat lower than the 1952-60 growth rate. Gila River shows a considerably lower growth rate than for 1952-60, 1.2%. Salt River, however, shows a somewhat higher growth rate than for 1952-60, 2.7%. The two reservations thus have contradictory trends for 1960-70 as compared with 1952-60. The 1970-72 growth rates are also opposite in direction: that at Gila River increases (to 1.7%), while that at Salt River decreases (to 2.2%). Nevertheless, the 1970-72 growth rate at Salt River is still higher than that of Gila River.

Differences in growth rate, 1970-72. I will first attempt to account for the growth rate differences between Gila River and Salt River for 1970-72. Birth and death data are available for both reservations for 1970-71 (and also 1969 for deaths only), but unfortunately the data for Salt River are combined with Fort McDowell and can not be separated except by estimation procedures. Since I have estimated the population for Fort McDowell in 1970 and 1972 (see Appendix F) and it is considerably smaller than Salt River, I will use the data on births and deaths for the latter two reservations combined as if they represent Salt River, pointing out where differences between Salt River and Fort McDowell may occur.

For Gila River, the annual rate of natural increase for 1970-71 was 1.66%. The derivation of this rate is shown in Appendix F, and is for an adjusted number of births which corrects for births to on-reservation residents erroneously reported off-reservation in areas adjacent to the reservation. The annual growth rate for 1970-72 (Table 44) was 1.7%. Thus, for all practical purposes, the growth rate at Gila River can be accounted for by natural increase alone.

At Salt River-Fort McDowell, natural increase for 1970-72 was 2.03% annually, while the growth rate (Table 44) was 2.2%. The difference in natural increase between Gila River and Salt River is 0.37%; the difference in annual growth rates between Gila River and Salt River is 0.54%. Thus, approximately 0.17% of the Salt River increase is from net migration. Given a population of about 2000 at Salt River, this means that four more persons returned to the reservation than left of the unknown number that migrated on or off-reservation.

Most of the greater growth at Salt River appears to have resulted from a greater natural increase. The crude birth rate at Gila River was 25.4; at Salt River, 30.1. The crude death rate at Gila River was 8.8; at Salt River, 9.8. (These rates are based on the adjusted number of births and deaths for 1970-71, which include vital events erroneously reported as occurring in areas adjacent to the reservations).

From Table 36, it may be determined that women aged 15-44 are 22.5% of the total population at Salt River (without Fort McDowell), while they are only 18.9% of persons of all ages at Gila River. Thus, even if the birth rate of women 15-44 (known as the General Fertility Rate, or GFR; see Appendix A for more information) were the same at both reservations, the larger proportion of women 15-44 at Salt River would produce a larger proportion of children, and a higher crude birth rate, than at Gila River. It turns out, however, that the General Fertility Rate is slightly higher at Salt River-Fort McDowell: for the adjusted number of births, it is 135.3 at Gila River and 140.7 at Salt River-Fort McDowell. (This rate includes one or two births to women less than 15; the rate has been calculated on the enumerated population at the reservations, which is too small, rather than the adjusted population which appears in Table 44. See Appendix F.)

Another measure which corrects for the difference in proportion of women of childbearing ages in different populations is the Total Fertility Rate (or TFR), which is the sum of the age-specific birth rates of women in a population (in which case it is referred to as births per woman), multiplied by 1000. (For more information, see Appendix A.)

While it seems possible that when age and sex differences are equalized the crude birth rate at Salt River-Fort McDowell is really higher than that at Gila River, given the inaccuracies of the data involved (two populations undernumerated at different rates, and two sets of birth data which may be underreported at different rates) and the small numbers involved, it seems safer to account for the higher crude birth rate at Salt River-Fort McDowell by the presence there of a greater proportion of women 15-44 than at Gila River. However, if the higher General and Total Fertility Rates at Salt River-Fort McDowell are true, I believe that they could be accounted for by better economic conditions at Salt River-Fort McDowell (discussed below).

The greater proportion of women (and men) 15-44 at Salt River-Fort McDowell as compared to Gila River (see Table 36) could also result from better economic conditions, as off-reservation migration (much of which is to find employment) is not as great at Salt River-Fort McDowell, presumably because of the greater proximity to the diversity of employment in the Phoenix urban area.

Turning to mortality data, the 1.1 per thousand difference in the crude death rate between Gila River and Salt River-Fort McDowell is probably not significant because of the inaccuracy of the data. However, to see whether the difference could be ascribed to the different age structures of Gila River and Salt River-Fort McDowell, I calculated the age-adjusted death rate for both places by the indirect method, standardized on the death rates of Costa Rica for 1963 (see Appendix A). This lowered the Gila River death rate by 1.2 per thousand, to 7.6, and the Salt River-Fort McDowell death rate was lowered 0.9 per thousand to 9.0. The difference is thus widened by standardization for age. However, at Gila River, 66.4 deaths were expected, and 60 recorded; at Salt River-Fort McDowell, 21.6 deaths were expected and 23 recorded. Since these are small numbers, I do not feel the deviation from expected is particularly significant.

Overall, then, I feel that what looks like a difference in natural increase between Gila River and Salt River is in part spurious, because of the multifold inaccuracies of the data, and in part the result of a higher crude birth rate at Salt River produced by a greater proportion of women of childbearing ages in the population than at Gila River. The growth rates of the two reservations should thus probably be closer by perhaps half.

Differences in growth rate, 1960-70. In this section I will try to account for the lower Gila River and higher Salt River growth rates in comparison with 1952-60 and 1970-72, as well as the difference between the growth rates for the two reservations for 1960-70 alone.

In attempting to determine why the Gila River growth rate was lower in 1960-70 than in 1952-60 or 1970-72, we face the same problem as for 1952-60, that the number of birth and deaths (except for 1970-71) for reservation residents is not available. Again we must use the number of Indian resident births for Pinal County to give an approximate idea of the trend at Gila River. Figure 7 shows that 1961 was the high point for Indian births in Pinal County, with a drop from 1962-64, and fluctuation at slightly below the 1955-60 level for 1965-70. By 1965-70, however, the on-reservation population had increased considerably over that of 1955-60. The similar mean annual number of births for these five-year periods (1955-59, 228.64; 1965-69, 222.4) means that either the birth rate was lower in 1965-69, or that a considerable number of Indians (the most significant group we are concerned with being females of childbearing ages) left Pinal County from 1962 to perhaps 1970.

It would appear that migration was perhaps the more significant of the two factors. The Arizona State Department of Health (unpublished figures) estimated a 1.4% annual growth rate for the Indian population of Pinal County from 1960-63, when the number of births was at a peak. That such a relatively low rate could be the result of natural increase alone seems unlikely after a growth rate of 2.10% for 1952-60.

Moreover, the number of births in Maricopa County rose rapidly from 1960-65, and fluctuated at a high level for 1966-71 (Figure 7). Such as increase in the number of births could only be possible through migration, and some of the migrants must have come from Pinal County and hence the Gila River Indian Reservation, by virtue of proximity to Maricopa County, in which Phoenix is located.

Although off-reservation migration thus seems to have played a considerable part in reducing the growth rate for Gila River, there is also evidence for a population increase, and perhaps lower birth rate.

The number of Indian deaths for Pinal County generally rises for 1960-70 (Figure 7). It seems unlikely that the death rate would be increasing at this time, so the increase in deaths must result from an absolutely larger population of Indians in Pinal County.

The number of children in the 0-4 age interval (1965-70 birth cohort) in the 1970 Census (Table 36) also seems quite small in relation to the next age interval, representing persons born 1955-65. The 0-4 age interval is 47.4% the size of the 5-14 interval; with a continued high birth rate, the 0-4 interval would be expected to be at least 50% of the 5-14 age group. Nevertheless, underenumeration of infants and small children may distort this relationship, so the evidence for a lower birth rate at Gila River from 1965-70 is not conclusive.

I feel that the low growth rate for 1960-70 is primarily the result of greater off-reservation migration during the period as compared with 1952-60 and 1970-72.

For Salt River, the birth data for Maricopa County from 1960-70 are not very useful for attempting to determine the pattern, as Maricopa County Indian births reflect an apparently increasingly larger off-reservation population (Figure 7). If decline in the birth rate were the main reason for the lower 1960-70 growth rate at Gila River, the growth rate at Salt River should also decline during this period, but it does not. However, the number of persons in the 0-4 age group at Salt River (92) is only 44.0% of the 5-14 age group (209). The population by single years of age 0-4 is unavailable; thus it is not possible to determine to what extent this may be a result of underenumeration of infants and young children at a rate greater than the rest of the population. However, since the 1960-70 growth rate at Salt River is higher but the number of children 0-4 implies a low birth rate or underenumeration, it would appear that the lower than expected number of persons 0-4 at both Gila River and Salt River is the result of age-specific undernumeration rather than a lower birth rate than occurred during 1955-65.

It would thus appear that at the same time that Gila River experienced a lower growth rate than 1952-70 because of net out-migration, Salt River experienced a higher rate than 1952-60 through net in-migration.

In 1964-65, Marvin Munsell spent a year at the Salt River Indian Reservation, gathering very detailed data, on which the Salt River population estimates for this period are based (Munsell 1967). His data provide a birth rate of 31.8 and a death rate of 20.1, for a natural increase of 1.17%. As this rate of natural increase is lower than the estimated annual growth rate for 1960-70, there is support for the assumption that considerable in-migration was taking place at Salt River for this period.

In order to support the assumption of net migration gain at Salt River and net migration (but not population) loss at Gila River, there must be reasons for preferring to live at Salt River, compared to off-reservation or Gila River.

It should come as no surprise that many Indians prefer to live on-reservation. In spite of the limited political power they have been allowed by the government, an Indian on a reservation is numerically a majority, unlike his minority status when residing off-reservation. In some ways, living on a reservation is cheaper: medical care is available at little or no cost, and all income earned from activities on-reservation is exempt from state (but not federal) taxes. There are no property taxes. There is often no rent to pay. Thus it can be assumed that a similar proportion of persons from both Gila River and Salt River prefer to live on-reservation, but in many cases can not because of the lack of on-reservation employment, and its relatively greater availability off-reservation.

Lack of habitable housing is another reason why persons may have to move off-reservation. From 1960-68, a period of considerable housing construction occurred at Salt River. Munsell, in fact, worked on a housing project in 1964 (Munsell 1967:27). In 1970, 23.7% of the existing housing units at Salt River-Fort McDowell had been built from 1960-68 (representing 58 units; USBC 1972:H-35, Table H-2, 1973:182, Table 15). However, during the same time, 25.2% of the housing units existing in 1970 at Gila River were built and an additional 5.4% were built from 1969-March 1970, when none were built at Salt River. The construction at Gila River represented 283 units. Thus, if housing were a reason for greater reservation in-migration, Gila River should have the greater rate of in-migration.

But at Gila River, 1950-59 was also a fairly active period for home construction, as 22.2% of homes occupied in 1970 were built during that period. The corresponding figure for Salt River is 13.4%. At Salt River, 64.8% of all occupied housing units in 1970 were built before 1950, while the corresponding figure for Gila River is 47.2%. Having to wait longer than at Gila River, perhaps once new housing was built at Salt River under various federal and other programs, people returned to Salt River to reside in the new homes, with others perhaps living in quite old houses, in the expectation that they would be able to move into a new home in a short time.

At Gila River, even though more of the housing occupied in 1970 was built from 1960-70, and even though Gila River became the only Indian reservation to be included in the Model Cities Program, in relation to Salt River, Gila River suffered two disadvantages as a place of residence: geographic and economic.

In general, economic conditions appear to be relatively better at Salt River. Housing constructed during the 1960s costs more to obtain (as in the case of rents) and maintain (such as when garbage pickup is made, which costs money). Fewer people at Gila River could afford the new housing then at Salt River.

In 1973, unemployment at Gila River was 18%, while it was 7% at Salt River (BIA 1973:7). Unemployment and underemployment in 1973 was 40% at Gila River, 29% at Salt River (BIA 1973:7). In 1970, median family income was $3417 at Gila River ($946 for the Maricopa County part of Gila River, including non-Indians), and $4780 for Salt River-Fort McDowell (including non-Indians). The proportion of families below the poverty level in 1970 was 58.6% at Gila River, (66.2% for the Maricopa County part of Gila River, and including non-Indians), and 42.8% at Salt River-Fort McDowell (including non-Indians) (USBC 1972:

P-77, 82, 1973:172).

The relatively better economic conditions at Salt River appear to reflect proportionally more employment. Employment should be greater at Salt River because the Salt River Reservation, adjoining the east side of Scottsdale, is closer to the Phoenix area than most of the Gila River Reservation--especially the Pinal County part, where most of the population lives. It is about 15 miles (24 km) from Salt River to downtown Phoenix, and the reservation adjoins three smaller cities, Mesa, Scottsdale, and Tempe. It is about 40 miles (64 km) from Sacaton to downtown Phoenix, and the Gila River Reservation adjoins the southwest Phoenix area, which is largely agricultural. Thus, a person can live at Salt River and still commute to a Phoenix-area job, while a person at Gila River must generally drive a longer distance.

Data on place of work show that about one third of the employed persons at Salt River-Fort McDowell (including non-Indians) work in Phoenix or Scottsdale, including 8.3% in the Phoenix Central Business District (Table 50). At Gila River, only 7.6% were reported to work in the Phoenix area, and none were reported to work in the Phoenix Central Business District or Scottsdale. The Gila River figure, however, is for the Maricopa County portion only, and includes non-Indians. No figure is available for the entire Gila River Reservation.

Persons at Salt River also have more automobiles perhaps because of relatively better economic conditions. This means more can commute to a job. These data appear in Table 51.

The economic situation at Gila River would probably be even worse without jobs provided by some factories located in several reservation industrial parks, notably a data-processing center, a diamond-cutting plant, and a tent factory.

However, in order to account for a reduced growth rate at Salt River from 1970-72 as compared with 1960-70, and a corresponding increase at Gila River, perhaps the housing at Salt River filled up by 1970 (as no new construction was reported in 1969 and the first three months of 1970), while construction continued at Gila River, perhaps enough to keep up with demand. The Gila River Indian Community General Community Plan (Van Cleve Associates 1972:14) mentioned an interest in applications for housing units in the northwest part of the reservation (which is closest to Phoenix) at this time. Other housing had been built at Sacaton, farther from Phoenix.

Significantly for the assumptions above, a housing survey at Gila River, summarized in the General Community Plan (Van Cleve Associates 1972:23) revealed that the primary disadvantage of on-reservation residence was housing, followed by unemployment. The major advantage of on-reservation residence was seen as low living cost (followed by peace and quiet). This would support the assumptions above that

1. Pima and Maricopa prefer to live on-reservation
2. They can not find sufficient employment on-reservation
3. The lower cost of on-reservation housing, and hence housing condition, is a result of economic deprivation
4. If new housing is built, but costs too much, it may be desired, but its occupants will not be permanent
5. New housing which only employed persons can afford may benefit mainly persons living off-reservation, who may then be able to move back to the reservation and commute to their job, increasing the growth rate of the on-reservation population
6. Salt River, which has a better location in relation to employment, even though not mainly on-reservation employment, should attract more on-reservation residents, because for a greater proportion of persons than Gila River it lacks a major disadvantage of on-reservation residence.

Summary. Thus, for 1960-72, I feel that the higher Salt River growth rate results in part from net in-migration because the location of Salt River is superior economically to Gila River under present conditions. It also appears that the Salt River crude birth rate is higher because of a greater proportion of women 15-44 than at Gila River. The General Fertility Rate may also be slightly higher, which may be a result of relatively better economic conditions than at Gila River. The differences between the annual growth rates for 1960-70 and 1970-72 for Gila River and Salt River taken alone appear to be related to the availability of housing, which affects the amount of migration to the reservation.

Note to Chapter Seven

1. Branigan's (1952:Figure[sic] 16) report of Indian deaths in Pinal County for 1949 presents only the "average" (presumably mean) age at death for selected (but leading) causes. Nowhere could I find a statement of the number of Indian deaths in Pinal County for all causes, much less the leading causes. This is unfortunate, since these data are available even now only by tabulating each death certificate, an extremely time-consuming project which I was not able to do, and hence lack mortality data before the Arizona State Health Department produced printouts of death certificate data (about 1959).

CHAPTER EIGHT

SUMMARY, COMPARISONS, DISCUSSION,
AND CONCLUSIONS

Let us summarize the demographic history of the Pima and Maricopa, compare it with other American Indian populations, and use the resulting conclusions to examine certain generalizations about population current in anthropology and demography.

Summary of Pima and Maricopa Population from 1700-1972

In Table 52 are my estimates and adjusted figures of Pima and Mariccpa total population for selected years from 1700-1972. The annual growth rate between each pair of years is also shown. The first figure for 1940 is the de jure Pima-Maricopa population, while the second is for reservation residents only. The population of the reservation (sans non-reserve dwellers) is shown after 1940 because it was impossible to obtain data on the total Pima-Maricopa population. After 1910, it was impossible to distinguish Pima from Maricopa in population data. Figure 8 shows Pima and Maricopa population, combined and separately, at various years, as a percentage of the population of 1700 (i.e., at contact).

From Table 52 and Figure 8, we observe that the combined Pima-Maricopa population experienced two declines in its known history. The first, of long duration, occurred from 1700-1882, while the second was a short-lived decline from 1890-95. The population was very similar in size in 1882 and 1895, and thus the Pima-Maricopa combined population had two nadirs. At nadir, the population was about 1/4 that of 1700, giving a depopulation ratio of about 4:1. Looking at the Pima alone, there were three declines of population. The first decline bottomed at about 1775, after which increase occurred until 1846. After 1858, decline occurred until nadir in 1882, then a small increase, and the third decline to (and second nadir of) 1895. The nadir population was only about half that of 1700, or a depopulation ratio of 2:1. The Maricopa alone essentially follow the Pima-Maricopa pattern, with constant decline to 1882, after which a fairly stable population size seems to have been maintained. The Maricopa suffered considerably more severe depopulation than the Pima. Their nadir population was about 1/20 the 1700 population, for a depopulation ratio of about 20:1. Thus, the Maricopa went from relative equality of numbers with the Pima in 1700 to about 1/10 of the Pima population at nadir. The factors producing this discrepancy are discussed below.

Population from 1700-75

This was the period of greatest population loss for the combined Pima-Maricopa population. Over a period of 75 years, population size decreased by an annual growth rate of about -1.0%. This rate was exceeded only from 1858-70, when it attained -1.5% yearly, but the remaining population decreased only 17% in size during this 12 year period. It is not possible to determine how constant the rate of population decrease was throughout 1700-75. I would imagine that it exceeded -1.0% during the early years of contact, or whenever epidemic diseases were introduced, and during other years was less than -1.0%. The main factor producing population decline during this period was the introduction of exotic diseases by the Spanish, to which the Pima and Maricopa had little immunity. This situation was aggravated by Apache and Yavapai raiding, producing a contraction of Pima and Maricopa territory. For the Maricopa, losses through warfare and captivity with the Quechan and Mohave also appear to have acted directly to produce significant population loss.

Population from 1775-1858

During this period, the combined Pima-Maricopa population still suffered a considerable loss of 28.5% of the 1775 population size in a period of 83 years, or a -0.4% annual growth rate. But while the Maricopa lost population, the Pima gained. Presumably the Pima had by 1775 developed some immunity to the recently introduced epidemic diseases, and there is no reason to assume that the Maricopa did not as well. Thus, to account for the discrepancy between the Pima and Maricopa, we must examine factors other than epidemics. One possibility is that the Maricopa did not adopt wheat as early as the Pima. However, the main difference was more likely a result of the intensity of warfare between Maricopa with Quechan and Mohave. Certainly, loss of males in battle had some influence on population, but probably more important was loss of women and children as captives. These captives then were passed on into Mexico, and captives taken by the Maricopa were also forwarded to Mexico for service as domestics. To a considerable degree, depletion of women and children from a population is much more crucial to preventing growth than depletion of males, for one male can inseminate many women, but a woman can produce, generally, only one child at a time, and this time is considerable. Loss of children as captives deprives the population of persons who have not yet replenished the population through reproduction. The motive for intensification of Yuman warfare was Spanish trade, the Spanish desiring captives for domestic service, and the Yumans desiring horses and Spanish material goods.

While Maricopa population loss from 1700-75 was 60%, at an annual growth rate of -1.2%, population loss from 1775-1858 was apparently greater, being 75% at an annual growth rate of -2.0%. It may seem surprising that the 1775-1858 population loss was greater than that of 1700-75, since during the earlier period epidemics must have been more severe, but during the later period warfare and captivity intensified, and this was the time when the populations forming the Maricopa left the Colorado River and lower Gila River to join the Pima. Moreover, the Maricopa may well have been experiencing epidemics to a greater degree than the Pima from 1775-1858. The disruptions caused by warfare could well have adversely affected the Maricopa food supply, and while there may not have been starvation, the population would have been weakened, and thus subject to diseases which the Pima could resist. A group such as the Halchidhoma, trekking from the Colorado River to Sonora to the Gila River would have little time for planting. There thus appear to be good reasons why this period saw a greater Maricopa population decrease than from 1700-75, and why the Maricopa decreased in numbers while the Pima increased.

Population from 1858-82

Both the Pima and Maricopa populations reached their lowest points by the end of this period. The combined population was 19.5% lower than in 1858, for a -0.9% annual growth rate, nearly as high as during the initial contact period of 1700-75, although over a shorter time. The greatest loss occurred from 1858-70, when the annual growth rate was -1.5%. This resulted primarily from the introduction of new diseases, or the reintroduction of old epidemic diseases by the constantly increasing numbers of whites who arrived in the area after the Civil War. The Pima-Maricopa population may have been too small to have sustained epidemics from 1775-1858, so that the same old epidemics of smallpox, measles, and other childhood diseases may have been reintroduced and initially caused considerable losses, as the Pima and Maricopa may not yet have developed immunity comparable to a white population. Thus, the loss was greater immediately after initial Anglo contact (1858-70) and less in the following years (1870-82). Five serious epidemics occurred from 1859-69, and while five also occurred from 1869-80, they were not as serious. It also appears that fertility declined at this time for several reasons: the (re)introduction of venereal diseases, poor maternal nutrition, and possibly less interest in reproduction in a time of stress. By the 1870s, the Pima and Maricopa were apparently becoming more immune to epidemic diseases, but faced the new problem of loss of water to whites above the reservation. Since the Pima and Maricopa could not raise enough to eat, some starvation occurred, but the major effect was to weaken the resistance of the population to diseases that ordinarily would not cause so many deaths. Had it not been for the taking of Pima and Maricopa water by whites, I believe that Pima-Maricopa population would have begun to continuously increase from 1870-1974.

Population from 1882-90

I feel justified in stating that Pima-Maricopa population had the potential to increase after 1870 because it did so from 1882-90 in spite of several limiting factors. The annual growth rate, 0.4%, although moderate, was nevertheless considerable for the period before the development of medicine as we know it today. This increase occurred in spite of two major epidemics, which, however, were fewer in number than during the previous period. An important factor at this time was the end of raids on the Apache and Yavapai, reopening erstwhile Pima territory and its wild plant and animal foods to exploitation by the Pima and Maricopa. The Apache and Yavapai had been restricted to one reservation and were closely watched by the federal government and not permitted to leave the reservation. Crops were also more abundant during this period, as compared with 1870-82, when there was usually a drought. However, agriculture was still reduced to one crop because of appropriation of Gila River by whites above the reservation. Thus, had they not been able to exploit wild food sources over a wide area, it appears that Pima-Maricopa population would have been stable or decreased during this period. Pima-Maricopa knowledge of wild food sources, retained even in spite of their reliance on agriculture, proved to be a lifesaver.

Population from 1890-1910

Nevertheless, although Pima-Maricopa population had the potential to increase, this was denied by further appropriation of Gila River water by whites, so that by 1910, even raising one crop was impossible for all but a few Pima and Maricopa. From 1890-95, there was actually a population decrease of 2.7%, at a growth rate of -0.5% annually. There was no reason for this to occur other than that the Pima and Maricopa had water taken from them, could not raise enough to eat, and fell to a variety of diseases that would not have caused population decline in a well-fed and well-housed population. The loss probably would have been greater except for an assumed development of considerable immunity to epidemic diseases among the Pima, and perhaps some smallpox vaccinations, which also may have reduced deaths somewhat during the 1870s and 1880s. From 1895-1910, however, in spite of many adverse factors, Pima-Maricopa population began to increase, and has continued to increase to the present. A number of factors, none of them of major significance in themselves, but together of sufficient strength to stop population loss, acted to promote Pima-Maricopa population increase. These included belated ration issues by the federal government, off-reservation work in Arizona and adjacent states, the drilling of water wells on-reservation, permitting a few to get a crop, and vastly increased attendance at off-reservation boarding schools by Pima and Maricopa children, freeing their parents of the impossibility of finding enough food.

Population from 1910-40

Throughout this period, Pima-Maricopa population was characterized by a moderate annual growth rate of 0.4%. The major impetus to population growth during the period was the beginning of effective public health measures, especially immunization of children against smallpox, diphtheria, whooping cough, and typhoid fever. However, tuberculosis and infective diseases of children, such as infant diarrheas, were still a serious cause of deaths, and the population thus increased at a rate well below 1% annually. Interestingly, during the depression of the 1930s, fewer births occurred, as can be determined from the age distribution of the 1970 Census of Gila River Reservation and Salt River Reservation residents. A considerable number of off-reservation residents returned to the reservations, representing loss of off-reservation employment, and the economic situation of the Pima and Maricopa apparently discouraged childbearing. Thus, the annual growth rate for 1930-40 appears to be more like 0.25% than the approximate 0.5% which characterized 1910-30.

Population from 1940-72

During this period, population figures are only available for the reservation population, but they undoubtedly represent well over half the total Pima-Maricopa population. At this time, population began to increase considerably, with the greatest annual growth rate attained in 1952-60 (2.2%), and a somewhat lower rate since (1.6%). Again, the Pima and Maricopa appear to have followed the same pattern as the general United States population, in that during the Second World War childbearing was seriously reduced, while after the war, and especially in the 1950s, unprecedented increases in the number of births occurred. However, besides a higher birth rate, the Pima-Maricopa population increase can also be attributed to a lower death rate. The Indian Health Service, part of the Public Health Service, assumed control of federal Indian health programs in 1954 from the Bureau of Indian Affairs. New treatments for serious diseases became widespread after the Second World War, even among the Pima, most notably successful treatments for tuberculosis and pneumonia, two of the leading causes of death for the Pima and Maricopa in 1930. Besides elimination of these two as significant causes of death by 1960, infant mortality also declined considerably from 1930-60. In fact, by 1960, accidents, heart disease, and cancer had become the three leading known causes of death among the Pima and Maricopa. Thus it is not surprising that in 1970-71, the Pima and Maricopa on-reservation population had a birth rate of 26.2, a death rate of 9.1, and a natural increase in population of 1.75% annually, above the level of the United States population as a whole. If approximately 10% of all Pima and Maricopa were living off-reservation in 1972, and this proportion may in fact be more, about 275 years after contact, Pima and Maricopa combined population had regained about half its size of A.D. 1700, the Pima regaining well over half, but the Maricopa never really recovering after the severe depopulation suffered from 1700-1882. Given relatively similar histories since 1860, this is not surprising, since we would expect the birth rates and death rates of the Pima and Maricopa to be relatively equal. Thus, even today, there is probably no more than one Maricopa for every ten Pima.

Consistency of Qualitative and Quantitative Data

As I outlined in the introduction, one of my tests of data accuracy was to compare qualitative data, such as reports of epidemics, crop conditions, warfare, etc., with the quantitative data and then determine if the two sets of data agreed as to the trend (and degree of the trend) of Pima-Maricopa population during a given time period. In nearly the entire period covered by my research (1846-1974), qualitative data agreed with quantitative data as to the trend of Pima-Maricopa population. For 1846-90 and 1910-40, the two sets of data were in agreement. For 1890-1910, the two sets of data indicated contrary trends, but the main problem was the serious age-specific and sex-specific underenumeration in the 1890 and 1895 census rolls of Pima-Maricopa population. When these rolls were adjusted for underenumeration, the trend became apparent. There were no qualitative data available for 1940-74. The magnitude of change did not always agree, but reasons for this were found, and they are discussed in the previous chapters. I do not believe, of course, that I have found the exact number of Pima and Maricopa living at any time, and some of my estimates and adjusted figures are less accurate than others. Nevertheless, I feel that the population trends and their relative magnitudes, as shown in Table 52 and Figure 8, are correct based on the information available to me. The population estimates for a specific year are probably subject to as much as ±10% error since 1846, and I remain more cautious of those estimates for years before 1846, especially the Maricopa. Still, the data are of sufficient accuracy to permit comparison with other American Indian populations, and to examine certain generalizations common in anthropology and demography. This will occupy our attention in the next few sections of this study.

Demographic Consequences of Euro-American Contact on American Indian Population

As I have mentioned in the Introduction, it is not easy to find evaluated population data with any historical depth for American Indian populations. Thus, in this section we will compare but a few of the many American Indian groups, and all are from the western United States. I have also included the Australian Aboriginal aggregate population. Tables 53-57 show the data as they will be used in this study. A few comments on the sources are appropriate, and indeed, necessary, before proceeding to discuss any general statements about American Indian population. The data for the Pueblo (Table 53) are from Dozier (1970:130 and passim) and include both Eastern and Western Pueblo. The estimates are based primarily on Hispanic sources and the RCIA. Nevertheless, Dozier did not take these sources at face value, and produced his own estimates, in which he modified the basic data to fit his understanding of the strength of various factors affecting population. Thus the figures have been subjected to some adjustment. The Navajo data (Table 54) are from Johnston's (1966:135-36, 138-39) exhaustive study of that population, and are based on Spanish sources, the RCIA, and reports of the Bureau of the Census. Again, Johnston did not accept the figures at face value, but made his own estimates and adjustments of existing data. Jorgensen (1972:37, 91) has provided a fairly detailed series of population figures of the Ute (Table 55), especially for the late nineteenth and twentieth centuries. These figures are essentially the enrolled population of Ute. For California, I have used a combination of sources. Most of the figures (Table 56) are from S. F. Cook's (1943a:4) study of The Conflict between the California Indian and White Civilization. However, Cook (1964:72) later more than doubled his estimate for 1770, and that figure has been used here. Cook's (1943a) figures exclude Indians living along the Colorado River in California (e.g., Mohave, Quechan) and those in the Great Basin area of California (e.g., Modoc, Paiute). Cook's (1964:68) new estimate of 1770 population excludes essentially the same groups. For 1905 and 1955, I have used the figures given by Kroeber (1957:218, 221). Although these figures appear to include the groups excluded by Cook, 1905 and 1955 do not really enter into the main part of this discussion, and thus are included for illustrative purposes. I doubt that the inclusion of several groups left out by Cook significantly changes the magnitude of the figures. Figures for 1800-1900 estimated by Merriam (1905) are not shown, but while differing absolutely from Cook's figures, they do not produce a different trend of population for California Indians (which was continuous decline until 1900). Finally, the Australian Aborigine figures are from two sources. I have accepted Yengoyan's (1972:86) report of 250,000-300,000, here averaged to 275,000, over F. Jones's (1970:3) estimate of 215,000. Both Yengoyan and Jones report 60,000 in 1921, apparently based on the Australian Census, and Jones (1970:3) has estimated 80,000 in 1961. However, we do not know the Australian Aboriginal nadir population, for Yengoyan (1972:86) reports that the population continued to decrease until the 1940s, at which point a turnaround began, and increase occurred. If we assume that the population decreased from 1921-41 at the same rate as from 1788-1921 (about -1.1% annually), we obtain an estimate of about 48,000 Australian Aborigines at nadir population, with a depopulation ratio of about 5.7:1.

Unfortunately, I can not at present carry out a formal test of hypotheses regarding American Indian population decline in relation to contact. The sample is neither adequate nor random, and there are questions as to the relative accuracy of the data presented here. Nevertheless, we can begin to come to some preliminary conclusions about the course of American Indian population and show where further studies are needed.

The Model of Constant Decline

Most studies of American Indian population either imply or assume that all American Indian populations followed a course of continuous decline after contact until a low point was reached. The population then either began to recover or stabilize, or in some cases, its lowest level was extinction. Thus, studies of American Indian populations have generally compared an estimate of precontact or contact population to the population at the time of writing of the study, or the nadir population (Dobyns 1966, Mooney 1928). It is only recently that the nadir population has been employed (Dobyns 1966) with any regularity, and while this is an important advance, this method still ignores what happened between precontact times and nadir (and since). Bennett (1966:425) has suggested the value of looking at population curves, or trends, rather than absolute numbers, and such an approach has been incorporated in this study. However, enough data are available so that we can not only discern population trends of specific North American Indian populations, but also the relative magnitudes of these trends. I will discuss magnitudes below; here we are concerned with whether there is any general trend of population followed by these American Indian populations after time of contact.

The Maricopa, Pueblo, Ute, California Indians, and Australian Aborigines all follow the continuous decline model of population dynamics: steady decline to nadir, then some increase. This is best illustrated in Figure 8 and may also be observed from Tables 52, 53, and 55-57. However, the Pima did not follow this pattern, having experienced three periods of population decline, separated, of course, by periods of population increase (1775-1846, 1882-90, and 1895-1972). As already mentioned, because Pima population in 1882 and 1895 was about the same, but was higher in 1890, the Pima actually experienced two nadirs. Even when the Maricopa are included with the Pima (Figure 8), there are still two periods of population decline (1700-1882 and 1890-95). The severity of population decline among the Maricopa in 1775-1858 more than made up for Pima population increase during the same period, eliminating one of the periods of population increase experienced by the Pima.

The Pima are not the only population who fail to fit the continuous decline model. As shown in Table 54, the Navajo nadir population occurred at contact or before, and there was only one brief period of decline from 1860-70, but even at the end of the decline, Navajo population was still several times higher than at contact.

With these exceptions to the model of continuous decline already, I have no doubt that more will be found. Moreover, even some of the populations included here which follow the model might be found to be exceptions were more population data available from the earlier periods. The importance of this finding is that if not all American Indian populations experienced a continual decline to nadir, then the introduction of epidemic diseases by Europeans was not entirely responsible for reducing these populations to their lowest point. It was thus also not the actual living conditions of Indians when Indians possessed their land and other resources that led to population decline. The Pima and Navajo show that a population largely under its traditional culture could recover from the effects of previously unknown diseases and increase at a respectable rate for the time (below 1% annually). Therefore, once the initial effect of low immunity to newly introduced diseases wore off, other factors had to maintain an environment in which population decline could occur. Since many American Indian groups were subject to armed attack by the United States Army and civilians, this undoubtedly had some effect. But the prime factor, as Merriam (1905:606) recognized, was

> . . . not . . . the number directly slain by the whites, or the number directly killed by whisky and disease, but a much more subtle and dreadful thing: it is the gradual but progressive and relentless confiscation of their lands and homes, in consequence of which they are forced to seek refuge in remote and barren localities, often far from water, usually with an impoverished supply of food, and not infrequently in places where the winter climate is too severe for their enfeebled constitutions.

Thus, while in the main it was ultimately disease which caused decline in American Indian population, and to a lesser extent, armed conflict, much of the decline was made possible because Indians had been driven from their land or robbed of their other resources. With inadequate food, poor housing, and insufficient clothing, as well as the mental suffering caused by destruction of a way of life, the weakened condition of many Indians made them easy prey for disease. Once the initial shock effect of the introduction of new diseases was over with the afflicted populations developing immunity, many American Indian populations should have increased in number. That they experienced further decline can be considered the result of their deprivation of resources by the ever-advancing and increasing white population of the United States, and not their lack of immunity to introduced diseases, or their living standard before their resources were taken. If white populations had lived under the same conditions as dispossessed American Indians, I believe whites would also have died in comparable proportions.

How Universal Are Certain Pima-Maricopa Population Trends

We will next discuss the validity of some generalizations based on Pima-Maricopa population dynamics by attempting to determine whether other American Indian populations provide support for such generalizations. As shown in Table 52, the two most severe periods of Pima-Maricopa population decline occurred from 1700-75 and 1858-82, especially 1858-70. These are the periods of initial contact with the Spanish (in the former case) and other Euro-Americans (in the latter case). We may thus ask whether American Indian population decline inevitably follows each initial contact with an immigrant population. California Indians also appear to have suffered the same pattern, although the timing was slightly different (see Figure 8). From 1770-1832, there was a decline to about 36% of the population at contact, with an annual growth rate of -1.7%. Decline continued from 1832-48, but at a lower rate. With the beginning of predominantly non-Hispanic Euro-American contact in 1848, population decline again occurred, at a very high annual rate of -4.9% until 1870. Although the rate of decrease may also have been this high at some time from 1770-1832, it may well be that the effect of Anglo contact on California Indian population was much more severe than that of the Spanish and Mexican immigrants (Cook 1943c:24-25).

The Ute and Australian Aborigines also show population loss immediately after first contact (Tables 55 and 57; Figure 8). However, other populations shown in Figure 8 do not follow the pattern. The Pueblo show the expected decline after first sustained contact, when the Oñate colonization mission arrived (about 1600), and there is continued decline even after the return of the Spanish population to the Rio Grande Valley in 1696, after the Pueblo Revolt of 1680, although at a lesser degree. But with the Anglo contact of 1846, there is no visible decline, and in fact, the population was about to begin a slow increase which lasted until about 1900. The Navajo, as always, are an even greater exception to the pattern experienced by the Pima. The initial Spanish contacts (1540, 1600) appear to have had little adverse influence on Navajo population, in that it increased from time of contact to 1860. Our starting point, of course, is 1600, which is when a semi-sustained contact with the Navajo began, although they had been in contact with sporadic Spanish exploring expeditions as early as 1540. But Johnston has nothing to say about Navajo population from 1540-1600 since there are no estimates of Navajo population made by observers until 1626 (Johnston 1966:127, 136). We can only assume that he felt the effects of the sporadic contacts of 1540-1600 to be insignificant. The only time Navajo population did decrease was not immediately after Anglo contact in 1848, but during the period when most Navajos were rounded up and sent to imprisonment at Fort Sumner in eastern New Mexico. Thus, the Navajo population decline occurred when they first arrived at sustained, daily contact with Anglos, since the Spanish were never successful in establishing missionaries among them, or settling Spanish persons in Navajo territory. Consequently, we may say that based on the data included here, American Indian population generally declined immediately after sustained contact with Europeans. By sustained contact I mean permanent settlement by Europeans or Euro-Americans in or near the territory of Indians in question. The intensity of contact, as measured by both the number of immigrants and how long they had been in the area, affected the degree of population decline after contact. Among the Navajo, contact was so insignificant until the 1860s that Navajo population did not experience decline until then. I would feel safe in saying, however, that all American Indian populations experienced population decline at some point after European or Euro-American contact.

For those populations subject to both Hispanic and Anglo contact, it would appear that decline under Anglo contact may have been more severe. The Pima and Maricopa experienced a greater rate of decline from 1858-70 (-1.5%) after Anglo contact than from 1700-75, after Spanish contact (-1.0%), as did the California Indian population (-1.7% under the Spanish and Mexicans vs. -4.9% under the Anglos). Perhaps more significantly, Zubrow (1974) found that before 1800, there was not a significant relationship between New Mexico Pueblo population change and climate (the assumption being that periods of drought would produce population decline and periods of above normal precipitation would produce population increase). After 1800, there was a significant relationship between climate and population change, with the acquisition of Pueblo resources by Anglos depriving the Pueblo of enough to eliminate their relative security against bad crop years. This is in spite of the estimate of Pueblo population increase from 1850-1900 and little decrease from 1800-50 (Table 53). Still, many factors must be considered in determining whether population decrease was greater as a result of Anglo contact as compared with Hispanic contact, such as weighing the importance of the annual growth rate against the length of decline. The important point is still that many populations whose resources were not expropriated by the Spanish lost their means of livelihood under the Anglo invasion. As expected, in California, those Indians who fell under the control of the Spanish missions, and hence lost their resources, experienced a greater population loss than those groups not under mission control (Cook 1943c:92).

As mentioned in the summary of Pima and Maricopa population above, from 1775-1858, Pima population increased while Maricopa population greatly decreased, and this was attributed to the much greater intensity of warfare between the Maricopa and their enemies than between the Pima and their enemies. It thus appears that warfare can be an important factor in population decline, contrary to the assumptions of some (Polgar 1972:206). However, it appears that it is not the deaths of males in battle that lead to population decline, but the disruption of the society which favors the development of epidemics through destruction of the food supply and a lowered living standard. In those populations where captives are taken and there is no replenishment from captives coming in, as among the Maricopa, the situation can be extreme population loss. Even losses from deaths in warfare can be significant. Cook (1943c:8-9) found that among the non-mission Indian population in California, 7.4% of the total population decline from 1848-80 could be attributed to physical conflict, based on reports of the number of deaths in various sources. Among certain tribes in northwest California, the proportion rose to 12%, while during the Hispanic period (1800-48), it was 11%-12%. For specific groups, the proportion varies somewhat more. While only 0.3% of the Maidu and Wintun aboriginal populations were killed in warfare, the corresponding figure for the Wappo was 21.0%. This is for 1800-48 (Cook 1943b:11). Dumond (1965:304, 306-7) has presented data suggesting warfare as a significant influence on population decline in Europe during the fall of the Roman Empire and especially in China during changes of dynasties and the Taiping Rebellion. Thus, while warfare may have been overemphasized in the past, we must not go to the other extreme and deny its influence in those specific cases where its effects were significant.

Assessing Overall Population Decline

As I have mentioned above, comparing the precontact or contact population with the nadir population (the depopulation ratio) does not tell in much detail the story of population decline in a given group. Nevertheless, as a summary measure of population decline, it is of great value. Similarly, the annual growth rate (which of course will be negative) from contact to nadir is also useful as a summary measure of the rapidity and severity of decline, as it is expressed as a function of time. I have found both measures to be useful in expressing depopulation. For example, we may encounter two populations, both of which decreased in size by 80% from contact to nadir, for a depopulation ratio of 5:1. But one of the populations may have declined to nadir in 100 years, while the other population took 200 years. While both groups lost the same proportion of population, the first group experienced a much more severe population loss, since it occurred in half the time.

I would expect that populations subject to greater disruption during contact would experience greater population loss, as measured by the depopulation ratio and annual growth rate. The main factors acting on population in a contact situation would be disease, warfare, and loss of resources. Captivity could be included under warfare, while famine could be included under loss of resources (i.e., food). Resources would include such things as land, water, crops, and the biota. It is also possible that the birth rate (or more accurately, the General Fertility Rate or child-woman ratio) could decrease as a result of contact, but the only information I have is from Cook (1943a:11), who found that in Mission Indian populations in California from 1800-32, the crude birth rate did in fact decline, but not because of fewer births per woman; apparently mortality was greater for women than men, and thus as the sex ratio increased, the birth rate fell, rather than the General Fertility Rate.

In Table 58 are shown the population at contact, nadir population, depopulation ratio, annual growth rate, and number of years from contact to nadir for some Native American populations from the western United States, and also Australian Aborigines. I would expect those populations that had to contend with warfare in addition to disease and loss of resources to have declined more than those populations that did not face warfare or on whom attacks were milder. Similarly, of two populations with no or relatively equal losses from warfare, the population with greater loss from epidemics or greater loss of resources should have declined more. What is really needed is a quantitative assessment of the factors leading to population decline for each of these populations, but my present unfamiliarity with the detailed history and data sources for populations other than the Pima and Maricopa prevents this. Thus, ideally, we should weight the intensity of warfare, disease, and loss of resources for each group, produce a combined score, and test to determine whether populations with the highest scores suffered the greatest population loss. At this point, only a qualitative assessment of the factors leading to population loss is possible.

As seen in Table 58, both the Maricopa and the California Indians are similar in possessing a high depopulation ratio and high negative annual growth rate. The California Indians lost almost the same proportion of population as the Maricopa, but in a considerably shorter time. Both populations suffered severe epidemics, intensive warfare, loss of captives to a foreign population, and loss of resources. Thus all three factors seem to have been present at high levels, and the degree of population decline is the highest of the populations shown here. We would expect the other populations shown in Table 58 to have experienced fewer factors leading to decline, or if all three factors were present, they should have been less intense.

The next highest depopulation ratio occurs for the Pueblo, while the next highest negative annual growth rate is for the Ute. That the Ute suffered a high negative annual growth rate should not be surprising. They were also subject to epidemics, intensive warfare, and loss of

resources, having been reduced in territory from about
half of Utah and Colorado to a much smaller reservation
area (Jorgensen 1972:Maps 1 and 2). However, white contact
with the Ute was not important until after 1850 (Jorgensen
1972:29) and even then was not as intensive as Anglo
contact with California Indians initiated during the Gold
Rush (and begun even earlier in the coastal areas by the
Spanish). However, it is surprising that the Pueblo lost
a greater proportion of their population than the Ute,
although over twice the length of time. Perhaps the figure
for the Pueblo is too high, or for the Ute too low, or
both. Nevertheless, the Pueblo were in more intensive
contact with the Spanish than the Ute. They thus may have
suffered greater loss from epidemics. Moreover, the Pueblo
revolted against the Spanish in 1680, and there were thus
some deaths from warfare, as well as some movement west to
the Hopi and Navajo. This was a considerable disruption
and could have increased the influence of epidemics.
However, during the Anglo period the Pueblo were never
subjected to the same degree of armed conflict suffered
by the Ute, and offhand, I would say that the Pueblo were
able to retain a greater proportion of their resources than
the Ute. But comparing early Hispanic lists of the larger
number of Pueblo villages with the present number, and the
documented northward contraction of the Pueblo settlement
area to the northern Rio Grande during the Hispanic period
leads to credence of a considerable population decline

before Anglo contact, probably because of the intensity of Spanish contact, including establishment of missionaries and churches in Pueblo villages, and Spanish attacks against Pueblo Indians. I would certainly expect the Pueblo to have suffered greater population loss than the Pima, who were not in as long or intensive contact with the Spanish, and Table 58 shows that this is the case.

The Australian Aborigines perhaps experienced a greater depopulation than the Ute, but less than the Pueblo, but at an annual growth rate close to that of the Ute. It is interesting to note that the Australian Aboriginal population at contact has been estimated as about the same as that of California Indians, although the population density in California was much greater. Here may lie the key for accounting for the lesser Australian population decline. California Indian populations, being denser, may have been more severely affected by epidemics, and loss of resources, such as fish or seafood, may also have been more crucial. Surely, California was much more fully explored and settled by whites than Australia, and thus contact was more intensive. In Australia there was a larger area to retreat to so that even until recently there were places not coveted by whites.

Finally, as expected, the Pima and Maricopa combined and the Pima alone suffered the least of the populations shown here (in relative terms), excluding the

Navajo. The Pima were not subject to Spanish attack except for a very short time, and in a restricted area. They experienced epidemics, but did not lose the greater part of their resources until 1870.

This discussion is intended to be mainly suggestive, and contains only the barest mention of the factors involved. Further studies should examine the degree of influence of specific factors on different populations, such as:

1. Where the number of immigrants is greater, but the length of contact is equal, is the native population loss greater?

2. Where a factor producing population decline (such as disease, warfare, or loss of resources) is more intense, is population decline from that factor greater?

3. Where the combined effect of factors producing population decline is greater, is decline greater?

4. Where population decline is longer, and the same size immigrant population is present, is decline greater?

To really test these statements, as well as others regarding the effects of contact on population decline, would require a well-designed cross-cultural study, meeting requirements as to randomness of sample, use of appropriate techniques of analysis, and verifiable hypotheses. The hypotheses presented above may look simple, but because of the inaccuracy of American Indian population data, they are necessary to assess data inaccuracy as well as test the importance of the factors producing population decline.

Pitt-Rivers and Ethnic Intermarriage

According to Pitt-Rivers (1927:262, 275), when a population that has experienced decline from diseases newly introduced by contact begins to stabilize or decrease, this does not represent developing immunity to the diseases that had been introduced, but rather interbreeding with the immigrant population. Those populations that did not interbreed with their conquerors were considered by Pitt-Rivers to have become extinct, and he gives the Tasmanians and Australian Aborigines of Victoria State as examples. However, the Pima and Navajo show that this is not the case. The Pima began to increase at the beginning of the twentieth century without large-scale intermarriage. Even today, although there are no good data, the Pima are almost entirely full-blood. The Navajo are also well-known for their preference to marry within their ethnic group, and their increase in population after the 1860-70 decline cannot be attributed to interbreeding with whites.

The Demographic Transition

According to Wrong (1967:17-18), the demographic transition is "the dominant organizing idea or theory in the field of population study since the discrediting of earlier efforts . . . to formulate universal laws of population growth and change." Certainly, one can hardly find a book on population, world ecology, modernization, or economic development that does not mention the demographic transition. Briefly stated, the demographic transition is an evolutionary sequence of birth and death rate levels which vary so as to produce differing levels of population growth during three (or sometimes five) stages. In the three-stage version, populations are assumed to begin with high and essentially equal birth and death rates; hence, no population growth occurs. In the second stage, population rapidly increases because death rates are lower but birth rates remain high. In the third stage, birth and death rates are once again approximately equal, but at a much lower level than during the first stage. The population has then completed the transition to "modernity." The five-stage model merely makes separate stages of the period between stages one and two, when death rates are declining but still fairly high, and the period between stages two and three, when death rates have declined to their lowest level and birth rates are nearing them.

Besides describing changes in birth and death rates, statements of the demographic transition (e.g., Wrong 1967:17-24; Thomlinson 1965:21-25; Stanford 1972: 70-73) usually attempt to state factors which are believed responsible for the transition. In the first stage, it is assumed that the death rate was so high in populations without scientific medicine that the best the birth rate could do was keep up with the number of deaths. The second stage begins when improved nutrition and medical advances are introduced to a population. The third stage is reached with "industrialization" or "modernization." This is often as far as the discussion goes, but some have elaborated on the third stage to state that economic self-interest leads to fewer births. As upward social mobility becomes more possible and material goods increase in availability as a result of industrialization, families are reputed to decline in size because children require funds that could otherwise be devoted to increasing social status and acquiring material goods (Wrigley 1969:191).

The demographic transition has been rightly criticized both as a description of what occurred in Europe (Wrigley 1969; Wrong 1967:19-23) and as a "theory" with predictive value for other parts of the world. One of its weaknesses is that it inaccurately and incompletely describes the changes in population which took place in Europe since the eighteenth century and then raises this to a generalization, with the expectation (or hope) that the pattern will be repeated in other parts of the world which are considered to be at earlier stages of the transition. Anthropologists should be especially suspicious of the demographic transition because it is presented as a universal evolutionary sequence. In many ways, the demographic transition is much like nineteenth century cultural evolutionary sequences, or what twentieth century antievolutionists believed were nineteenth century cultural evolutionary sequences. The demographic transition proposes that all populations will go through all stages of the sequence. It is based on the history of European populations, and European and Euro-American populations are considered the most evolved or modern; in other words, Europe and North America set the model for the rest of the world. That other populations may take different directions is not conceded.

More specifically, Pima and Maricopa population history provides little support for the demographic transition. Let us examine the three stages of the demographic transition and see to what degree the Pima and Maricopa followed them. First, the initial stage consists of high and equal birth and death rates and hence stable population size. For the Pima and Maricopa, however, most of the time either births or deaths dominated, producing either increase or decline, and not stability. From 1700-75 and 1858-70, Pima deaths considerably outnumbered births, and decline occurred (Table 52). From 1775-1858 and 1882-90, Pima births outnumbered deaths, even before Euro-American medical techniques were in use among the Pima (other than some smallpox vaccination from 1882-90). From 1775-1846, the Pima annual growth rate was 0.15%, while from 1882-90 it was 0.38%.

Looking at other populations, before the arrival

of modern medicine, the Navajo increased throughout most of their known history, the only exception being a short period from 1860-70 (Table 54). For American Indians in general, Vogel (1970:139) feels that the comments by early Europeans on the good health of American Indians were true, in that Europeans, coming from much more densely populated areas, experienced higher death rates. Thus, many American Indian populations could well have been increasing at a time when European populations had not yet reached stage two of their transition.

In other parts of the world, other populations have also apparently increased before the introduction of Euro-American medicine. In northwest Thailand, Kunstadter (1972:330, 348) found that population increase had been occurring since 1870, in spite of at least one smallpox epidemic. Others have related population increase before the introduction of modern medicine to the introduction of new crops. Bowers (1971:30) feels that the introduction of the sweet potato to certain ecological zones in New Guinea has permitted a population increase which began in 1870. Although Chinese population experienced growth before European contact, Ho (1959:183-84) feels that the sixteenth century and later introductions of maize, potatoes, sweet potatoes, and peanuts enabled Chinese population to continue increasing. The potato has even been credited as a factor producing population increase in Europe (i.e., stage two), especially in areas marginal for European grains such as wheat, barley, oats, and rye (Langer 1963; Wrigley 1969:168).

According to work by Birdsell (1957), Dumond (1975), and Polgar (1971, 1972), the problem for hunting and gathering populations may not have been keeping the birth rate high enough to compensate for deaths, but rather keeping the number of births down. Sahlins (1972:1-41) and Woodburn (1968) have shown that hunters and gatherers were not always one step from starvation but rather often enjoyed sufficient food without seeking it every waking hour. Assuming a female reproductive period of 15 years, reduced to a mean of 12 because of maternal mortality, as well as 2 years between births, a woman could produce six children of which perhaps only three would live to reproduce. This, however, would still produce a 50% increase in population in one generation. Thus, with accidents and warfare relatively unimportant causes of death for hunters and gatherers, population size was limited mainly through the use of abortion and infanticide. Among hunters and gatherers, the necessity for limiting the number of children was the inability of a mobile woman to care for more than one unweaned child at a time (Dumond 1975:718). We might thus expect sedentary agricultural populations to have even higher annual growth rates than hunting and gathering populations, and this appears to have occurred. Polgar (1972:204) estimates that until the Neolithic, population increased 0.003% annually, while

Dumond (1975:718) feels the rate was somewhat less, 0.0007%
to 0.0015%. During the Neolithic, Polgar (1972:204)
estimates the annual growth rate as 0.08%-0.12% and Dumond
(1975:718) as 0.15%-0.4%. Still, Dumond (1975:718)
mentions certain factors which he believes acted to limit
the size of at least some farming populations by lowering
the birth rate. Some persons never marry in some farming
populations, especially those with impartible land
inheritance. Negotiations over marriage between landholding groups can delay age at marriage. Finally, because
of the greater density of farming populations, epidemics
may have been more frequent and severe, although this
factor may not have really become important until the
development of preindustrial cities (Polgar 1964). Dumond
(1975:719) assumes mortality among farming populations was
about the same as among hunters and gatherers.

The Pima should have had a high birth rate before
contact. Although abortion and infanticide were practiced
under certain circumstances, and there was a prolonged
breastfeeding period (Russell 1908:186), there was no
reported postpartum sexual abstinence or other restriction
on marital sex. Everyone reportedly married, there were
no negotiations over marriage, no preferred types of
marriage, a minimum of restrictions on whom one could
marry, and limited polygyny. From 1700-75, Pima population
declined from epidemics. The deaths of many persons should
have relieved any pressure on land, if there was in fact

any before 1700, which does not seem likely. I believe, however, that the apparent nonfunctionality of Pima clans and moieties may be related to this population decline. Before 1700, with an assumed high birth rate, land may have been scarce enough that its use was regulated by clans or moieties. But with the great population decrease of 1700-75, the clans and moieties, whose main function may have been to control access to land, may have atrophied. The Maricopa appear to have had a more functional clan organization than the Pima and this may result from being outnumbered by the Pima. Through clan membership, the Maricopa may have been able to regulate access to their lands.

After 1858, the demand for grain by transient and resident Anglos led to production of grain for sale by the Pima and Maricopa. To do this, the Pima may well have needed more workers. However, it is unclear whether this need would have been met by having more children or employing more Papago during the harvest season. Certainly, there were advantages to hiring Papago: they brought products desired by the Pima, such as agave, acorns, and salt, and had to be fed only during the harvest, while a child had to be supported all year, but beyond a certain number, children were economically valuable only at the harvest. Thus, the Pima birth rate may have increased after 1858, but I think it unlikely.

As a result of the above objections, we see that

the first stage of the demographic transition is a fiction devised by demographers who knew little about population before the eighteenth century in Europe. Since they did not know what had occurred, it was safest for them to assume stability. But the Pima and certain other American Indian populations show that population increase occurred during what was supposed to be the first stage of the demographic transition. Nevertheless, even though Pima population increased before the introduction of modern medicine, it seems unlikely that the annual growth rate could have exceeded 1% (cf. Wrigley 1969:205).

We now turn to the second stage of the demographic transition, which states that the death rate decreases when health advances, mainly the prevention or treatment of disease, either are developed by a population or are introduced by another population. However, among the Pima and Maricopa, population increase occurred before the introduction of scientific medicine. Although the 1775-1858 and 1882-90 increases were followed by declines, the beginning of the continual increase to the present of the Pima and Maricopa began about 1895. During 1895-1910, the annual growth rate was 0.6%, and this was before much use of modern medicine among the Pima and Maricopa (the only exception being smallpox vaccinations). The Pima-Maricopa are not alone in this. Even in Europe, where the demographic transition supposedly took place, population increase cannot be attributed entirely to decreased mortality from medical advances. Other factors, such as the introduction of the potato as a staple crop (which led to earlier marriage and higher fertility), food imports from colonies, and emigration all played a part (Polgar 1972:207). Nevertheless, we can state that the greatest (but not the only) population increase among the Pima and Maricopa (and probably most if not all other American Indian populations) came during the 1950s, when public health measures were intensified and medical care improved, so that certain causes of death were eliminated as significant. Clements (1931:418-19) recognized this when he stated: "If the death rate from tuberculosis and pneumonia can be materially lowered among Indians, the most serious checks to the increase of the aboriginal population will have been removed." Among American Indians, 1952 saw the start of drug therapy against tuberculosis and the use of antibiotics against pneumonia (Adair, Deuschle, and McDermott 1957:90), and as Clements had predicted, Pima and Maricopa population took off at that time in spite of a high accidental death rate.

It thus would be better to revise the second stage of the demographic transition, saying that when modern medical treatment and sanitation are introduced, a population will experience its highest known annual growth rate.

The third stage of the demographic transition has produced the most heated discussion among demographers, especially in relation to areas outside Europe and North America. Some demographers are amazed that these populations have not yet attained the third stage by reducing their fertility in order to compensate for the lowered mortality which has resulted from the introduction of public health programs. This situation is what has become known as the population explosion.

The Pima and Maricopa can shed some light on this situation. According to Coale (1964:53), in an exploding or developing population, more than 40% are under age 15, only 2%-4% above age 65, and the median age is less than 20 years. To this we may add a natural increase of over 2% annually. By these standards, the Pima and Maricopa are experiencing a population explosion. Persons under 15 comprised 43.0% of the 1970 Pima-Maricopa on-reservation population, and persons 65 and over (not over 65 as specified by Coale) contributed only 6.8% to the Pima-Maricopa on-reservation population (Table 36). The median age was 18.9, and the annual growth rate for 1960-70 (not the natural increase) was 1.6%. For comparative purposes, the 1970 Arizona white population contained only 29.2% persons less than 15, 9.5% persons 65 and over, and had a median age of 27.3 (USBC 1971b:Table 20). It is important to understand that the Pima and Maricopa are a "modernized" group integrated into the industrialized economy of the United States. Very few derive a living from subsistence farming because of the unavailability of water. The Pima and Maricopa thus rely largely on low and unstable wage income, lease income, and welfare (Munsell 1967:216-69). Yet they obviously are not a population typical of the third stage of the demographic transition. If the demographic transition is correct in ascribing declining birth rates to the possibility of upward social mobility, however, it is not surprising that the Pima and Maricopa have high birth rates. Their position in the economy is such that there is little real chance to acquire more than enough for daily needs. The Pima and Maricopa were cheated of their most valuable resource, the waters of the Gila River, and have little control over their remaining resources. Restrictions on tribally-initiated and run development are considerable, with already established non-Indian firms being encouraged to avail themselves of the tax advantages and captive labor force of reservations. Off-reservation, Pima and Maricopa face discrimination in hiring, and those few who do obtain employment paying a decent wage or salary are often expected to act like whites if they expect to be promoted or retained, often to the extent of shifting their social associations from predominantly Indian to white. Thus, given the overall economic position of the Pima and Maricopa, limiting the number of children may not be advantageous, and may even be disadvantageous. Munsell (1967), for the Salt River Pima-Maricopa, and Robbins (1968), for the Blackfeet, have shown that these two groups have ways of coping with the low end of the economy. When personal or family income is relatively high and stable, households tend to contain a nuclear family. But when income is relatively low and unstable, families and other relatives move in together to form extended family households. Each member contributes some income or labor to the household, which functions as an economic unit. Thus, one person will have a car, another welfare income, another some lease income, while other members will engage in seasonal or part-time wage labor, which does not provide a stable income. Thus, by pooling resources, the members of the household attempt to obtain a stable (but nevertheless it is still a relatively low) income. In this environment, children may not be seen as a disadvantage. When someone falls on hard times, he or she must have relatives to rely on--brothers, sisters, sons, daughters, parents, even grandparents and grandchildren. If there are no children, one may have to rely on non-relatives, who may owe their first priority to their own relatives. If one has children, it is hoped that one of the children may somehow obtain a good living, in which case the parents hope not to be forgotten. Even though the parents may not live with the child, they may receive economic assistance, as Shaw (1974:150) recounts in her life story. Thus, Ward (1962:94) is correct in stating

> that without the thrust of growth there is no particular reason why people should want smaller families. Children may not die; they cannot be

educated; meanwhile they work. A certain fatalism prevails. It is only when hope and expansion begin that the choice of a smaller family makes sense.

A further point about Pima and Maricopa fertility is that when economic conditions are better, fertility is higher than when they are bad, as during the depression of the 1930s, when fewer Pima were born. During the Depression, we may assume that more Pima and Maricopa had low and unstable incomes, and thus there were more multifamily households. This in itself could act to in part reduce the birth rate by reducing the amount of privacy available to household residents. In better times, with more families having relatively high and stable incomes, there would be relatively more single family households, and thus more privacy for family members.

During a depression, the Pima and Maricopa would be less involved in an industrial economy, and during better times, more involved, questioning the idea that birth rates decline as involvement in an industrial economy proceeds. All this has relevance to populations in other parts of the world which have high birth rates. The industrialization and "modernization" of these areas is different from the indigenous industrialization of Europe and North America. One of the advantages of locating industries in the developing world is that lower wages can be paid. Moreover, local resources are exploited for the benefit of the highly industrialized countries, and people in less industrialized countries participate in a world economy by becoming both consumers of manufactured goods, made from indigenous resources, which were exported, and imported in the form of goods made somewhere else; and as cheap labor to manufacture goods which can be sold in highly industrialized countries. The economic "development" of the less industrialized countries has in fact led to their underdevelopment, for they play specific roles in a world economy controlled by centers of economic and political power in the highly industrialized countries (Frank 1966, 1967; Jorgensen 1971:84-90). The reasoning behind the third stage of the demographic transition, that people will have fewer children when they can improve their socioeconomic status, may or may not be true. But if this is in fact why birth rates decline, it is preposterous to expect high birth rates to decline at present, because the "development" of areas with high birth rates has not led to the possibility of socieconomic advancement for the vast majority of the population.

Returning to the Pima and Maricopa, it is probable, however, that the birth rate of 1970 is lower than in previous times, but not because of the demographic transition. Table 59 compares Pima-Maricopa population with Navajo population for several dates. Although the Pima and Maricopa were about one-half the Navajo population of 1870, they are now no more than one-tenth. Yet the Pima and Maricopa had few restrictions on reproduction. However, two factors may have been working to promote Navajo population growth (Johnston 1966:150; Kunitz 1973:2-3, 5). The Navajo, unlike many American Indian populations, were able to expand their territory during much of the nineteenth century. Since the Navajo were a very dispersed population, it is also assumed that they were less subject to the effects of epidemics than more densely settled populations. The Pima and Maricopa were earlier deprived of their resources by whites, and were more densely settled. Thus, the Pima-Maricopa birth rate may have been as high as that of the Navajo, but the death rate may have been higher, producing a lower growth rate. If this is so, it could account in part for the difference in growth between the Pima-Maricopa and the Navajo. But we also must assume that the Pima-Maricopa birth rate declined at some point or points, for Navajo population has continued to grow faster than Pima-Maricopa, while death rates (Pima-Maricopa, 9.1; Navajo, about 6; Kunitz 1973:Table 8) are at least similar enough that mortality cannot account for the entire difference in the annual growth rate (Pima-Maricopa, 1.8%, 1952-72; Navajo, 2.4%-3.3%, 1950-75). If the depression economy of the late nineteenth century lowered the Pima-Maricopa birth rate like the depression of the 1930s, there may have been a real decline in the Pima-Maricopa birth rate. Certainly, the decreased child-woman ratio in 1890 and 1895 compared with 1860 suggests this (although also the possibility of higher child mortality). Thus, part of the difference between Pima-Maricopa and

Navajo population growth may have been a lower Pima-Maricopa birth rate during at least the twentieth century.

With the Navajo, the remaining questions are as to the factors which have acted to maintain a high birth rate and whether the birth rate has in fact been constantly high. If the economic value of children is great, a high birth rate could well be maintained. For example, the Navajo use young children as shepherds. With compulsory schooling, shepherds are lost to education, and a supply of young children may be seen as a necessity. This, of course, could not be the whole story of high Navajo birth rates, but suggests that economic factors may be important.

It has been suggested that the Hopi, who have not grown as fast as the Navajo, and who are growing at a lower rate at present, have had higher death rates than the Navajo in the past, because the Hopi are a much denser population, and thus more subject to epidemics. More recently, the Hopi have become more involved in wage work off-reservation, and have been described as a population approaching the third stage of the demographic transition by having fewer children in order to increase social mobility and acquire material goods (Kunitz 1973:vii, 8-9), while the Navajo, being less involved in off-reservation migration, have been described as undergoing a slower demographic transition.

However, it seems likely that in the nineteenth century, the Hopi, faced with a scarcity of farmland, may well have limited population growth by reducing the birth rate, while the Navajo, who could expand their territory, did not need to reduce the birth rate. Thus, while the Hopi death rate may have been higher than that of the Navajo, the birth rate may also have been lower. Moreover, Wrigley (1969:81-89) found that high mortality in epidemics can lead to lower fertility by delaying age at marriage, shortening a woman's childbearing years through earlier death, and reducing the number of children surviving in a population. The greater reported degree of off-reservation migration by the Hopi compared with the Navajo shows a possible greater pressure on reservation resources. I doubt that in most cases this migration results from choice, but rather from necessity. The present economic situation of the off-reservation Hopi is not such that it would make possible a middle class life style, and with it the desire to limit the number of children in favor of socioeconomic advance or acquisition of expensive material goods. Off-reservation Hopi[1] males had a 1969 median income of $4989, compared with $6424 for Arizona white males and $5150 for Arizona Spanish-surnamed males. Off-reservation Hopi females earned a 1969 median income of $3174, Arizona white females obtained $2284, and Arizona Spanish-surnamed females $1788 (USBC 1972a:576; 1973:162, 166). The Hopi female income is higher than that of white females, but I believe this reflects the greater necessity for some Hopi women to find work, and I doubt whether female income is pooled with male income in the majority of cases.

In considering all of the above objections to the demographic transition provided by the Pima-Maricopa and other populations, I conclude that the demographic transition is of no value in describing Pima-Maricopa population dynamics, nor American Indian population dynamics in general.

American Indian Urban Migration

The meager data available to this study of the Pima and Maricopa suggest that women were more greatly involved in urban migration than men. The Papago and California Indians also show this pattern. Further study should be directed toward determining whether this pattern is typical of American Indians, and if it results from less discrimination against women.

In 1968, the on-reservation Papago sex ratio was 100.0 (Rund, Siegel, and Rumley 1968:9, N = 5372), while the off-reservation sex ratio was 96.2 (Rund and Rumley 1968:10; N = 4144). Cook (1943e[1971]:558-59) found that California Indians in cities had a sex ratio of 79.8, while those living outside the county or counties of their pre-contact territory showed 89.0, and those living in the county or counties of their precontact territory had a sex ratio of 107.2.

Malthus

After the demographic transition, the ideas of Malthus are probably the most common topic of discussion in demography. Arguments rage about what Malthus did or did not say or mean, and his statement of the relationship between differential rates of increase of food supply and population has been discredited, but there is truth in his view that population size ultimately depends on food supply. However, before this point is reached, other factors often intervene. It would appear that political factors are more important than natural factors in impeding access to resources, including food. For the Pima, but not Maricopa, for example, 1775-1846 was a period of population growth, but even after this period the Pima still apparently had enough land, water, and food, for they could sell considerable surpluses to whites, and constantly increased the area cultivated. But by 1870, white appropriation of Pima-Maricopa water was beginning to decrease the food supply, and by 1890, after further losses of water to whites, the Pima and Maricopa could no longer support their population with their remaining food supply. But this was not because Pima and Maricopa population had grown too large; it was because an immigrant population had taken the resources of the Pima and Maricopa, which resources had been adequate for Pima-Maricopa needs. Thus we cannot say that Pima-Maricopa population was or is too large; on the contrary, the United States white population was apparently too large because it found it necessary to expropriate the resources of the American Indians.

It is this sort of situation, on a larger scale, that is at the heart of the population explosion argument, in which persons in the highly industrialized nations claim that the less developed nations should reduce their population growth or the world as a whole will face too great a pressure on resources, or preceding it, large-scale war. To this persons in less developed nations reply that there are surpluses in the world today and all that is needed is redistribution of them. To some extent, both views are correct, but they are speaking of different things. The highly industrialized countries are thinking only of their welfare by considering the effects of world population on world resources. Obviously, if population pressure becomes too great, the industrialized nations could suffer either a lower standard of living (such as if the less developed countries prevented access to their resources) or armed conflict, which could end disastrously should a nation with nuclear weapons decide to use them in such a conflict. The less developed nations, which already have to live with the conditions the highly industrialized countries fear, are concerned with the present situation of inequality of distribution of resources and income, and feel that if the highly industrialized countries want to use the resources and labor of the less developed countries, the more developed countries should at least pay a sufficient price so that people in the less developed countries can live a decent life. The highly industrialized countries tell the less developed nations that if they would only reduce their population growth rates, they would have enough to go around. In fact, an increasing amount of land in the less industrialized countries is devoted to commodity crops for export at the expense of food crops for local consumption (Barraclough 1975). Thus, given the present world economy, it is hard to believe that a starving inhabitant of Bangladesh would have enough to eat, or for that matter that all Pima and Maricopa could afford a middle class life style (assuming they want it) if they had a mean of two children per family instead of a higher number. As long as inequalities in the distribution of wealth remain both among nations and within nations, the question of family size is largely academic: one can be poor with only two children as well as with ten.

Population Size and Sociocultural Evolution

Cross-cultural studies of sociocultural evolution by Carneiro (1967) and Naroll (1956) have attempted to quantitatively relate population size to the number of cultural institutions or traits, such as organizational traits, craft specialties, team types, occupational specialties, and organizational types.[2] Table 60 shows Pima and Maricopa populations in 1700, 1775, and 1846 and the number of various types of institutions or traits predicted from the formulas derived by Carneiro and Naroll. The Pima appear to have been only little affected, while the Maricopa were considerably so, possibly losing half of their institutions from depopulation alone. It was not possible for me to carry out a count to determine to what extent the predictions were validated, but disappearance of institutions can occur for causes other than population decline, such as disruption of the society through loss of resources so that it can no longer support its culture.

Methodology

The importance of methodology to demographic studies of American Indians should by now be apparent. In order to obtain accurate data on the aggregate American Indian population, we must have accurate studies of the groups comprising it (Haviland 1966:433; Kroeber 1939:131-32). I believe that this study shows the importance of obtaining and evaluating for accuracy all population estimates and censuses for an American Indian population. With the considerable inaccuracies in many of the data, only by examining all available figures does the situation become clearer. This is especially important because most American Indian populations are small, and there is much random variation that in a larger population would be considered evidence of data inaccuracy. In this regard, testing the sex ratio for its probability of random occurrence is very useful, and has been done in this study. Lovejoy (1971:104) has used χ^2 in a similar way. The use of the census rolls, either from the Bureau of Indian Affairs or the Bureau of the Census, and preferably both, is the best way to evaluate data accuracy. Here data anomalies can be uncovered by means of the age distribution by sex. It is better to have two rolls than just one, and the more the better. With two rolls, the cohort survival ratios can be calculated, and much can be learned of the accuracy of the censuses being compared. Having evaluated the censuses in this way, age-specific and sex-specific underenumeration should become apparent, and in some cases, it may be possible to determine whether certain geographic areas have been left out. The rolls can also be evaluated by age heaping. Knowing that in uncertain cases ages are usually estimated to the nearest year ending in 0 or 5, the age digits at which heaping occurs can be used to determine when the roll was first made. Perhaps the most accurate way to determine accuracy of the rolls would be to make a card (preferably computer card) for each person listed on a roll, and attempt to match persons from one roll to another. This would also allow some measure of the death rate. Unfortunately, time did not allow me to do so for this study.

Regarding estimates, this study shows that they are neither always too high (Kroeber 1939:180) nor always too low (Dobyns 1966:406, 414-15), but sometimes too high and sometimes too low. But certainly the view that all estimates are too high must be discredited; how can a person deliberately exaggerate the size of a population whose true size he does not know?

Finally, in demographic studies of American Indians, and other peoples of the world who have not until recently been well-censused, we are just not dealing with data as accurate as most demographers would like, and we cannot investigate in as much detail the demographic features of these populations. But for American Indians at least, we can certainly determine population trends, and even their magnitudes. Certainly for the nineteenth century, and even more so for the twentieth century, we can get some idea of the actual size of the populations, with perhaps less than 10% error for certain years.

General Conclusions

Based on the above discussion, let us advance certain conclusions regarding American Indian populations, and population in general. These are conclusions, however, only in the sense of being concluding hypotheses about American Indian (and world) population that are in need of further rigorous quantitative testing.

1. There is no general population curve (or "demographic transition") for American Indian populations, but all suffered at least one decline of varying severity as a result of European or Euro-American contact.

2. Even American Indian populations not involved in warfare with European or United States governments or their citizens, and not removed from precontact territory, could suffer 50% population loss. With warfare and removal, depopulation was even worse.

3. The crucial factor in reducing American Indian populations to nadir was not newly introduced diseases, for after some immunity was developed, some populations were rebounding, but rather loss of resources to Europeans and Euro-Americans, which created a situation of poverty. Before the introduction of public health measures, this permitted population decline to occur by making the people susceptible to diseases that a better standard of living (such as traditional American Indian culture provided) could have prevented. Whites also would have succumbed to disease in large numbers under such conditions.

4. Before the twentieth century, the level of mortality appears to have been more important in setting the growth rate, while since the beginning of the twentieth century, and especially since the Second World War, the level of fertility appears to have had greater influence on the population growth rate.

5. There was not a relative equality of the birth rate and death rate among American Indian populations in precontact times, nor, for that matter, in postcontact times. Thus, population increases occurred before the introduction of Euro-American medicine, and the first and

second stages of the demographic transition are shown to be false assumptions.

6. The Pima-Maricopa birth rate has been sensitive to economic conditions, at least in the twentieth century, but in opposition to the relationship specified by the demographic transition. When economic conditions were bad, the birth rate declined, while when economic conditions were relatively good, and the Pima and Maricopa were more integrated into the surrounding industrial economy, the birth rate increased.

7. The demographic transition and the ideas of Malthus regarding population and food supply are not useful in explicating Pima-Maricopa population change.

8. Loss of population may have played a part in atrophy of traditional institutions and other cultural traits among American Indians. In some societies, such as the Maricopa, half of the institutions of particular types (e.g., occupational, labor teams) could have been lost.

9. Population estimates are neither always too high nor always too low, but rather sometimes too high, sometimes too low, and once in a great while, just about right.

A vast body of demographic data on American Indians is yet unexplored. I believe that the census rolls of American Indians will acquire a significance for the historical demography of Native Americans that church registers of vital events now have for European historical demographers. But generalizations such as those above can be subjected to verification only when enough evaluated data are available so that a valid sample of American Indian populations can be drawn. It is my hope that in a period when the goals and effects of fieldwork are being seriously questioned, historical demographic data on American Indians will receive the attention they have so long deserved, and that hopefully this will lead to more accurate collection of demographic data, respecting the right to privacy of the persons being enumerated, whether by official sources or researchers.

Notes to Chapter Eight

1. All Hopi residing in the United States minus those on the Hopi Reservation (but excluding the Joint Use Area). Thus, Hopi residing on other reservations have been classified here as off-reservation.

2. Organizational traits (Carneiro 1967:234-35) are a list of 354 traits referring to such aspects of culture as "subsistence, architecture, economics, political organization, religion, etc. . . ." They are expected to be cumulative, i.e., the larger the population, the more traits are expected. The formula relating the two is $N = \sqrt{P}$, where N = number of cultural traits and P = population (Carneiro 1967:236). A craft specialty (Naroll 1956:694) is "A social pattern of manufacture (or repair) of a durable artifact for the use of some hale adult member of the unit studied other than the maker (or repairer)." The formula is $C = \sqrt[6]{P}$, where C = number of craft specialties and P = population. A team (Naroll 1956:696) is "a group of at least three people with clearly defined membership and formal leadership in regular use." The formula (Naroll 1956:700) is $T = 2\sqrt[5]{P}$, where T = number of team types and P = population. Note that the number of types of teams and not the number of teams is employed (Naroll 1956:698). The formula for the number of occupational specialties is $S = 2\sqrt[3]{P}$, where S = number of occupational specialties and P = population. For the number of organizational types, $r = 1.5\sqrt[4]{P}$, where r = the number

of organizational types and P = population. These
formulas, of course, are quite crude, but nevertheless
can give some idea of the loss of institutions or traits
suffered by the Pima and Maricopa as a result of
depopulation alone.